Henry James
The Indirect Vision
Second Edition, Revised and Enlarged

by
Darshan Singh Maini

U·M·I Research Press

Ann Arbor / London

Produced and distributed by
UMI Research Press
an imprint of
University Microfilms Inc.
Ann Arbor, Michigan 48106

Library of Congress Cataloging in Publication Data

Maini, Darshan Singh.
 Henry James : the indirect vision / by Darshan Singh Maini.—2nd
ed., rev. and enl.
  p. cm.—(Studies in modern literature ; no. 83)
  Bibliography: p.
  Includes index.
  ISBN 0-8357-1838-7 (alk. paper)
  1. James, Henry, 1843-1916—Criticism and interpretation.
I. Title. II. Series.
PS2124.M27   1988
813'.4—dc19   87-24871
                                                                          CIP

British Library CIP data is available.

Studies in Modern Literature, No. 83

A. Walton Litz, General Series Editor

Professor of English
Princeton University

Consulting Editor:
Daniel Mark Fogel

Professor of English
Louisiana State University
Editor, *Henry James Review*

Other Titles in This Series

88~5352

Henry James
The Indirect Vision
Second Edition, Revised and Enlarged

For
Adeline R. Tintner
and
Daniel Mark Fogel

Contents

Preface

In presenting a revised and enlarged edition of *Henry James: The Indirect Vision,* I have chiefly been guided by the desire, since I started working on it some seventeen years ago during a Fulbright assignment at Harvard University, to place the book before a wider and expanding readership. Watching the Jamesian scene closely, I find the new James reader almost always something of a monk in the rigour and pursuit of his labours, and almost always something of an "insider," and the current critical assault in its complexity and dimensions, may well rival the pleated mysteries of the Master's own handiwork. With the critics basing their readings and interpretations on a variety of new approaches—rhetorical, textual, hermeneutical, structuralist, semiotic, poststructuralist, postmodernist, phenomenological and so forth—James in particular appears to have become an increasingly exciting and provocative writer, whose depths may never be quite sounded and whose quiddity may never be fully comprehended in terms of the traditional responses. Amazingly enough, he strikes one at once as Victorian, modern and postmodern in a manner that subsumes both thought and style, taste and ambience. So, despite such an impressive collage of critical comment, the unique charm and the abiding mystery of James still hold and still compel. If his appeal has a touch of the romance of high reading, the industry of the new critics has a matching magnificence.

In revising the twelve essays of the original volume (Tata McGraw-Hill, New Delhi, 1973) and in adding three new pieces on love and sex, politics, and criticism, I have taken note of fresh critical statements, formulations, discoveries and departures with a view to authenticating some of my earlier impressions and views, and also to using, where necessary, acquired insights. It has been well said that Henry James serves as a literary barometer for our times. To respond, then, to his overtures is to register one's reactions to the pulse and beat of changing thought.

Books on James, as well as all manner of essays and critiques, have steadily continued to swell the Jamesian theme since the revival of the early forties, and though the wave appeared to have nearly spent itself around the end of the sixties with the decline of the New Criticism establishment, James understandably surfaced again when the structuralists and the postmoderns and the phenomeno-logists began to carve up the critical empire, colonize the minds of new readers, and upset some cherished assumptions and tenets. This was quite natural, for perhaps no other novelist inveigles both reader and critic into the labyrinths of fabulation so compulsively and rewardingly as James does. Each theory of art and fiction seems destined to seek him out, as though to test its truths and its effects. James thus emerges as a measuring instrument to show how and where a theory is vindicated or springs a leak. To be sure, each great writer could be used illustra-tively to support this thesis or that, but where James suggests a different dimension is in his own premonitory and penetrating awareness of most of the insights that have only become available in recent years. This is not really to claim for him a clairvoyant status, but to aver that he was so endowed as to have come instinctively close to the mystery of the art of the novel. In a fashion, he constituted its *nirvana* in the sense both of its "transcendence" and its "death."

Again, since the setting up of the Henry James Society and of its organ, *The Henry James Review,* in November 1979, there has been a qualitative leap in the area of Jamesian studies. It has since then been possible to extend the whole range of emerging argument even to some of the Master's marginalia and forgotten pieces, not to speak of the established classics, which continue to receive informed, and at times, worshipful attention. The James fraternity now harbors all manner of academic pundits and purists and all manner of reluctant admirers and celebrants. Such an assembly of minds has brought to bear upon his works a singularly significant hermeneutic, whose full meaning is now beginning to unfold.

This returns me to the raison d'être of this book. With the *Jamesiana* being an overworked and saturated industry, one is nonetheless obliged to add a postscript to the proceedings. All that I can recall today is that it appeared important to me at the time of writing to offer a personal response to a writer who had, over the years, coerced my imagination and beckoned me into those outlying and strange high-lands of the imagination, where only the Jamesian "writ" obtained, and where to seek admittance was but to seek one's own self and validate one's own vision of life, man, and society through the energies of art. And a variant reading of a Jamesian novel or tale, which the "blessed" complexity of his style and technique made imperative, added to the thrill of discovery and validation.

James, as I seek to show in these essays, was a master of "indirection," invading the mind in a soft, sly, and insinuating manner. Indeed, one of the conditions for enjoying his work is to let the imagination take its own time to come to terms with him. He sounds the richest chords when the playfulness of the author begins to act like a bait and rouse the reader's response to the pitch of desire and understanding. It is a slow gathering of essences and effects, but it is only the incremental weight of such impressions and the long, leisurely stay in such arbours that finally permit one to peep into the encoded message of the Jamesian canon.

A word about the scheme of this book. From the beginning, the idea was to isolate some of the major themes and techniques that, to my mind, constitute the essence of Henry James. Naturally, when a writer happens to be that prolific and that complex, it is not possible to touch in detail upon each and every significant novel or story, though it is, by implication, possible to spread the argument to cover his entire *oeuvre*. Admittedly, then, scores of things have had to be merely hinted at or simply taken for granted. And since these essays had to be both brief and concise in terms of the economy of this volume, I naturally turned more to the novels than to the *nouvelles* and tales, though in some cases the latter too were taken note of, when they helped to illustrate a particular point in some special way. Accordingly, in each essay I take up three or four novels and tales for a somewhat extended treatment. This obviously does not cover the illustrative potential of other equally relevant and engaging texts in relation to the subject of that particular essay. The object was merely to indicate the direction in which a particular problem could be pursued or worked out. There is, as we know, no finality in matters of interpretation, and in any case a writer like James would always seem to be mocking our efforts should we ever presume to be in possession of "the story in it."

Of the essays included in this volume, the following appeared in journals and critical anthologies, though they were subsequently revised in the light of later perceptions. The essays on the Jamesian woman and the Jamesian style were published in *The Indian Response to American Literature* (USEFI, New Delhi, 1967) and *The Indian Journal of English Studies* (Orient Longmans, Calcutta, 1968) respectively; the essays entitled "Love and Sex in Henry James" (*Proceedings of a Symposium on American Literature,* edited by Marta Sienicka, Adam Mickiewicz University, Poznan, 1979), "The Politics of Henry James" and "Henry James: The Creative Writer as Critic" (*The Henry James Review,* Spring 1985 and Spring 1987, reprinted by permission of the Johns Hopkins University Press),were the outcome of a continuing engagement with the *daemon* of Henry James. Here, they are included under slightly new titles in keeping with the spirit of the volume. In addition, I have made use of my article, "Henry James and the Dream of Fiction" (*The American Review,* Winter 1985), particularly in revising the introductory chapter called "The Altar of the Master." To all the editors of these volumes and journals, I owe special thanks.

To the list of those friends and colleagues who find specific mention in the preface to the 1973 volume for various acts of kindness and consideration, I wish to add the names of some kindred spirits encountered since then—Professor Charles R. Anderson (Johns Hopkins), Professor Seymour Chatman (Berkeley), Professor Leslie Fiedler (S.U.N.Y., Buffalo), and Professor James W. Tuttleton

(N.Y.U.). All of them have, in one way or another, helped enlarge the Jamesian circle. Of my Indian colleagues, two James scholars, Dr. Ranjit Kapoor (Punjabi University) and Dr. Malashri Lal (Delhi University) have promoted the Jamesian debate at this end.

I owe special thanks to Dr. Amritjit Singh (Rhode Island College) for his unfailing support, and to Mr. J. S. Ranajee (Cheyney University) for many a "Jamesian" favour, and to Mr. John M. Pickering of the Pennsylvania State University Press for his sustained faith in the virtue of this volume.

Finally, in dedicating this book to Adeline R. Tintner and Daniel Mark Fogel, I salute two friends from the dividing generations destined to carry the Jamesian flag far enough to leave us all beholden and hopeful.

D.S.M.

Chandigarh
June 1987

1

The Altar of the Master

In a letter to William Dean Howells on the occasion of his seventy-fifth birthday, Henry James wrote: "Your really beautiful time will come." Commenting on this in an essay on Howells, Lionel Trilling observes: "The really beautiful time has come to James, but it has yet to come to Howells, and probably it will be a very long time coming."[1] And Professor Trilling is right; James's finest hour has come in a manner so memorable that one cannot but marvel at the miracle achieved. It is as if some special destiny governs the fortunes of men of genius, and the muses will not suffer neglect or injustice, particularly where a ravenous and unrequited imagination is on the prowl. Indeed, when a body of work solicits attention and exacts tribute, as of necessity, one may know that its moment of recognition has arrived. That James's hour should have come so soon—within a generation's time after his death—only shows that his is a type of imagination that is apt to elicit a delayed response even at the best of times.

The James "revival" that began rather gingerly and tentatively around the mid-thirties with the publication of the Henry James issue of *Horn & Hound* (1934) was in full cry a decade later, and since then has assumed such gothic proportions and aspects as to entice both reader and scholar into a fantasy of criticism. The rationale of this remarkable upsurge, which has few parallels in the history of revivals, has been examined by, among others, Malcolm Cowley, Clifton Fadiman, Paul Rosenfeld, Q. D. Leavis, R. P. Blackmur, Leon Edel, Marius Bewley and Maxwell Geismar in some detail, yet all the explanations offered—the American campaign to claim back its fugitives, the swing from naturalism to symbolism, Eliot's "metaphysical" James of the later phase battening on the Donne revival, the discovery in James of "New Criticism" virtues like ambiguity, irony, rhetoric, form and "distancing," a "change in sensibility," the appeal of James's "international" tales in the wake of the U.N. spirit, the cold war ethos and climate, and so forth—do not appear to have resolved the complexity of the problem. Each critic naturally viewed the matter in the light of his own reading of the Master's work, and of his own ideological perceptions. And since nearly all the major novels and stories admit of several equally convincing, if not valid, interpretations, one is not surprised to find the critics supporting diverse and contradictory views regarding the true basis of the "revival." Whatever the reasons, one thing is pretty obvious; *Jamesolatry* or the canonization of James was not an esoteric indulgence merely, nor an academic conspiracy of bourgeois-liberal renegades, whom Maxwell Geismar is pleased to call "Jacobites" in his bitter but pertinent book. Apparently the eclipse of James in his later years and his denigration in the committed thirties, the sudden "discovery" in the period of the cold war—a thing that ominously synchronized with the novelist's birth centenary—and his partial dethronement once again since the youth revolution of the last decade seem to support the thesis that the "cult" had strong politico-cultural overtones. This is, to an extent, true, though there is an element of oversimplification in it. There is, as I see the matter, something deeper, more fundamental involved in the process. The problem is essentially psycho-epistemological. In a manner, it could be described as a shock of recognition that resulted from a muffled sense of identity. Perhaps it will be true to say that there is a moment in the *Zeitgeist* which compels a given response, and though it may spend itself soon, it is not the less authentic for that reason. What really matters in the end is the validity of the literary and aesthetic experience that is James, and no one who has had a feel for his fiction can ever remain insensitive to the unique blandishments of his muse. Even when he knows the Jamesian siren is driving him to the rocks, he may not deny the call, which has an ineluctable appeal.

What, one may ask, is the nature of this appeal or fascination? Perhaps it is best described as the Shakespearean element in James's imagination—the element that finds an exact metaphor or rhetorical correlative for the idea or emotion born in a certain context. For I take James's gift for rhetoric[2] as his supreme virtue, and there is passage after passage in his stories and novels which has a Shakespearean flavour and ambience. Of course, the sheer intensity of James's "grasping" imagination, when on the hunt, is finally a disquieting feature, inasmuch as it dislocates, disperses and liquefies reality in an effort to transcend it—a thing that never happens in Shakespeare—yet the quality of the imagination at its finest has such a magnificence about it as to make it one of the rarest poetic imaginations in the world. James will, assuredly, never be as popular as Shakespeare, or even Dickens for that matter, not only because his involved technique and style discourage the common reader, but also because his themes and moral concerns, even when they have a Shakespearian aspect, do not finally add up to a cohesive, integral, humanist world-view, despite some opinions to the contrary.[3]

Could it also be that the appeal of James to a war-weary generation that had gone sour on ideology was an appeal to what Irving Howe in another context calls, the "pastoral"[4] element in man's nature? That is to say, it is a harking back to those untrammelled states of consciousness where the mind chafes at all kinds of restrictions, and feeds instead on fantasy and dream. The retreat from action to myth, though retrogressive, when disengaged from reality, is then a requirement of the human psyche which must enact its own consolations in periods of both bafflement and ennui. In other words, what James seems to offer to the reader of the tired mid-forties and the politically neutralized fifties and early sixties is something which a part of our mind always solicits—a life of the uncovenanted consciousness, owing allegiance to nothing outside of its own earned insights. Such a view of life can easily slide into rank solipsism, as it seems to do in the later James, but this is not to deny the presence in us of a strong desire to draw the finer breath of life at the higher altitudes of thought, even if, in the end, we have to draw that breath in pain. It is an enduring dilemma of man. It is in that sense that we find a Hamlet seated in us, that we hear a James whispering soft endearments in our ears. But even as we must exorcize this ravaging ghost, we cannot but recognize its authentic nature, its ravishing power.

Let me concede one thing straightaway. James is a "minority" writer, stipulating an elite readership. And he is so not by choice or election, but by temperament and necessity. This is a somewhat different question from the one relating to the elite view of culture, such as James shares, by and large, with T. S. Eliot. For there will always be, whatever the nature of our society or world, an aristocracy of the mind, unrelated to wealth, position or heredity. Such an aristocracy will keep cultivating gardens of sensibility and tending private altars without necessarily imbibing patrician and elite values. This may suggest a compact of snobbery between writer and reader, and one does indeed have an uncomfortable feeling of belonging to an ingrown freemasonry where Henry James is concerned, not unlike the one contemplated in "The Great Good Place" (1900), but this, I repeat, is eventually a matter of sensitivity rather than of mere social superiority. Ralph Touchett, who appears to speak for James in *The Portrait of a Lady* (1881), was no doubt thinking of that pristine and inviolate pride of the spirit when he defined Isabel Archer's affluence in terms of "the requirements" of "the imagination."[5] Such a pride may not be confused with *hauteur,* for it stems not from contempt but from integrity. There is indeed an archetypal literary sensibility that abides amidst all changes, just as there is an archetypal moral sensibility such as we find in the young lady from Albany, or in a Milly Theale, or a Strether. The appeal, of course, is strongest where a reader has, like James himself, a feminine sensibility grown rich in psychic or interior life. Such a reader feels drawn to those Jamesian orchids of the imagination, for he has often raised a few of these exotic flowers in the nursery of the mind. Thus, in a manner, James was, and continues to be, an elite writer. Even in his palmiest days, he remained inaccessible to the common reader, just as in his leanest period, he continued to ensnare the imagination of the initiates whose palates had been broken to "the sacred fluid"[6] of his later fiction. James is indeed a period wine like Proust, and yields his full flavour only in slow and measured and protracted sips. This is, admittedly, in the final analysis a grievous fault, for by dealing with privileged human beings—privileged in money as well as in the goods of the spirit and the imagination—he restricted the area of experience to the lords of life[7] either way. Necessarily, such a view tends to underwrite preciosity, abstraction and pyrotechnics in art; inhumanity, sterility and dilettantism in life. But this, as I have said earlier, does not alter the fact that there is in our psyche an element that craves such an indulgence. James brings to the surface this "secret sharer" in us.

Significantly enough, James, like Keats, could foresee the interest of posterity in his work, though it must have been cold comfort to a writer who was human enough to demand immediate rewards in terms of recognition, money and fame. Even in the midst of the "havoc wrought" upon his fortunes with the failure of *The Bostonians* (1886), *The Princess Casamassima* (1886) and *The Tragic Muse* (1889), he had the wit to write to Howells: "Very likely too, some day, all my buried prose will kick off its various tombstones at once."[8] And we find some fifty or sixty years later a series of endless explosions so that even his squibs and "amusettes" have been teased out of shape to make them yield their powder. James, it appears, has had a kind of posthumous revenge for the neglect he suffered during his later years; the mathematics of evaluations work out admirably in the end. His mortification on this score was indeed responsible for the large number of stories he wrote about writers and artists. In "The Real Thing" (1892), there is, in parenthesis, a reference to a neglected genius, Philip Vincent, "the rarest of the novelists," who in the declining years of his life is at last recognized by "a higher criticism."[9] In "The Next Time" (1895), another Jamesian novelist, Ray Limbert, suffers acutely because, for all his sops to "the bitch goddess" of success, he cannot propitiate her; his fineness or "the purity of his gift" still leaves him far *above* the level of general acceptability. As the narrator ruefully remarks: "You can't make a sow's ear of a silk purse! It's grievous indeed, if you like—there are people who can't be vulgar for trying."[10] Undoubtedly, a soured psyche is enacting here, as elsewhere in these stories, a flawed aesthetic at times, but this does not diminish the force of James's recurrent motif in his fiction of the tragedy of refinement in a world of compulsive compromises and brutalities.

Another remarkable thing about James's prescience is that there is hardly a Jamesian sin or lapse or weakness which the novelist himself has not recognized in his letters and criticism, or dramatized in some form or other in his fiction. From his first important novel, *Roderick Hudson* (1875), to one of his greatest novels in the final phase, *The Golden Bowl* (1904), particularly in the stories and novels dealing with the psychology of art, James raises endless queries and doubts en route in regard to the health and even validity of his own aesthetic. One may not accept the popular Follett theory about *The Sacred Fount* (1901) being a full-blown parody of his own later style, for, as Leon Edel rightly argues, so highly solemn and prim a writer—almost a Pope of fiction in tail-coat and top hat—was not likely to mock his own craft in such a sustained manner, yet the entire corpus of Jamesian writing is a witness to the fact that James could, both consciously and unconsciously, turn the hose obliquely in his own direction, not in puckish delight, as Charles Lamb could do, but in honest doubt and bewilderment. Which of course does not diminish the gravity of those lapses and limitations. It only serves to underscore Clifton Fadiman's point that James's "insight was so tireless that it was bound to comprehend finally his own prejudices."[11]

There have always been, since James's "metaphysical" fiction of the later phase, two images of the novelist. For some contemporary readers and writers of authority he remained a pompous, priggish, unwieldy man of letters whose peculiarly pale and cadaverous creations created in them violent spasms of disgust and nausea. There was, they felt, something unclean about this kind of fiction. Some have even gone on to call him "a sissy's sissy," a cosmopolitan momma's boy, "the ultimate international wimp" as David Kirby laments in a review of a recent book on James.[12] A few, more tolerant, marvelled at his spiderish industry, but finally dismissed him, as Somerset Maugham did, as a social twitterer serving trivia with awesome solemnity. Thomas Hardy noted in his diary that James had "a ponderously warm manner of saying nothing in infinite sentences."[13] And we know how H. G. Wells, to whom James continued to pay court despite his acute differences with him over the nature of art and fiction, ridiculed him in *Boon,* comparing his later style to the manner of "a hippopotamus balancing a pea on its snout," or of "a leviathan retrieving a pebble."[14] Hugh Walpole who otherwise admired the Master, and in "Mr. Oddy" presented a sympathetic portrait, pictures him as "a quite legendary figure, a sort of stuffed waxwork from whose mouth a stream of coloured sentences, like winding rolls of green and pink paper, are for ever issuing."[15] But there is another image too, that of a novelist of genius scaling breathless heights of the temple of fiction, leaving his compeers such as Howells, Stevenson, Conrad, Ford Madox Ford and Edith Wharton in a warm glow of admiration and envy. Which of these two pictures has come to stay is not difficult to guess. Thanks to the labours of recent critics, James is at last beginning to be seen as more than "a supersubtle carver of cherry-stones."[16] He is tragically flawed, but he is also tragically great.

The fact is, few novelists in the world have been the object of so much adoration and derision as Henry James. If some critics and readers have tended to see him as the high priest of fiction whose tireless insight into the processes of fabulation on the one hand, and into the deepest recesses of the human psyche on the other, makes him the ultimate novelist, other critics and fellow novelists have turned away from him in dismay and despair. There is, indeed, something so unique about the cut and quality of his imagination as to lead the acolyte into the inner sanctum of art, and the mocker into a rash of bewildered comment. And in this ambiguity, oddly enough, lie both James's appeal and his fate as a novelist.

That the Master's "ghost" continues to surface in modern and, lately, in postmodern fiction in a most disturbing manner only testifies to his "presence" in various disguises. Where such an influence is openly and candidly acknowledged by way of a late tribute, as in the Jamesian novels of Louis Auchincloss and of so many other contemporary novelists, it is a question of a shared dream of fiction, a question, above all, of both taste and tradition. But where it erupts fitfully, agonizingly and covertly as in the metafiction of a Barth or a Barthelme or a Nabokov—and also in their critical comments etc.—it comes closest to Harold Bloom's Freudian theory of "the anxiety of influence" which, advanced in relation to poetry, and somewhat extravagant in its arcane calculations, has a singular validity where a poetic novelist like James is concerned. For the sophisticated parodists of metafiction cannot somehow exorcise Henry James much as they try to devalue and dismiss his work. Parody is, in any case, a wry salute to an acknowledged guru, and the pastiche a way of meeting the assault of influence. The long engagement with the "ghost" of Henry James appears to have pushed all such fabulists into yet another "jolly corner!"

James criticism, having run a fairly full course from the ideological inter-pretation (Van Wyck Brooks, Stephen Spender, Leslie Fiedler, Irving Howe, Quentin Anderson and Maxwell Geismar) and the ethical-cultural (F. R. Leavis, Lionel Trilling and Dorothea Krook) to the bio-psychological and Freudian (Anna Robeson Burr, Saul Rosenzweig, Leon Edel and Edmund Wilson), has lately been concerned with the mythic, imagistic, textual, rhetorical, stylistic, structuralist, poststructuralist, reader-response and phenomenological aspects of James's fic-tion (Austin Warren, R. P. Blackmur, Wayne C. Booth, David Lodge, Ian Watt, Tzvetan Todorov, Susanne Kappeler, Paul B. Armstrong and M. A. Williams). Other notable critics like Joseph Warren Beach, F. O. Matthiessen, Marius Bewley, F. W. Dupee, Oscar Cargill, L. B. Holland, J. A. Ward, Sallie Sears, Tony Tanner, Charles R. Anderson, Arthur Mizener, Robert Gale, Adeline R. Tintner, James W. Tuttleton, Richard A. Hocks, John Carlos Rowe, Daniel Schneider and Daniel Mark Fogel have used some of these criteria and methods in varying degrees, and have taken us into the James territory as far as we could go without loss of credibility. But there are some writers on James who, having run off the tangent in the manner of the Master himself, have caused a kind of critical vertigo. James does lure away an unwary reader or critic into such fantastic alleys, and therefore it is all the more important that we have our critical freedom in attendance, as we follow some Jamesian will-o'-the-wisp. James in his own way tried to nail down "the publishing scoundrel," though he didn't quite imagine the scoundrelly critic who would chase him out of a book if only to prove his thesis!

There is, I admit, great difficulty in pinning down James in some of the stories and novels of the later period. The text often bristles with such twists, dodges and blinds that we may never with any degree of certitude pronounce the final verdict. But this is not to say a critic should himself resort to ambiguity in dealing with it. There is perhaps no such thing as open-ended criticism. It may be the business of the writer not to resolve but to dramatize ambiguity, as J. A. Ward[17] observes, but the critic must, as far as possible, state his position, if only to prove the integrity of his own response.

Has the "cabbalistic" James, then, left a key to his hidden code in the works themselves? Or, is there indeed a key at all which will help unlock all the secrets of his pleated and plated craft? He himself dramatized the issue in an ironic vein in "The Figure in the Carpet" (1896). He has, however, elsewhere observed that where a critic is concerned with the entire body of a writer's work, his first duty is to "seek out some key" to the author's method, "some utterance of his literary convictions, some indications of his ruling theory."[18] This indeed is unexceptionable so far as it goes. However, where a writer's output is as staggeringly high and complex as James's, and where even ideas are so costumed as to appear to lose their lineaments at times, it may be fatuous to look for a master key. At best, one can hope to locate a few signs within the general code of "the indirect vision,"[19] as James styled it.

2

The Progress of an Artist

And the great domed head . . .
. . . .
. . . drinking the tone of things
And the old voice lifts itself
weaving an endless sentence.
Ezra Pound

Where a writer has left behind, to use Leon Edel's felicitous phrase, "an imperium of letters,"[1] raised over a period of nearly half a century of creative career, it should be easy enough to draw the outlines of his portrait, but the difficulty arises when we try to find the right style for it. There are so many evasions and silences, jumps and breaks, detours and decoys in this story that the "essential" James remains, despite Professor Edel's heroic evocation of the man and his industry in five insightful psychographs, something of an enigma. The portrait done by Sargent, and presented to James by his admirers on his seventieth birthday along with "a golden bowl," is perhaps the nearest any painter has come to finding the stance of his psyche—a portrait that James himself liked immensely. Here we see not the "bearded Buddha" or "the sea captain" of Lamb House, not even "a lay cardinal," but a patrician turned ambassador in the employ of a penetrating imagination. There is about the finished picture a high tone, a "rotundity of aspect," even a hint of "the portentous," to use Jamesian lexicon. This is perhaps what he wished to be, this was his *persona,* his willed mask. Whilst the "Roman" face suggests at once a packed power and an egg-shell delicacy, the penetrating eyes slightly clouded by a masterful dream[2] seem to pierce the void beyond. Even the profile done by Jacques Emile Blanche, though a more rotund presence, recalling a Victorian *paterfamilias,* yet has an intensity of gaze bordering on abstraction. And this too is the impression created by the pair of eyes in a photograph taken by Katherine E. McClellon in 1905 during James's celebrated visit to America after a lapse of years. Undoubtedly, the passion that lit up the face and the eyes was a passion that James called "the madness of art."[3] It breaks through the veneer of Victorian placidities that seem to drag down the bust to a type. Something of this impassioned truth and something of this orotund stuffiness are to be found all along in James's fiction, though as we shall see, the development of the novelist shows a marked swing in the direction of the discovery of self through the sacrificial processes of life and art.

It is one of the commonplaces of James criticism to suggest that since his lean life lacked colour and drama and storm, James, making a virtue of necessity, made art do the job of felt experience, and what is more grievous, erected an aesthetic on that basis. There is a lot to be said for this point of view, but the more important thing to remember is that the dramatization of those insufficiencies in novels, fantasies and fables shows a remarkable integrity of understanding and analysis. It may be truer to say that the real James is more to be found in his works of art than in his autobiographies, memoranda and letters. As he himself noted, "the artist is present in every page of his book from which he sought so assiduously to eliminate himself."[4] Perhaps it would be better to say that the man behind the book is consumed in the process and absorbed, rather than eliminated. It is the job of criticism to collate surmises and hints, and thus reconstruct the image out of the gathered essences. In James's view, "a writer who gives us his works is not obliged to throw his life after them, as is very apt to be assumed by persons who fail to perceive that one of the most interesting pursuits in the world is to read between the lines of the best literature."[5] Again, in his story, "The Death of the Lion" (1894), the narrator tells the nosey journalist, Mr. Morrow, to leave the convalescing novelist, Neil Paraday, alone. "The artist's life's his work," he observes, "and this is the place to observe him. What he has to tell us he tells us with this perfection."[6] Similarly, the autograph-hunting American young lady, Miss Hurter (*sic*), is advised to "succeed in never seeing him at all" in real life, for "the more you get into his writings, the less you'll want to."[7] Obviously, James is suggesting here and in so many other places, the significant extension of the artist's life into his work, the apotheosis of the self in art. This would, in a way, appear to contradict James's well-known Flaubertian dictum about objectivity and impersonality in art. But a little careful consideration will show that though James hated the idea of the omniscient author breathing down the neck of the reader, he did not believe with T. S. Eliot or the New Critics that a work of art ought to be so sovereign an artifact as to obliterate all traces of the identity between the man who suffered and the artist who created it. This, as he knew, was never a fact, for one could always feel the feathered presence of the man in the wings of the story. Thus, it is through our understanding of the numerous alter-egos James has set up in his fiction, as also through our interpretation of hidden codes and signatures, that we can best trace the history of his artistic and spiritual growth.

However, the stories and novels which dramatize James's hungers and conflicts and dreams are, on the whole, ideational extensions of his situations rather than transcriptions of the known facts of his life. In one sense, such highly organized fantasies as "The Altar of the Dead" (1895), "The Beast in the Jungle"

(1903), "The Great Good Place" (1900) and "The Jolly Corner" (1908) are essentially poems in that some of the real aches and absences are compounded in the crucible of the mind, and reshaped by the emblematic imagination of the writer. Yet to understand them, we have to understand the hidden compulsions of James's private life.

The James family is surely one of the most brilliant but baffling consanguinities of literary souls in existence. The father, Henry James Senior, whilst affirming the Christian ethos and pieties both in private conduct and in his writings, had brought up his children in an atmosphere of debate, inquiry, understanding and freedom. Himself a creative sceptic and a dissenter of utopian cast who believed in the sovereignty of the spirit, and passed from Emersonian affirmations to Swedenborgian sallies of the soul into the unknown, he wanted each member of the family to grow into knowledge as a result of his or her own achieved perceptions. Perhaps that is why the children received little of both formal and Sunday-school education. Instead, they were given at an early age, particularly William and Henry, a feel of European life so that the little New Englanders could measure for themselves their ancestral Calvinistic ethics against the backdrop of classical continuities. For William, the future world-renowned philosopher and psychologist, the European experience never became a cause of alienation, for the appeal of the American soil to this pragmatic imagination was an abiding reality. For Henry, the novelist, it constituted a fundamental change in his modes of comprehending reality and mastering it. It also meant for him a way of dramatizing the inherent ambiguities of his personal situation. We shall see this in great detail when "the International Theme" is taken up for discussion and analysis.

Henry's unconscious and deep-seated jealousy of his more successful and brilliant elder brother has, in the view of some critics, sparked off many a James story. Leon Edel invokes the Jacob-Esau[8] analogue, and goes on to interpret an earlier tale like "The Romance of Certain Old Clothes" (1868) in the light of this "complex." He even sees in the cruel and acidic Dr. Sloper of *Washington Square* (1880) hints of William James's personality. Maxwell Geismar, comparing the attitudes of the two sons towards their mother, calls William "open, easy and affectionate," and Henry, "formal, evasive, reticent," and refers to the signs in the latter of "an arrested oedipal development."[9] S. Gorley Putt concentrates more on "the geminian split in Henry's sense of experience,"[10] and traces the twinship and cousinship theme in several of James's novels and stories. All this would suggest the presence of dark, compulsive forces which decoyed the Jamesian imagination into peculiar mazes and traps. In short, the eruption of the dark element in James is not a metaphysical question as in Conrad or in Kafka,[11] but a psychic phenomenon.

Undoubtedly, the most damaging psychic wound in James's life was caused by that "horrid even if an obscure hurt"[12] which he suffered at the age of 18 in a fire accident. Since the novelist himself has clouded the issue in his characteristic evasive manner, it is not surprising that what was perhaps only a "slipped disc" or a temporary injury to his genitals has led critics to speculate about his castration and impotence. Whatever the nature of the accident, it certainly caused a deep dent in his unconscious, and lacerated his sensibility. Some of the earlier stories in particular carry the mark clearly enough, though Leon Edel sees in the missing fingers of the ghost in "The Jolly Corner" a symbolic eruption of "the obscure hurt." The more important thing, however, is the flawed nature of the aesthetic scaffolded on this grievous "fixation." It is an ersatz aesthetic, substituting art for immediacy, and making the artist a castrated monk, safe from the fleshly attractions of life. Maimed in body, health was to be recovered only in a life of the spirit embalmed in art. As R. P. Blackmur put it: "Like Abelard who, after his injury, raised the first chapel to the Holy Ghost, James made a sacred rage of his art as the only spirit he could fully serve."[13] Let it, however, be understood that this is clearly a case of "ingrown virginity," and that the elderly spinster in James later calls to question this unwholesome worship in "The Beast in the Jungle," "Mona Montravers" (1909), *The Sacred Fount* (1901), *The Ambassadors* (1903), etc. Also challenged in some later stories, though never quite repudiated, is the aesthetic built round the concept of the art as goddess and the artist as a vestal virgin.

Another "nuclear" incident of his early life is the tragic death of his cousin, Minny Temple, the eternal bride of his imagination. Her spiritual essence is not only poured into two of his finest heroines, Isabel Archer and Milly Theale, it also becomes a normative gauge of Jamesian ethics. Minny was never a fever in his blood—indeed, James seldom ran a temperature where women were concerned—she was more a silent flame he had lit up in the fastnesses of his heart. She was an image of nostalgia, James's "Bright Absentee," to use Emily Dickinson's phrase. Writing to his mother on Minny's death in his letter of March 26, 1870, he said: "As much as a human creature may, I fancy, she will survive in the unspeakably tender memory of her friends. . . . Twenty years hence what a pure eloquent vision she will be."[14] In a letter to William James, he wrote: "Her image will preside in my intellect."[15] His imagination was, therefore, to dwell for ever on "the woman lost," and perhaps one reason why James was so much occupied with the theme of death in his fiction may well be the ravishing nature of death he associated with Minny's demise. Leslie A. Fiedler, Maxwell Geismar and other critics have noted the impulse towards *thanatos* in him. In fact, toward the end, the sepulchral imagination of James is fully engaged. The symbolic turning of the face to the wall by the shattered Milly Theale in *The Wings of the Dove* (1902) certainly suggests, apart from her alienation, the idea of death as a paramour. We are again reminded of Emily Dickinson, another virgin burning to the wick, and craving a similar ravishment.

James's love-life (if, indeed, he had any) as we piece it from his letters, autobiographical writings and contemporary sources, is again not half so well realized as from those stories and novels wherein he is either rationalizing his uneasiness and failure of nerve in his relations with Miss Constance Fenimore Woolson as in "The Aspern Papers" (1888) and "The Altar of the Dead," or voicing the long ache not of unrequited but unsolicited love, as in "The Beast in the Jungle," "Mona Montravers," "The Bench of Desolation" (1909), "The Velvet Glove" (1909) and, above all, in *The Ambassadors*. We hear of James's possible affairs with Sarah Wister, Edith Wharton and others, but it is obvious that no woman ever really brought him to the boil. There was always something Prufrockian about him in the manner of the hero of "Crapy Cornelia" (1909), an inhibitive element that turned his passion into thought, and his thought into psychic self-abuse. He simply did not appear to have the daring of his emotion, and that accounts for the warm but simulated embroidery of sentiment woven by him in some of the stories about the "missed" life. There is, however, never a doubt as to the essential sincerity of his lamentation over the waste in his emotional life. Strether's famous advice to little Bilham in *The Ambassadors* about the need to make the best of one's youth, and John Marcher's horror at the discovery of his ineluctable void in "The Beast in the Jungle" are nothing but the wailings of a heart grown cold in the service of pure form and propriety. The desire to warm his hands on the fire of life, to use a phrase from Landor, is perhaps the single greatest motif in his later fiction. Herbert Dodd wasting away his years on "the bench of desolation," and the telegraphist girl trapped "in the cage" of her sexual inhibitions and fantasies are terrible pictures of emotional erosion and subversion. Again, Traffles in "Mona Montravers" contrasting "the sense of decency" with "the sense of life" appears to be speaking for James when he says to his wife: "What do we know about the sense of life—when it breaks out with real freedom? It has never broken out here, my dear, for long enough to leave its breath on the window-pane. But they got it strong down there in Puddick's studio."[16] Also, the way repressed sexuality erupts in his later novels such as *What Maisie Knew* (1897), *The Awkward Age* (1899) and *The Sacred Fount* (1901), and makes James appear a desperate *voyeur* and an old snooper stuck up on nymphets and nubile girls, would suggest the nature of the ravages caused. Again, the letters addressed late in life to the young American sculptor, Hendric Christian Anderson, to Dudley Jocelyn Persse, and to the *Times* Correspondent in Paris, Morton Fullerton, do suggest a streak of homosexuality in James, and the story "The Pupil" (1891) has lately been interpreted in that light; but I think the erotic imagery and idiom of the letters again merely point out the yearning in James for human and youthful rather than physical intimacy in a world of diminishing relationships and increasing brutalities. It would also be stretching the meaning of "The Great Good Place" to affirm that the desire for a monastic man's world as expressed in that story stipulates pederastic urges. The pictured utopia rather expresses man's archetypal longing for getting "inside the whale."

This "stag" club idea also would then seem to connect with James's view of marriage as an impediment to artistic life. No doubt in "The Lesson of the Master" (1888) and other similar tales James voices such sentiments, and in some of his letters seems to regard marriage as some kind of an extravagance and a "luxury." Also, there is hardly a happy marriage in his entire fiction, and two of his greatest books, *The Portrait of a Lady* and *The Golden Bowl,* give harrowing pictures of emotional spoliation and spiritual travail in married life. But I do not believe, as Leon Edel does, that "the marriage tie, to Henry's vision, was a tie which enslaved"[17] eternally, or that it impoverished the life of the spirit always. Nor do I feel that women were to James merely "lovely creatures to be admired . . . and nothing more."[18] In fact, the institution of marriage as such is never questioned. On the contrary, the nuptial imagery of his novels and criticism strongly suggests his belief in the mystic consummation of man and wife. I think Laurence Bedwell Holland to be essentially right when he observes that James's own unwillingness or failure to marry does not diminish the value of marriage per se in his scheme of things. James associates "the form of marriage with commitments of the profoundest sort,"[19] as he puts it. If an Isabel Archer or a Maggie Verver has a shattering experience in marriage, it is in marriage too that she grows rich in suffering, graduates to a higher consciousness, and discovers her true self. It's the paradox of marriage that it releases the spirit even as it constrains life. The form imposes order on the chaos of passion, and alone gives it significant meaning. This, as we shall see, is also a point emphasized repeatedly in James's poetics. Again, women are not presented in his work as mere social entities good for mild, delicious dialogues. In fact, his best prose is inspired by their mystic charm and promised fulfillment. There is even a kind of "female principle" at work in his fiction which rests on the view that whatever happiness can be wrested from life comes through contact with these light but luminous "vessels" of eternity, these "doves" and "princesses" of paradise.

If a Euphemia ("Madame de Mauves," 1874) turns the marriage into a steel cage, or a Madame de Cintre (*The American,* 1877) shuns it and enters a convent, the fault is found not with the form but with the rigid puritan ethics of the American woman, with the heartless code of honour of the French nobility.

There is one more incident of James's life which is truly of a traumatic nature, and has profoundly affected his later fiction. I am, of course, referring to the *Guy Domville* affair. James had always hankered after the stage, and when after the "failure" of his naturalistic novels, he turned to the theatre, he was as much exploiting what he called "the mercenary muse" as fulfilling a deep requirement of his artistic soul. But the opening night incident in London in January 1895 when James was booed and jeered at by "a brutal gallery" led to an agonizing reappraisal of his artistic purposes. Writing to John Hay, he observed: "The theatre indeed is a black abyss of platitude and vileness."[20] In part, what really happened had been seen in a flash of apprehension by James a few hours before the spectacle of his disgrace. Writing to Minnie Bourget who had wished him luck, he remarked: "It is five o'clock in the afternoon, and at 8.30 this evening *le sort en est jeté*—my poor little play will be thrown into the arena—like a white Christian virgin to the lions and the tigers."[21] What I wish to emphasize here is the nature of the sexual imagery, suggesting an unconscious compounding of the two grievous tragedies of his life, theatrical and sexual. However, it was James's unique achievement to tease a victory out of defeat. The "dramatic" form of the later novels such as *The Other House, The Spoils of Poynton, What Maisie Knew* and *The Awkward Age*, as also the psychological drama of the great triptych, *The Ambassadors, The Wings of the Dove* and *The Golden Bowl*, owe their artistic triumph partly to the training he acquired in the writing of his still-born plays. His genius was not essentially theatrical but poetic, and the novel alone offered a form which could at once comprehend poetry and drama. Had James succeeded on the stage at this time of his career, it is doubtful if he would have returned to what he called, "the other ink, the sacred fluid of fiction." He ruefully acknowledged the point in "The Next-Time," where the narrator tells us that after his failure to write best-sellers, his friend Limbert had to return to "the sincerities of his prime." For him, then, "the only success worth one's powder was success in the line of one's idiosyncrasy."[22]

Here was then a classic example of an emotionally starved psyche finding its passional correlative in art. If James does bounce back to life, it is via art, despite his questionable aesthetic.

James's literary career has traditionally been divided into three phases or periods: 1870–1880 (the period of apprenticeship and "the International Theme"), 1881–1895 (the period of maturity, moral realism and naturalism) and 1896–1904 (the period of indirection, symbolism and metaphysical concerns). Philip Guedalla's well-known quip about the three dynastic Jameses—James I, James II and the Old Pretender—appears to have been based on some such conventional, but simplistic, division. There is evidently some attraction in the arrangement, for the three periods correspond to the three phases of man's life—youth, middle years and old age. And this kind of division is applicable to most writers, for the very processes and abrasions of life involve changing insights into the meaning of society, self and existence. James criticism has not been slow to use the Shakespeare analogy, and to show, with considerable force, the similar nature of the dialectics of growth in two of the greatest masters of the imagination in the English language. Evidently, then, James's arc of understanding describes an archetypal pattern. However, it must be remembered that the qualitative leaps in his visions and techniques present enormous difficulties of interpretation. His antithetical mode of comprehending and presenting reality combined with his nuclear obscurities, ellipses and elisions often leaves us guessing as to the meaning of the change. This may be so because of James's radical scepticism which in the end seems to challenge the very show a loving imagination has created. Taken that way, the idea of growth itself may be suspect. All that we can do, therefore, is to stop for breath at a few levels in the spiralling house of his fiction.

Some of the major themes and even techniques of his fiction abide till the end, though they acquire fresh dimensions and aspects en route. Thus, such themes as the international question, the felicities, enticements and treacheries of art, appearance and reality, innocence and experience, the sin of human manipulation, the discovery of the self through suffering and travail, the growth of consciousness into conscience are to be found all along in his fiction in one form or another, though one major theme of his later years—the ache of the missed intensities of life—naturally does not fully surface till the onset of what Maxwell Geismar wittily calls James's "menopausal mood."[23] Similarly, the values of moral beauty and decency, renunciation and sacrifice, freedom and accommodation, as he sees them,[24] are enshrined in his work from *Roderick Hudson* to his unfinished novel, *The Ivory Tower* (1917), and these are never subjected to irony, which, otherwise, is a pervasive instrument of both fun and cognition in James. Also, we are left in no doubt in regard to his distaste for vulgarity, provincialism, shabbiness and adventurism. Again, the characteristic technique of "the commanding centre" or "the point of view" first seen at work in *Roderick Hudson* remains with James intermittently till the end, though in the final phase he moves on from the technique of the single point of view, as in *The Ambassadors,* to the technique of multiple points of view, as in *The Wings of the Dove* and *The Golden Bowl,* a shift perhaps from monism to pluralism or relativism in terms of philosophy. Also, the narrators, "reflectors" and confidantes, though they become more and more subtle as their tribe multiplies, are there to be seen in some of his earliest stories, *nouvelles* and novels. The prose style does change considerably, as I hope to show in a separate essay, though the later dense and metaphorical style is stipulated by James's rhetoric in the earlier books. What is really new in the final phase is the "Manneristic" style of the architectonics employed by him to achieve a break-through in vision. How one views this depends upon the nature of one's response to the problem of complexity and obscurity in literature and art.

Though there have always been ardent admirers of the novels and tales written by James in the first, experimental phase, the popular critical kudos have gone to the James of the middle period, with *The Portrait of a Lady* assuming the dignity and weight of a classic. To this period also belong the three "naturalistic" novels, *The Bostonians, The Princess Casamassima* and *The Tragic Muse,* which, particularly the first two, have now been securely placed as important landmarks in the James canon, thanks to the restorative and balanced criticism of F. R. Leavis, Lionel Trilling, Marius Bewley and others. Dr. Leavis, in particular, regards this phase as "the highest plateau" on the Jamesian landscape, for he finds the moral realism of the Master as profoundly structured as the realism of George Eliot. He finds in him those great ethical and racial continuities that make up "the Great Tradition." Correspondingly, he regards the James of the final phase depleted in inner resources, and striking out for ambiguities and inflated rhetoric to hide the poverty of his perceptions. The moral concerns of the later books lose themselves in the sandy wastes of intellection and ratiocination. What Dr. Leavis and some other critics miss in them is the clear, sun-lit quality and sparkle of the earlier books, their settled serenity and spiritual beauty. This view of some of the great earlier and middle-period novels is shared by several notable critics; what is not granted by the more informed James criticism since F. O. Matthiessen's designation of the later period as "the major phase" is the thesis that James's later books are merely cloudy integuments of a mind in disarray, the work of a tired craftsman whose hand has lost its uncommon cunning. It is exactly in the deepening and widening of the moral insights, and in the evolvement of the "mannered" and indirect style that it finds the later novels and tales truly great and magnificent. I am essentially in sympathy with the view of Matthiessen and later critics, though, like some of them, I am distressed at times by Jamesian pyrotechnics, particularly in *The Sacred Fount,* and in later inflated and overrated tales like "The Great Good Place," "The Figure in the Carpet," etc. They are unique in that no one else in the history of world fiction could have written them, but their very singularity or originality, if you like, finally reduces their value. Their purely ideational character does not always authenticate them as typical human experience. They are ideas on verbal stilts—magnificent trick-work, but non-starters otherwise. However, such novels of the later phase as *The Spoils of Poynton, What Maisie Knew, The Awkward Age,* apart from the three great masterpieces, are, despite some arid patches, the work of a Shakespearian imagination at the height of its powers. In fact, I find such a summation of all the Jamesian endowments of vision and craft inevitable in the novels of the final phase. All the needles since his earliest creations clearly pointed in the direction his muse was destined to take. And there was perhaps yet another James burgeoning in *The Ivory Tower,* poised for a social vision of reality achieved after his visit to America in 1905, but we may not go beyond the surmise that he had had at last a glimpse of the dark pit of piled, ill-gotten millions on which the superstructure of Western culture stood. Perhaps "the imagination of disaster" which had realized the destructive evil of dark sexuality in such novels as *The Other House* and *What Maisie Knew* was finally groping towards its passional correlative in the pervasive evil of dark finance.

What then, one may ask, is the form or style of James's evolution? Does he remain an acute case of arrested, baulked and fixed personality as Maxwell Geismar believes, or does he, despite his crippling insufficiencies, keep moving in an essentially creative manner? If we examine the huge corpus of his writings from the point of view of the kinetics of art, we cannot help but notice the energies that agitate and enliven his creations. There is all along a feeling of swing and stir, of a breeze felt in the face. To be sure, there are a few dead kittens around, but the abiding impression is one of flow and movement and flight.

At the outset of his career, we find James's imagination quivering at the thought of the romantic reaches and promises of life. *Roderick Hudson,* the first ripe fruit of his artistic engagement, is all aglow with the heat of emotion. If the raging, destructive passion of the young American sculptor is distrusted by James because he finds its explosiveness inimical to the health of the artist who must cultivate "coolness," it is also precisely the existence of such a raging passion that makes art possible in his view. This paradox of art—the packing of passion in ice—gives the novel its tension and poetry, though it is nearly ruined by melodrama in the end. Christina Light, nevertheless, remains one of the most alluring products of the romantic imagination. She keeps James's conduits open for the emotions to seek transcendence. Similarly, *The American* is more than an international tale, it is a magnificent exercise in the reality of romance. Christopher Newman is a voyager in the deeps of life, and though his boat is severely rocked in the end, he too has seen in the face of Madame de Cintre the trembling possibilities of a mystic shore, real enough to beguile his fancy. This extra-sensory apprehension of reality is beautifully described by James in his preface to *The American* written for the New York Edition of 1905, when he contrasts "the real" with "the romantic." "The real," he says, "represents to my perception the things we cannot possibly not know, sooner or later, in one way or another. The romantic stands, on the other hand, for the things that with all the facilities in the world, all the wealth and all the courage and all the wit and all the adventure, we never can directly know, the things that can reach us only through the beautiful circuit and subterfuge of our thought and desire."[25]

However, James does acknowledge the paucity of the facts of life in these earlier novels, and in the preface to *Roderick Hudson* admits the meagreness of illustration which is sought to be compensated through embroidery and intensity. As he puts it: "The damage to verisimilitude is deep."[26] In *The Portrait of a Lady,* which marks the beginning of the middle phase, James has already struck a happy balance between romance and reality. The observed and felt facts of life are now more densely woven into the tapestry, and "the watcher in the window" takes in an eyeful of details. Isabel Archer's romanticism is tempered with irony, though its essential beauty still moves us deeply. It is not surprising that his movement now is further and further in the direction of realism. If *The Portrait of a Lady* was written under the influence of the moral realism of George Eliot and the affective realism of Turgenev, his next two novels, *The Bostonians* and *The Princess Casamassima,* in particular, sought to absorb the naturalism of Zola and Maupassant. The evocation of Boston in the one, of London in the other, is based on the concrete, observed and felt facts of the case. However, James's poetry is in constant attendance even here, and *The Princess Casamassima* and a part of *The Tragic Muse* have some splendid moments of the poetic truth that seems to undercut the naturalism of these novels. Nevertheless, it is for their social structuring and knotted realism that they have been acclaimed by F. R. Leavis and Lionel Trilling.

The novels and tales of the final phase once again swing back to romanticism, though this romanticism in its Gothic structures and "Mannerist" style is different from the impressionistic romanticism of *Roderick Hudson* or of *The American* or of *The Portrait of a Lady.* Now the observed facts of life are passed through distorting mirrors and multiple prisms, and the refracted images are teasingly tenuous and ambiguous. Dream, fantasy, symbol and myth reinforce reality, and the language becomes highly metaphorical and involved. The shift is from the concrete to the apprehended, from solidity to ambience or psychic atmosphere. It is in these final novels of "the crowded consciousness" that we feel James has pawned the imagination perhaps to some higher purpose. It will be wrong to assume that since the imagination at times takes the bit in its teeth and sheers off in the direction of pure thought or pure fantasy, all reality also slips through and is lost. Actually, James has only shuffled the cards of reality in a bid to achieve the breakthrough. He grievously overplays his hand as, for instance, in *The Sacred Fount,* but this does not invalidate his pictures in other novels of this period. Obviously, James felt, as Shakespeare did in his romances of the final phase, particularly in *The Tempest,* the need to radically readjust his sights to come to terms with reality. The truth in the end is veiled, and the mystery abides. The hand that seeks to break the code needs must turn to hieroglyphics.

This kind of development is perhaps best described in the idea of "the dialectic of the spiral return" pursued by Daniel Mark Fogel in his *Henry James and the Structure of the Romantic Imagination.*[27] It is a circular movement where the union of romance and reality is consummated as an act of the imagination. To put it differently, there is in the final phase a coalescence of the poet and the novelist, of the *vates* and the fabulist. The interpenetration of the two basic modes of comprehending the human reality is then achieved through a sacrificial aesthetic and an evolved dialectic.

Before I sum up James's progress as an artist, it is important to know why there is a shift in his vision and in his perspective toward the end. In Michael Egan's view, "a fundamental shift in sensibility and aesthetic"[28] is clearly visible after 1895, by which time Ibsen had begun to exert a powerful influence on James. That "the Ibsen factor" is now a recognized premise in any interpretation of the final phase may not be disputed, but that it's so central and so crucial is not easy to establish. Whether "the golden bowl was struck in Norway"[29] or not, the fact remains that the Master was now beginning to assemble all his powers of penetration and statement to be spiritually ready for the scuffle with reality, albeit in his late "indirect" manner.

If Egan insists upon Ibsen's influence, Richard A. Hocks sees the benign ghost of William James secretly at work in the novelist's thought. He interprets William's pragmatism as a very different kind of set of values from what it purported to be at the putative and functional level. "In fact, one could," says Hocks, "call it the epistemological assumptions of realism pushed to their very limit," and he adds, "Pragmatist thought is essentially circular in mode."[30]

However, the concept of circularity that Fogel and Hocks advance in their own way is challenged in some respects by Ralf Norrman in his prickly and provocative book, *The Insecure World of Henry James* (1982). Norrman argues that the Jamesian world is, at heart, full of epistemological confusion, if not chaos, and that his whole theory and practice of "chiastic inversion," in pattern, in structure, and in language has a tremendous leak. This is really not a new charge, though James's celebrated ambiguity is increasingly receiving a new kind of attention, as in *The Concept of Ambiguity* (1977) by Shlomith Rimmon.

Stephen Spender has observed[31] that there are two modes of experience and development in literary and artistic life, from romance to realism as in the case of Goethe and Yeats, and from realism to some kind of romance as in the case of Shakespeare, Henry James and T. S. Eliot. It may perhaps be truer to assert that every writer or artist needs a transference from one form to the other in order to achieve a totality of vision. But in doing so he does not dispute the validity of the earlier mode; he only subsumes it under the new. Yeats, for instance, does not cease to be romantic in the later poems, nor does Keats, who too was moving from "feathers to iron" in the end. Similarly, James has not forsworn the realistic modes of understanding reality; he has added "invention" to "observation," and not moved from "observation to invention," as Mr. Spender opines. For Henry James in particular, the wheel of experience comes full circle when he shifts from the romanticism of the earlier novels to the realism of those written during the middle years, and then swings back to a new form of romanticism in the productions of the final phase. We may say that in the end he at once comprehends the reality of romance and the romance of reality.

3

A Theory of the Novel

Of all the major novelists in the English language, few have left behind such an acute and sensitive body of comment on the theory, soul and genius of the novel as Henry James has. Other notable practitioners of the craft like D. H. Lawrence, Virginia Woolf and E. M. Forster have certainly examined in some depth the nature or character of the genre that solicited their imagination and drew them to it as to a flame, but none of them, I think, has James's monkish and passionate concern with the dialectics of the novel. This, however, is not to suggest anything like a doctrinaire approach, or even a complete or consistent view of fiction in James, for as we shall see, some aspects of his admirable theory seem to have been stretched with a view to accommodating or justifying his own fantastic experiments in form. What's more, his own practice or exercise appears, particularly in his later works, to run counter to some of his cherished ideas in regard to the health of the novel. When James the theorist and James the novelist coalesce as in *The Portrait of a Lady,* we find him proving the truth of his "theory" on the pulse, as it were, but when the execution outdistances, and indeed invalidates it, as in *The Sacred Fount,* we are left with a maverick on our hands. James's perceptive paradox of the form being best preserved when it is violated is well illustrated in the great triptych of the final phase, but this does not allow us to equate anarchy with resilience. In sum, then, his "poetics" constitute, despite some obvious shortfalls, the most insightful single attempt ever made to understand the psyche of fiction. We do not have here the Aristotelian logic, clarity and hardness, because James's criticism is essentially impressionistic and "manneristic," as is his art. But we do have here a rare intelligence at work, scaffolding more a *vision* of the novel than its geometry or science. I think Robert Marks is only partially correct when he remarks that James "found the philosophy of fiction a chaos and left it a science."[1] He did find it a chaos, but he left it, not a complete aesthetic, but a complex of great insights and impressions.

It should be obvious from the above that James took no special care to develop through his critical writings a consistent, demonstrable theory of the novel as such. However, it is possible to distill such a "theory" from the mass of comments when we sift and collate them. A few running threads will be found in almost everything he wrote concerning the subject—essay, review, preface, notebook, letter, tale or novel. Thus we can, I trust, gather a fairly viable pattern of his philosophy of fiction from the following writings: his seminal essay, "The Art of Fiction" (1884); his reviews of the works of the French novelists such as Flaubert, George Sand, Emile Zola, Guy de Maupassant; his comments on the Russian novelists such as Turgenev, Tolstoy and Dostoievsky; his views on the English novelists such as Scott, Dickens, Trollope, Stevenson and Arnold Bennett; his critical biography of Hawthorne; his recently revived essay called "The Future of the Novel" (1900); his memorable address, "The Lesson of Balzac," delivered in America in 1905; his controversial correspondence with H. G. Wells; his notebooks published since his death and his stories of writers and artists, etc. It is, I admit, a complex pursuit, but the lineaments of the "theory" may not be realized otherwise. It may also be pertinent to add that my concern here is not with James the critic as such, but with James the artist who brooded over the mysteries of his craft to seize upon the essence.

Before James settled down seriously to the business of writing fiction, he had been, as we know, doing a considerable amount of reviewing. In all those formative years of his literary life, he continued to examine deeply and steadily the undercurrents that fed fiction and made it a unique artistic experience. Something in the novel set his soul aflutter, and though he was to experience its "mystic" delight only when he was himself fully immersed in the element, he could clearly savour, at the start, the taste of this inebriating brew. However, the novel, which was to become for him an instrument of visionary quest, remained, he ruefully acknowledged, a "pudding" or a "dessert," almost a bauble, in England and America. Even more distressing, it was not only regarded by Victorian parents as something really "disreputable," but also "false," a thing untrue to life—a view shared even by some of the practicing novelists of the day. Mark Ambient's wife, agonizing over her husband's fictional ethics in "The Author of Beltraffio" (1884), regards the novel as an exercise in wickedness. As Ambient tells the narrator: "Yet her conception of a novel—is a thing so false that it makes me blush. It's a thing so hollow, so dishonest, so lying, in which life is so blinked and blinded, so dodged and disfigured that it makes my ears burn. It's two different ways of looking at the whole affair."[2] Considering "this old evangelical hostility"[3] to the novel, James could not but look with envy and nostalgia in the direction of France where the genre had been for long *discutable,* a conscious and sovereign work of art in its own right. It was thus one of his deepest desires to see it established as a compeer of painting and sculpture in the English-speaking world. That is why form assumed for him almost spiritual dimensions.

Though the novelists before James fully realized the comic, satiric and homilectic potentialities of the novel, not many saw it as a qualitatively new genre, singularly suited to the rendition of the involved, confused and tortured relationships of an industrial society in transition. That is what Dickens realized in his final phase with the darkening of his vision. James never quite understood till perhaps the unfinished *Ivory Tower* the revolutionary role of the novel as a mirror of bourgeois consciousness, but he did view it as the finest instrument capable of registering moral and spiritual changes in men and societies. The way it could orchestrate the entire span of psychic and social life gave it a marked edge over other forms of literature. In fact, he could distinctly feel its modernity and its catholicity. It was a form that comprehended at once fable and drama, poetry and music, painting and architecture. It was, so to speak, the most complete genre yet invented. Conrad also fully understood this, as did D. H. Lawrence, who, in his characteristic manner, declared that the novel "was the highest form of human expression so far achieved."[4] Thus, for James too, it came to mean perhaps the ultimate art. Why it took so long to come of age, he did not quite care to go into, though he did observe: "It arrived, in truth, the novel, late at self-consciousness."[5]

Though James couldn't have foreseen the fantastic experiments in this genre in all their aspects leading to the "Antinovel" itself, he did seem to comprehend its very special place as an instrument of perception and cognition in a society threatened by internal contradictions of a stupendous character. To put it differently, something in the nature of the fictive process itself demonstrated the novel's worth as a phenomenological artifact duplicating reality through linguistic devices and narrational strategies, which, if understood in their evolved, organic and interlocking relationships, yielded insights into the human condition itself. The novel, thus understood, became *the ultimate form,* so to speak. It became a register of mankind's being, evolution and future. It showed how under aesthetic "heat" or pressure, it became a metaphor for life.

What impressed James most about the novel was its utmost freedom and resilience, its unlimited appetite for all forms of reality. It could literally appropriate the most intimate as well as the remotest shades of human experience. Above all, it could find a suitable framework to accommodate all kinds of complex and multiplying relationships. As he put it in "The Future of the Novel," it is "of all pictures the most comprehensive and the most elastic. It will stretch anywhere, it will take in absolutely anything. All it needs is a subject and a painter. But for its subject, magnificently it has the whole human consciousness."[6] Again, in the preface to *The Ambassadors,* he talks of the novel as "the most independent, most elastic, most prodigious of literary forms."[7] Obviously, James was thrilled by the artistic possibilities and complexities and challenges latent in it. He could almost see in it his own salvation. James's idea of freedom involved not only the choice of the subject or theme or what he called *donnée,* but also the novelist's manner of executing it. All we are concerned with is the end-product. What devices, sleights-of-hand, idiosyncrasies of style or subterfuges he elects to employ in the interests of both effect and authenticity are entirely his own affair. There is no limit to invention, no limit to artifice. No novelist may lay down a formula for "the good novel," he observes in "The Art of Fiction," which he wrote by way of a support and a rejoinder to Walter Besant's lecture on the subject. The novel, he says, "lives upon exercise, and the very meaning of exercise is freedom. The only obligation to which in advance we may hold a novel, without incurring the accusation of being arbitrary, is that it be interesting."[8] This is as large a charter for the novel as we could draw up, though it carries within it seeds of anarchy, if we understand "freedom" and "exercise" to mean uncontrolled fantasy. The idea of the novel's freedom from restraints is once again taken up in the preface to *The Portrait of a Lady*. "The house of fiction," writes James, "has in short not one window, but a million—a number of possible windows not to be reckoned, rather; every one of which has been pierced, or is still pierceable in its vast front, by the need of the individual vision and by the pressure of the individual will."[9]

The idea of the novel being, in the final analysis, a uniquely personal interpretation of life is present in James's work from the start. Each mind is peculiarly equipped to penetrate the protean human reality and scoop up as much of it as it could hold. At the bottom of it all is the Jamesian belief in three things: the idea of nescience or the fundamental unknowability of human reality, the idea of the relativity of human truth, and the idea of the human consciousness as a *tabula rasa*, a blank page to be inscribed or written upon. These "metaphysical" positions are not as much argued in James's critical writings as assumed. In the novels and tales, they are worked out in the plot and in the disposition of characters. For instance, the way irony works consistently in his books would suggest a settled scepticism in his attitude towards reality. All absolutes, whatever the field—ethics, religion or politics—are distrusted, and as every Jamesian reader would testify, there inheres in his philosophical stance a fundamental ambiguity. Again, such open-ended novels as *The Portrait of a Lady, The Ambassadors* and *The Wings of the Dove* lead one to believe that their author kept the complex of choices or the channels of action open, emphasizing once again the inscrutability of life and the mystery of character. As for the value of consciousness as a plastic plate acquiring multiple and diverse impressions, or as a musical instrument throbbing to all manner of wandering airs, we have only to look at the dramas of rich and crowded consciousnesses he has created in scores of novels and stories. Thus, I return to the point that to James the novel was a highly personal mode of comprehending reality and making it significant or meaningful. "A novel," he avers, "is in its broadcast definition a personal, a direct impression of life."[10] Obviously, he is, amongst other things, concerned with the cognitive character of the novel.

James also affirms in so many places the view that art lives upon selection and rearrangement. Life is all chaos and confusion, all welter and anarchy. If life were to invade literature with its terrible fluidity, promiscuity and irrationality in its primary form, no frame such as even the-stream-of-consciousness novel has devised could withstand the assault; it would buckle and go under. Form alone gives meaning to experience. In his unfinished novel, *The Sense of the Past* (1917), Pendrell, another Jamesian alter-ego, observes that "detachment and selection, prime aids of the artist, were the sacred sparenesses menaced by a rank growth of material."[11] Thus, the individual consciousness operating on the jungle of impressions and reactions has to snatch or track down significant moments, and then shuffle them about in a bid to create patterns that may endure. In other words, the felt reality has to be dissolved in the crucible of the imagination to acquire beauty and poetry and significance. James is also quite clear on the subject of typicality despite the fact that some of his own later compositions are anything but typical. "Art," he writes, "is essentially selection, but it is a selection whose main care is to be typical, to be inclusive."[12] What, in fact, he is asserting is a synthesis of the uniquely individual and the known universal in human experience. Thus, the novel is a rendered or pondered summary of life which admits of a great deal of the play of the mind and the imagination.

This emphasis on "selection" may not be confused with the imposition of a strict, preconceived pattern upon experience. Nothing was further from James's mind than the idea of a fixed mould, whether compositional or thematic. Within the broader categories of organic growth and related form, a novelist, in his view, was free to let his imagination blow, like the winds of heaven, where it pleased. "Catching the very note and trick," he writes in "The Art of Fiction," "the strange irregular rhythm of life, that is the attempt whose strenuous force keeps Fiction upon her feet. In proportion as in what she offers us we see life *without* rearrangement do we feel that we are touching the truth; in proportion as we see it *with* arrangement do we feel that we are being put off with a substitute, a compromise and convention."[13] Obviously, this does not invalidate James's idea regarding the necessity of imposing form upon the chaos of experience; it only strengthens the view that the novel must ultimately have the colour and aroma of life.

Though James emphasizes the fact of personal experience in the writing of a novel, he seems to view the subject from a larger angle. Experience for him means much more than one's individual involvement in or knowledge of a certain situation as could be gathered, directly and indirectly, frontally and tangentially. It would suggest the value of intuition, fancy, epiphany and the like in the making of one's experience, amongst other things. Elaborating the point in "The Art of Fiction," he remarks: "Experience is never limited, and it is never complete; it is an immense sensibility, a kind of huge spider-web of the finest silken thread suspended in the chamber of consciousness, and catching every air-borne particle in its tissue." A little later in the same essay, he talks of "the power to guess the unseen from the seen."[14] It will appear, therefore, that James is very likely writing here an apologia for the type of fantasies he himself came to write later in his career. Maxwell Geismar's objection that by "experience" James means here and elsewhere "experience in the mind of the artist," rather than general human experience is well taken up to a point, for there is a fatal tendency in the later James to equate ratiocination and abstraction with experience. This, however, does not mean that he undervalues the social and communal aspects of experience. In the preface to *The Princess Casamassima,* he writes: "Experience, as I see it, is our apprehension and our measure of what happens to us as social creatures—any intelligent report of which has to be based on that apprehension."[15] Only it will be nearer James's intention, if we were to see his extension of experience in the light of what constitutes "the romantic" for him in his memorable words on the subject in the preface to *The American.* The romantic imagination is always, after a stage, the imagination of proxy. James is rightly accused of offering ersatz or fake experience at times, but we must not forget that beyond a certain level, the imagination can with felicity appropriate the experience of others. Also, the life of the mind is an experience in itself, and this too is worthy of rendition in its own right.

James regarded the novel as an organic entity developing from a "germ" or a "seed" in accordance with the principles of its growth. It was Yeats's "great-rooted blossomer" whose leaf and blossom and "bole" formed an indivisible unity. Each part was related to the other parts and to the whole in a dark, fecund manner. That is why it is possible to regard the Jamesian novel as an expanding metaphor. James, therefore, discouraged the "old-fashioned distinction between the novel of character and the novel of incident," for, in his view, character and incident were umbilically tied to each other. "What is character," he asks, "but the determination of incident? What is incident but the illustration of character?"[16] This integral interplay of character and incident in his own works leads to what Leon Edel has appropriately called "psychological determinism."[17] The characters "live out their natures" in the course of the story, and the incidents are the end-product of the dreams and fevers and distempers thus worked off.

Similarly, James stipulates an organic link between form and substance, technique and theme. His whole industry, as we know, was geared to "the search for form," because to him no novel was worth its salt till it had evolved a viable framework which could carry the burden of its *donnée.* His criticism of the "loose baggy monsters" of Tolstoy and Dostoievsky, though ill-conceived on the whole, was nevertheless based on the view that where a novelist failed to impose a form upon his fluid material, the result was likely to be most discouraging, except in the case of a great genius who might, so to speak, prevent the book from falling apart by the sheer force of his native endowments. In any case, such a novel would be a *sui generis* case, a treacherous example for those less gifted. In a letter to Hugh Walpole written in 1912, he repeats: "Form alone takes and holds and preserves substance—saves it from the welter of helpless verbiage—the *found* form (because the sought for) is his absolute citadel and tabernacle of interest."[18] In an earlier essay like "The Art of Fiction," he uses a sartorial metaphor to describe the relationship between form and theme. "The story and the novel, the idea and the form," he says, "are the needle and thread."[19] Later, this relationship is viewed in the Prefaces in terms of "marriage" and "sacrament." The achieved novel then is a consummation in a "mystic" manner. The point is again emphasized somewhat differently in a letter to Auguste Monde in 1913: "I feel that in a literary work of the least complexity the very form and texture are the substance itself and that the flesh is indetachable from the bones!"[20]

James's view of the novel further posits the existence and necessity of "beautiful determinants." That is to say, each situation as it develops in the story is logically and intrinsically related to, and conditioned by, certain factors, and till a novelist has exhausted all the latent possibilities of their growth and expansion, he cannot be said to have completed the job. In the preface to *The Portrait of a Lady*, he observes in this connection: "These are the fascinations of the fabulist's art, these lurking forces of expansion, these necessities of upspringing in the seed, these beautiful determinations, on the part of the idea entertained, to grow as tall as possible, to push into the light and the air and thickly flower there. . . . "[21] This law of "internal relations" is James's sacred and prized contribution to the art of the novel, and as Dorothea Krook shows convincingly, it is "not only a logical principle," but also "a view of reality, a metaphysical principle."[22] It helps one understand "the indirect vision" of the later novels.

There is yet another aspect which deeply attracted James, and that was the moral energy of the novel. He briefly alludes to it in "The Art of Fiction," though the Prefaces and his practice would more significantly illustrate the point. In questioning Walter Besant's observation regarding "the conscious moral purpose" of the novel, he is not really disputing the need for impregnating the story with moral values, for that would make nonsense of all that he stands for in fiction. And when he quips: "You wish to paint a moral picture or carve a moral statue; will you not tell us how you would set about it? We are discussing the Art of Fiction; questions of art are questions (in the widest sense) of execution, questions of morality are quite another affair,"[23] he is simply dramatizing the view that a work of art being an aesthetic artifact, above all, should be free from ethical heroics or histrionics, which is not to say at all that it must not carry a positive sum of values and positions and directions. Obviously for James, the very structure of the novel envisaged moral engagement. In fact, he fully endorsed the view of one of the Goncourts who declared that "the novel is ethics in action."[24] The dynamics of fiction required the release of moral energies. It is exactly this side of James's fiction which a critic like F. R. Leavis celebrates as of enduring value. A novelist does not have to announce or parade his ethical imperatives; the genius of the novel subsumes them. Or rather the imperatives, if any, lose their rigidity in the heat of creation, and are mellowed down to settled moral serenities. The novel, in other words, would not accept a whip, a discipline which is not of its own choosing. That is perhaps what D. H. Lawrence also meant when he declared that one couldn't "fool the novel."[25] For whenever the natural, sympathetic flow of the story was interrupted with a view to diverting it elsewhere, the novel, if it had true moral energy, would carry on despite the novelist. Most often though, like a shot bird it would fall dead in its tracks. Essentially, the moral atmosphere of a work of art was all that really mattered for James in the end. And this depended upon the quality of the moral imagination that a writer brought to bear upon the story. He puts it eloquently thus: "There is one point at which the moral sense and the artistic sense lie very near together; that is in the light of the very obvious truth that the deepest quality of a work of art will always be the quality of the mind of the producer. In proportion as the intelligence is fine will the novel, the picture, the statue partake of the substance of beauty and truth."[26]

Again, James was distressed by the angular, linear, skimpy and dubious ethics of the English Novel. By contrast, he admired the freshness and openness of the French Novel in its treatment of sex on the whole. (This did not mean that he regarded the bed-room scenes as essential for the health of the novel. On the contrary, in his essays on Zola, Maupassant and George Sand he shows positive disgust for sheer carnality or animality in fiction.) It appears somewhat odd therefore that he himself should have acquired the reputation of a prude. The fact of the matter is that James's own fiction does skirt round the subject, which, in his shy and awkward manner, he describes as "the great relation between man and woman, the constant world-renewal."[27] The eruption of sexuality in his later fiction is no evidence of James's freedom from taboos as Leon Edel seems to believe; if anything, the manner of the eruption and the forms it assumes would strongly suggest the opposite. However, this did not diminish the value James attaches to the healthy airing of the subject in the novel. For he knew that the question of morality and the question of sex finally converged on the same axis. One was, in truth, a test of the other.

And finally, James's views on the artistic sovereignty and integrity of the novel brought him into a direct confrontation with H. G. Wells, who regarded it "about as much an art form as a market place or a boulevard."[28] In this entire controversy, Wells, then at the peak of his powers and popularity, displays a characteristic brashness and insensitivity, despite the fact that his basic position in regard to art as an aid to life was unchallengeable. Summing up the differences in his letter of July 8, 1915, Wells wrote to James: "To you literature like painting is an end, to me literature like architecture is a means, it has a use. I had rather be called a journalist than an artist, that is the essence of it."[29] That James created a mystique of the novel is true enough; what is not quite true is the assumption that he regarded it as an autonomous work of art unanswerable to social reality. His repeated emphasis on the aesthetic aspects in no way militates against the view that the novel ought to be an instrument of understanding and promoting social consciousness. If this were so, he could not have admired so handsomely the bounce and vigour of Wells's own earlier novels. It is precisely their social energies which appeal to him. "The particular intentions of such matters as *Kipps,* as *Tono-Bungay,* as *Ann Veronica,*" he writes, "so swarmed about us, in their blinding, bluffing vivacity that the mere sum of them might have been taken for a sense over and above which it was graceless to inquire."[30] He would very much have desired a more formal beauty than he could find in Wells's fiction, but he never disputed its social intentions. Actually, most critics of James, dismayed by some of his own extravagant fantasies in the final phase, tend to equate his lapses from social reality with his theoretical positions in art. The fact of the matter is that in so far as there is a theory of the novel in James, it is as breezy and bracing as one could hope to find anywhere. His own practice, even when it deviates grievously, does not alter its value or validity.

There is, as I suggested at the beginning, no hard-and-fast theory of the novel in Henry James. Throughout his long creative career as novelist and critic he continued to explore the "sacred" realms of fiction as a "pilgrim" in search of the truths that made life an art and art a life, and he ranged far and wide for the purpose. His frequent use of a mixed critical lexicon based on analogies and correspondences from painting, architecture, geometry, tapestry, music, etc. would testify to his unending quest. Since his comments and observations on the essence of the novel are scattered all over, he does seem to contradict himself here and there. However, as I see it, James's contrapuntal imagination seeks to reconcile polarities, and, therefore, what might strike us as contradictions are really different but not mutually exclusive approaches to the teasing problems of art. The structural and visionary unity which he sought in the novel could only be achieved if the various pulls and pressures were given a full play. The virtues which he admired in the novel may be stated as movement, density, vividness, intensity, resilience, economy, objectivity, coherence, moral energy, rhetoric and poetry. They may not add up to a regular theory or aesthetic; they do, however, represent the best there is to seek in fiction. James was not a very original thinker, but the majesty of his imagination was so striking as to give his thought a luminous quality. He was indebted a great deal to that "beautiful genius," Turgenev, to George Eliot, to Hawthorne, and to the French naturalists, but the novelist who ultimately led him into the inner chambers of the "House of Fiction" was Balzac. He himself affirmed that he had "learned from him more of the lessons of the engaging mystery of fiction than from any one else."[31] In some essentials, his artistic credo remained unchanged over the years. As early as 1874 he defined it in a pontifical manner, reminiscent of the early T. S. Eliot. "We confess," he wrote, "to a conservative taste in literary matters—to a relish for brevity, for conciseness, for elegance, for perfection of form."[32] As he grew richer in exercise and experience, he went on expanding the view, mending his fences where necessary. The novel in the end seemed to him invested with a special vision and a special destiny.

4

The Torment of Form

In any discussion of Henry James's methods and techniques in relation to his "search for form" in fiction, we have to keep constantly in view his stated and understood positions concerning the philosophy of the novel. It is not as if he took special care to always relate practice to theory, for, as we study his notebooks and prefaces, we are struck by the freedom he allows his imagination at the conceptual level itself. To be sure, most of the novels and tales are well-pondered, well-plotted even before they emerge from the "green-room," and earn their respective forms, but a closer study of the manner in which a given plot or story finally seeks out its own "redemptive" form will show the continual presence of what I may call the imponderables of art. And this kind of creative vagueness is stipulated at the start. It is not, it may be added, a vagueness of intention or design, but a vagueness of exercise. How a *donnée* or idea will gather the hum of associations and acquire relational complexities, how it will be ravished en route and yet remain essentially inviolate, how it will in the end be consummated in form and consumed in the text, are matters that James leaves to his trusted imagination. He knows that there is nothing more explosive than a besieged imagination, which, when baited and roused, will somehow storm its way through. The beautiful difficulties and muddlements which his muse solicits and erects are not wilful obscurities except in a few lamentable cases, but the obscurities that inhere in human situations, and that alone would allow the *donnée* to fully manifest itself. For, I do believe, all the devices and auxiliaries that James the strategist keeps in reserve will not avail, unless the imagination can finally rise to the challenge. In fact, as we shall see quite often in his later fiction, the idea overreaching itself puts the forged form to a severe strain, and sometimes runs away with the situation, so to speak. The imagination, in other words, is seldom subservient to form in James; it's the form that accommodates itself to the coercive imagination. The mystery of creation abides. In the end, the processes of fiction are as mysterious, if not irrational, as the processes of poetry.

Nevertheless, the "torment of form"[1] in James is so real and acute as to raise questions regarding its philosophy as such. It should not be difficult to see that this unsleeping concern with form has aesthetic as well as sociological aspects. In other words, the chiselled, rounded structures he seeks in fiction are not, ideologically speaking, different from the stratified, ordered structures he seeks in society. In either case, the painterly eye is pleased with symmetry, smoothness, elegance and finish, though it develops a kind of fatigue in the end, showing, as it were, the boredom of brilliance. No wonder that, for Mark Ambient, as the narrator of "The Author of Beltraffio" tells us, "the passion for form" amounted to "the real search for the holy grail," and "imperfection" struck him not only "as an *esthetic* but quite also as a *social crime*"[2] (italics mine). This is quite authentically the voice of James himself, though in ridiculing the narrow ethics of the Anglo-American readership in the person of Mark Ambient's aristocratic wife, he is also questioning the excesses of that aestheticism which is hoisted as a view of art and life by J. A. Symonds, Walter Pater and others.[3] The teasing ambivalence shows that while he was almost mystically drawn to form *qua* form, he was also quite clearly uneasy about this kind of pathological fixation. That is why in a later novel like *The Golden Bowl,* for instance, the form is stretched to the utmost in behalf of the form itself. The "exquisite treacheries," manipulated here through a salvaging exercise of "insidious recoveries" and "redemptive consistencies,"[4] of which James speaks in the preface to *The Ambassadors,* thus help preserve the essential form. If the structural mould is saved by delicate infringements, so is the marital mould, the most conventional, yet beautiful, of all social forms. The double "treachery" restores the form of things, so to speak. This, of course, is no apologia for adultery—always an ugly and typically European sin in James—but an eloquent plea for compassion and understanding. Similarly, "the exquisite treachery" to Woollett in *The Ambassadors* is matched by calculated breaches in the scenic structure of the novel, which otherwise has, as E. M. Forster puts it, the rounded shape of "an hour-glass."[5] Again, the question of form in society is viewed ambivalently in the novels and tales dealing with the International Theme. As we shall see subsequently, whenever a form begins to harden and show signs of arterio sclerosis, it subverts the form itself. This is true of form as structure of the novel and as structure of society. Our concern here is with James's architectonics, not with his ethics. What artistic or even artful devices he employs to secure the significant form is what I propose to touch upon briefly in this essay.

A James novel or *nouvelle* is often born in a vicarious, if not casual, manner. A loaded hint dropped by a guest at a party or dinner, a wayside remark, heavy and dark enough to cause ripples in the mind, a newspaper "story" rich in dramatic overtones, a friendly or professional confidence exchanged over a glass of wine, a salacious scandal in the air—all these formed his celebrated "germs" or "seeds." James had the unfailing impulse of a *raconteur,* and the moment an incident or idea stood up to command attention, he grasped it by the "tail," as he often put it. For the rest, he knew how to seize or even dream up the whole "animal," even though sometimes the "tail" wagged merrily, and the face remained smudged or blotted out. All that the imagination needed was a precarious perch to balance its wings. And the more precarious it was, the more it exulted in breathless possibilities. It may even be averred that the Jamesian imagination needed ever so little to set it off; it was indeed the condition of its exercise that it operate from a pin-head. A whole continent of dreams and desires began to take shape, once he felt the fluttering presence of a beautiful idea. If it moved him deeply as in the case of *The Ambassadors,* whose *donnée* rested on the advice given by Howells to a younger compatriot, Jonathan Sturges, regarding the need to live fully and authentically in youth, then the idea-turned-flesh acquired, even after a long period of hibernation, a sensuous beauty and a finished form. If, on the other hand, the idea merely appealed to his mind because of its erotic extravagance as in *The Sacred Fount,* or because of its geometrical neatness as in *What Maisie Knew,* or because of its sheer novelty as in "The Friends of the Friends" (1896), the result, even if some kind of a tour de force, had an air of abstraction, preciosity and manipulation about it. It appears indeed that as James's muse grew older, it needed something gnarled and twisted and Gothic to sustain it. He almost came to believe that any fantastic little idea that received a treatment of the grasping imagination could somehow vindicate itself, and achieve its artistic destiny. If the idea was intrinsically thin, a mere "conceit," "a little fancy"[6] as in the case of "The Altar of the Dead," or in that of "The Friends of the Friends," poetry then had to be pressed into service to carry it through. "The Altar of the Dead," at least as I view it, is a great poem, not a great tale; the dazzlement is of treatment and rhetoric rather than of the idea as such. In fact, most of the later tales are not great archetypes of social reality, but great artifacts of creative fancy. Their fugitive and fractured nature somehow diminishes their human appeal. James arrives at the theme not by some inner or spiritual compulsion, but by some outward or fortuitous circumstance.

Sometimes the idea of a tale or a novel first appeared to him in a crude or unattractive form, and as the notebooks reveal, he would then start processing it, passing it through filters and distilling its essence. Even when he had, at times, made what he probably considered a false start, he struggled with the ideal possibilities of the idea. Sometimes an idea dropped once is taken up years afterwards, as in the case of *The Sense of the Past.* It appears as if, in such cases, James took out cold and congealed bits of mutton from the deep freeze of the mind, and then slowly heated them over the fire of the imagination to recover something of the old flavour. In this process, something was inevitably lost or destroyed. It made such stories look academic and pale-faced, as mere exercises of the disengaged imagination. However, if the shy, maidenly idea was warm and sensuous and authentic at the start, its consummation years later was always an advantage, for it then appeared to have grown silently and invisibly in the dark chambers of the unconscious to a state where it was ready to burst out of the shell. This is true of all the three great novels of the major phase. To cite an example, *The Wings of the Dove* was conceived as early as November 1894, though when it appeared finally in 1902, the "germ" had lain in "the deep well of unconscious cerebration" for years, to appear later "with a firm iridescent surface and a notable increase of weight,"[7] to recall the words James used in the preface to *The American*. The *donnée*—a young person of twenty or so, aching to live but doomed to die, "a creature dragged shrieking to the guillotine"[8]—finally found its "objective correlative" and "the chain of events" actually some twenty-five to thirty years after it must have first flashed in his mind. For the story of Milly Theale, as we know, is built round the figure of his beloved young cousin, Minny Temple, who had died of consumption in 1870. What he wrote to his mother then: "Twenty years hence what a pure eloquent vision she will be,"[9] becomes, more or less on time, an artistic truth. There is a perfect telescoping of the two images, and the emotion, now "recollected in tranquillity," has a poetic serenity and beauty about it.

Another thing to note about the Jamesian *donnée* is the nature of its birth or origin. A novelist may proceed from a pure idea or concept to the complex of characters and incidents needed to dramatize it, or he may start with some concrete fact or detail, and work out the *donnée* in the superstructure raised upon it. James's notebooks clearly establish the primacy of the latter method, though in a few significant cases—*The Sacred Fount,* "The Coxon Fund" (1894), "The Altar of the Dead," "The Figure in the Carpet," etc.—he does reverse the order. In the preface to *The Portrait of a Lady* he writes: "I might envy, though I couldn't emulate, the imaginative writer so constituted as to see his fable first and to make out its agents afterwards: I could think so little of any fable that it didn't need its agents positively to launch it."[10] In such novels and tales as *The Spoils of Poynton, What Maisie Knew,* "The Turn of the Screw," "The Aspern Papers," "A London Life," "Brooksmith," "Europe," "The Birthplace," and a host of others, he had the primary facts of the case always in hand before he set out to "rear the edifice." Even when he started with an idea and not a given concrete story from actual life, as in *Roderick Hudson, The American, The Portrait of a Lady, The Bostonians, The Princess Casamassima,* etc., he visualized it, not as an abstract ethical, artistic or political principle for which a framework had to be devised, but as an idea that inevitably, from the start, attached itself to some concrete figure, fact or outline. In other words, he was not really moved by ideas but by characters and incidents and situations. Unlike his father and elder brother, he had little enthusiasm for pure thought, or even for great world-shaking ideas. T. S. Eliot's well-known statement that James had a mind so fine, no idea could violate it, may well be stretched to mean that no fine idea could violate a mind that gave little hospitality to pure thought.

James's use in his notebooks and prefaces of such words and expressions as "germ," "seed," "acron," "virus of suggestion," etc. would naturally suggest that he took an "organicistic" view of the novel. That is to say, for him, it was a living thing that grew tall according to its inner "logic." Each "germ" or "seed" stipulated, given a proper soil and treatment, a spontaneous and natural growth. The foliage and the fruit were inevitable once the "seed" was planted in the dark bed of the imagination and allowed to shoot forth in the sun. The *freedom* of the burgeoning blossom, however, was always related to the *necessity* of the conditions bearing upon it, and this dialectic process in itself involved control and restraint. However, in his excellent opening chapter entitled "The Organic and the Scientific" in *The Search for Form,* J. A. Ward shows how the "romanticist" or the "organicist" in James is both opposed to and dovetailed with the "neoclassicist" and the "formalist" in him. The rhetoric of organicism is constantly held in check by the rhetoric of classicism. The principles of "growth" and "freedom" are balanced against the principles of "symmetry," "economy" and "composition." James, says Professor Ward, constructs his novels "both from the outside in" and "from the inside out,"[11] thus creating that poetic "tension" which results from the interplay of contraries. The two contending forces of "explosion" and "containment," or of expansion and control, struggling for supremacy, jostle each other about in continual combat and achieve a truce only when the limits of form are reached. In his essay called "The Crown," D. H. Lawrence speaks of such an archetypal combat between the male principle and the female principle of life, with victory always in the balance. If the male principle is equated with the principle of "explosion" and the female with that of "containment," we have some idea of how a Jamesian novel seeks to win its delicate, but tensile form. If, in the end, some accommodation has to be made, on the whole it will be done on the terms of the "organic" and male principle of "explosion," for in James, as I have said earlier, the form is finally, if necessary, subordinated to the imagination. The original "germ" or idea has a kinetic potential that will not be denied. In the preface to *What Maisie Knew,* he compares it to a dog that has broken loose: "Once 'out' like a house-dog of a temper above confinement, it defies the mere whistle, it roams, it hunts, it seeks out and 'sees' life; it can be brought back but by hand and then only to take its *futile thrashing*"[12] (italics mine). Obviously, whatever collar or form one may force upon it, it will continue to strain at the leash. And in this straining and stretching lies the secret of its health and beauty.

James's perennial interest in antinomies and polarities—action and stasis, being and becoming, light and dark, life and art, theme and form, America and Europe—stems from his antithetical mode of comprehending human reality, which he sees as a pair of contraries forever seeking a dialectical fusion. In the preface to his book, *Rage for Order,* Austin Warren writes: "The title of this book couples together two contraries necessary to poetry or literature—intensity and calm, initial violence sought and achieved discipline."[13] This is indeed an admirable way of describing all those novels which, like the later poems of W. B. Yeats, have the effect of a flame packed in ice. Such a novel, for instance, is Emily Brontë's *Wuthering Heights,* in which the principle of storm and the principle of calm are not only thematically, but also structurally mated, much in the manner of a Jamesian novel. "The Jolly Corner" presents, for instance, a case where the storm raging in the soul of Spencer Brydon is dissipated to make room for what James calls "serenity of certitude." In the essay devoted to Henry James's "Symbolic Imagery in the Later Novels," Mr. Warren thus concludes: "The tension in James between the dialectic and mythic is an epistemological way of naming that rich interplay and reconciliation of impulses which constitutes his great achievement."[14]

Thus, the ideal form is envisaged as the one in which the "organic" and the "scientific" interpenetrate each other to form a dialectic unity. The form, then, emerges at once from the "logic" governing the novel's inner growth and the formal restraints put upon it from the outside. That is why, finally, the best analogy, in Professor Ward's view, is furnished by architecture, which as most modern architects view it, is an organic art comprehending the principles of both space and élan vital. In the preface to *The Portrait of a Lady,* James talks of "the house of fiction" and the manner in which the "single small cornerstone, the conception of a certain young woman affronting her destiny" is laid with a view to rearing "a square and spacious house."[15] Elsewhere also architectural idiom is used to describe the dynamic and living structure of the novel he has in view. Though the incidence of architectural imagery in the novels and tales themselves is, as Robert Gale[16] tells us, rather limited, its use, I think, is truly poetic in that complex human relationships are seen figuratively in terms of both formal elegance and functional accommodation.

To achieve the appropriate form—and each story has its own unique concerns—James employed a number of aids, agents and techniques. In his introduction to the collection of prefaces entitled *The Art of the Novel,* R. P. Blackmur lists nearly all such devices which a luminous intelligence needed to arrive at the truth of things. The finished, rounded form was but the ideal vessel containing that truth. At first sight, the formidable array of agents—narrators, reflectors, *ficelles, disponibles* and fools—the complex battery of aids—mystery, muddlement, melodrama, foreboding and the portentous—and such special techniques as the commanding centre, rotation of aspects, contrast and parallelism, foreshortening, framing and scenic disguise seem to crowd the Jamesian canvas to the point of confusion, if not chaos. However, as we learn to understand the spider-like industry of the artist, all these skeins and skills fall into their proper places in the scheme of things, and we are left wondering at the miracle achieved. Sometimes, of course, a *donnée* is not strong enough to carry the full burden of some of these devices, and the tale comes to grief, but even in their failure such Jamesian productions often impress us with the magnificence of their reach and exercise.

James, it appears, is particularly fond of neat, balanced, rounded structures in fiction, and to effect them one of the most important techniques he uses is what he calls "the planned rotation of aspects." He subjects a character, incident or issue not only to an intensive, but also an extensive treatment. Things, in other words, are seen horizontally and vertically, laterally and diagonally. Intensity is a matter of feeling and emotion, but amplitude is a matter of consciousness and vision. To see, therefore, a theme or a thing in the round is to see it whole to the extent that is is humanly possible to do so. The character or the incident in question is viewed from multiple angles. It's as if several pairs of eyes have to view the same thing in slow succession before the full meaning dawns upon the reader. It is rotated before the mind's lantern in such a manner that the first impressions are at once deepened and modified. New ironic shades and nuances keep subtly changing the picture, creating a vague restiveness and tension. We are never allowed to take anything or anybody for granted. This, of course, connects also with James's scepticism, but perhaps the more important impulse at work is the classical search for perfection, for each creative scepticism stipulates a lost ideal. Thus, the multiplying mirrors, which present a character or a situation in different lights and at different levels, keep the quest alive till the end. The spherical structure, when achieved, as for instance in *The Ambassadors,* in no way exhausts the possibilities of the chief protagonists; if anything, it really defines their deepest impulses, and is organically related to their gathering vision. That is to say, form and character create each other in the process of development, and do not spend themselves entirely in doing so. The way James goes over, behind, and around a character like Strether or Fleda Vetch or Mrs. Brookenham, or a situation such as we find in *What Maisie Knew,* in *The Other House,* in *The Golden Bowl,* shows his concern for the rotundity of things. This kind of quest does, at times, turn into an abstract game of chess, as in *The Sacred Fount,* in "Julia Bride" (1908) and in other stories, and then the rounded symmetry he seeks smacks of artifice and guile. In the unfinished novel, *The Ivory Tower,* he himself makes an acute observation about the obsessive regard for rotundity in art. Here, James is describing an ivory tower, "a remarkable product of some eastern, probably some Indian patience. . . . "

> The high curiosity of the thing was in the fine work required for making and keeping it perfectly circular; an effect arrived at by the fitting together, apparently by tiny golden rivets, of numerous small curved plates of the rare substance, each of these, including those of the two wings of the exquisitely convex door, contributing to the artful, the total rotundity. The series of encased drawers worked to and fro of course with straight sides, but also with small bowed fronts, these made up of the same adjusted plates. The whole, its infinite neatness exhibited, proved *a wonder of wasted ingenuity.*[17] (Italics mine)

This appears to me to be a fairly apt epigraph for some of the later tales.

To secure the effect of rotundity, James sets up a structure of multiplying relationships. New characters and situations are created around the central *donnée* in order to explore its furthest ramifications. Nothing is added which is not strictly germane to the scheme of things. He had indeed a horror of what he called *remplissage* or "stuffing," the Victorian novel's besetting sin. For him, everything had to fall into its slot to give off its sounds. The complicated web of relationships was intended, above all, to create an atmosphere of density and "saturation"—the colour of life itself. These relationships are seldom viewed only from the outside, as Dickens and Trollope seem generally to do. The mere comedy of social forms and the conflicts arising from them are not enough for James. His needling intelligence keeps probing the hinterland of baulked and botched relationships, the abrasive processes of distrust and decay, the tragic gaps in communication and understanding, the irrational impulses and motives masquerading as injuries, the repaired fences and earned recoveries, etc. In short, all the tangled and amorphous and mercurial states of consciousness are rendered poetically with a view to establishing the ambiguity and complexity of human relationships. The later novels in particular are rich in such psychic reverberations, though from *Roderick Hudson* onwards James's interest in the psychology of involved relationships is acute enough to push almost everything else into the background.

In trying to work out the full possibilities of a *donnée,* James often ran into compositional difficulties. As we gather from his letters and notebooks, one of his major problems was to confine himself to a set number of words. The magazine editors stipulated a certain length, and, despite his great regard for economy, he often overshot the mark widely. Thus, sometimes, a story turned into a *nouvelle,* and a *nouvelle* into a full-blown novel. Once an idea had taken root in his mind, he could not help but push it to its logical, perhaps even illogical, extreme. Each idea, he felt, had a cluster of covert connotations attaching to it, and it was the novelist's business to catch "the associational nimbus,"[18] as he put it. No wonder the sum of psychological correlations and intersections increased enormously as the story proceeded, full sail, toward its appointed port. The form obligingly stretched itself to accommodate the mass of meanings and relationships accreting round the *donnée.*

James's use of "difficulty," "mystery" and "muddlement" on the one hand; of "foreboding," "the portentous" and "melodrama" on the other, has often been misunderstood, and he is himself to blame for it, to some extent. By deliberately obfuscating a situation, as for instance, in *The Sacred Fount,* in "The Figure in the Carpet," in *The Sense of the Past,* etc., he seems to be using some of these devices to dress up an untenable, fantastic idea, which he knows is otherwise a non-starter. In such cases, the difficulty and mystery are not integrally related to the *donnée,* but are imposed upon it with a sleight-of-hand. It is, of course, possible to make out a perfect case for *The Sacred Fount* as an extended exercise in epistemology; in which case the obscurity is nuclear and thematically viable. But even then the impression of legerdemain and sophistry abides. The overtreatment itself makes it suspect. But in some of his more human and plausible dramas, he erects "beautiful" difficulties and muddlements as aids to a fine intelligence battling against the crass stupidity of the "fools" and the massed vulgarity of the snobs and the upstarts. The way James teases our minds into ironic insights, the way he draws a red herring across the track to beguile us into believing the opposite of the truth, the way we earn our return to sanity—all these things, done within the framework of the stipulated form, make a Jamesian novel or tale a delightful exercise. Though *The American, The Europeans, The Portrait of a Lady* and *The Bostonians* are full of these ingrained obscurities, the finest examples are to be found in such later works as *The Spoils of Poynton, The Ambassadors* and *The Wings of the Dove.* Occasionally, as in "The Turn of the Screw," the atmosphere of mystery and presentiment or foreboding is skillfully exploited by using oblique and ambiguous remarks, innuendoes, half-articulated and fractured statements, when, in truth, the tale is intended simply as an "amusette" and "a pot-boiler,"[19] albeit of a most sophisticated order. Whether the governess was a self-deluded, fixated creature or not, her Freudian critics surely are! The use of "the portentous" in relation to the dubious and evil characters such as Madame Merle and the Countess Gemini in *The Portrait of a Lady,* Mrs. Wix in *What Maisie Knew,* Rose Armiger in *The Other House,* etc., is more successful, I think, than the use of "melodrama" as such. In at least two of his earlier novels, *Roderick Hudson* and *The American,* melodramatic incidents towards the end do not serve a thematic purpose, as they do in some of the later novels of Dickens. The entire machinery of lost identities, recovered truths about paternity, skeletons in the family cupboard, is too old a fictional trick to serve the cause of the form dear to James here. Quite obviously, this is either a sop to the Victorian taste or, more likely, a failure of the imagination at a crucial point in two otherwise powerful and beautifully wrought books. The nearest James came to weaving melodrama into a complete vision of evil is in "The Turn of the Screw" and, more importantly, in *The Other House,* a "Greek" drama of swept emotions and "dark declivities," to use a Yeatsian phrase. If however, melodrama is given an extended meaning, as by Jacques Barzun in a thoughtful essay, "Henry James the Melodramatist," then James's dramatization of the Manichean evil in tale after tale makes him indeed a visionary melodramatist. But, as I have said above, he is, at least in several of his earlier stories and novels, quite content to use it as an easy device to induce stock responses. Where an artist uses melodrama as a *medium* of conveying the truth of evil and suffering, he has, like the cartoonist, used exaggeration or distortion as an essential part of his craft, but where it serves as a substitute for energetic solution of complexities, it becomes a theatrical ploy. Mr. Barzun quotes the well-known exchange of words between Kate and Densher, on which *The Wings of the Dove* closes ominously, as an example of the "melodramatic event in a usual sense."[20]

"As we were?"

"As we were."

But she turned to the door and her handshake was not the end. "We shall never be again as we were!"[21]

The effect here is not the effect of melodrama in the "usual" or theatrical sense at all; on the contrary, we have here one of the finest examples in James or anywhere of the use of "foreboding." The terrible finality of the tone suggests ironic shades of the deepest dye. As I show elsewhere in this book, the style of the clipped dialogue makes these lines Shakespearian in their tragic beauty and inevitability. Melodrama as such relies on expediency and ersatz satisfactions. There is no poetry or inevitability or even irony about it.

However, the question of melodrama in James, as Mr. Barzun rightly observes, is ultimately related to his love of the dramatic form in fiction. And we see in his restless search for the ideal form a continual move in that direction. Though the earlier novels are in essence more pictorial than dramatic, they abound in moments and scenes of high drama. James's muse exulted in intensities and confrontations and conflicts, and his native love and sense of drama found fulfillment in these epiphanies and scenes of explosive power—the vision of Christina Light as it flashes on Roderick Hudson in his Rome studio, Christopher Newman's agonized confrontation with the proud Bellegardes in their home, the climactic scene between the plain Catherine roused to spiritual beauty by love and her cold, pitiless, sadistic father, Dr. Sloper, exulting in his mordant wit, and a dozen such scenes. However, the structures of these novels are not fully dramatic; the tight scenic organization we find in the novels of the nineties is missing. As for the naturalistic novels of the eighties, their very spirit militated against the strict economy needed in the dramatic form.

However, after his failure in the theatre James turned to fiction once again to create a theatre of the novel. Even as he reviled the vulgar pit and the insensate treachery of the form, he could not throw the thing out of his system. Its aesthetic appeal held him in spell. Thus, by a supreme act of the will and the imagination he wrested a great victory out of a crippling defeat. The injured ego sought to vindicate itself through the very medium that had turned sour on him. The strictly scenic structure of such novels as *The Other House, The Spoils of Poynton, What Maisie Knew* and *The Awkward Age* makes them memorable dramas conducted entirely according to the principles of the theatre. Marianne Crawford once called the novel a "pocket theatre" that carried within its covers all the protagonists and sceneries and dialogues it needed. What James did was to make that loose description a living reality. For James, "an acted play is a novel intensified"[22] and the "the dramatic" constitutes "the sum of all intensities."[23]

But his greatest triumph in the form came a little later, when within the theatre of the novel he created a theatre of consciousness, a kind of ultimate theatre, where the show is hoisted by a dramatic imagination that has seized the essence of things. Its finest example is *The Ambassadors,* where, as Percy Lubbock tells us, James has made Strether's consciousness a revolving stage on which his crowded and anxious thoughts play out their part much in the manner of actors and their auxiliaries. This is a very unusual kind of drama, for the actual figures of the story exist for the reader only as they exist in one luminous consciousness. But this is precisely the manner in which James the playwright effects his own elimination from the scene, and lets the rendered show speak for itself. The very nature of the *donnée*—a vital change in the vision of the hero, or a silent revolution in the thought of "the ambassador"—makes it an unpromising subject for the usual type of drama. How could a writer capture and convey in visible images on the stage something that is by its nature secret, shy, inward and dark? As Percy Lubbock puts it eloquently: "Strether's predicament, that is to say, could not be placed upon the stage, his outward behaviour, his conduct, his talk, do not express a tithe of it. Only the brain behind his eyes can be aware of the colour of his experience, as it passes through its innumerable gradations; and all understanding of his case depends upon seeing these."[24] If one were to extend Lubbock's thesis, it may be possible to say that ultimately all drama is essentially subjective, not objective. The single consciousness whose "point of view" is dramatized may then be equated with the dramatist's consciousness which too is single and collates varied experiences on the stage in the same way as the single consciousness of the chief protagonist does on the stage of the mind. In the final analysis, as we shall see in the following chapter, no complete objectivity is possible, but James has undoubtedly taken the drama in the novel to the farthest point possible.

The dramatic novel, towards which James inclined increasingly as he mastered the mechanics of his craft, is in Edwin Muir's view "an identity of character and incident," and in Joseph Warren Beach's, "character in conflict."[25] The essence, says the latter, lies in showing or rendering rather than in narrating incidents. The older Victorian novelists told the tale in the manner of a master and a pontiff; they visibly delighted in revealing the hand that controlled the destiny of the characters. James, on the other hand, like Flaubert's "God of Creation," always sought to remain invisible, even though felt in every page of the book. In fact, the Jamesian "theory" of the novel, as we have seen, was from the beginning a theory in behalf of the dramatic form, though a much larger degree of freedom was still stipulated than the drama as such would allow. Characteristic action, intensity, stylized dialogue, economy, objectivity, conflict, all these virtues are fully aired in his essay, "The Art of Fiction." In short, the novel in James's view aspires towards the drama in the same manner as poetry aspires toward music. However, it may be noted that for him the drama is as much of character and incident as of thought and impression. The dynamism of thought is in itself a dramatic or dialectic phenomenon. When it is co-extensive with the outward movement of men and events, then the thought acquires a kinetic quality. The dialectic structure, whether of thought or of the novel, describes an arc or "trajectory" of "thesis, anti-thesis, synthesis," as Walter Isle, quoting Holloway, puts it in *Experiments in Form: Henry James's Novels, 1886–1901*. And he adds, "No matter how much the central situation in a novel is static, the structure is always to some extent dynamic and linear."[26]

An important aspect of the dramatic novel is the ultimate cohesion of form and theme. James brought this about by establishing two "centres"—"a centre of vision" and "a compositional centre," as Joseph Weisenfarth views them in his perceptive book, *Henry James and The Dramatic Analogy*.[27] In the earlier novels, he is more concerned with "the compositional centre"; the effort is to keep the physical structure from exploding because of the excess of imagination and romantic exuberance. All things and events as projected must go homing to the "centre," which like a king-pin holds the related parts. From *Roderick Hudson* to *The Princess Casamassima,* the "compositional centre" dominates, so to speak. But as we move into the dramatic novels of the nineties, we find the fusion of the "compositional centre" and the "centre of vision." Once again, *The Spoils of Poynton* is an ideal example of this kind of marriage. Fleda Vetch is not "the commanding centre" from the point of view of composition or structure only, but also from the point of view of the ultimate vision or meaning of the book. She has structured a vision on the Jamesian principle of sacrifice, and James has envisioned a structure that will hold because of its compositional asceticism. In short, Fleda, James's "super-subtle" heroine, makes a form of vision and a vision of form. This analysis applies with equal force and validity to Strether in *The Ambassadors*. He too literally creates the form of the novel in which he appears by uniting these two "centres." Where we have multiple points of view, as in *The Wings of the Dove* and in *The Golden Bowl,* we also have, by that very logic, the corresponding multiple "centres of vision."

And, finally, a few words about "foreshortening" and "framing," etc., which are important devices used in fashioning the form. In the prefaces, James refers frequently to "foreshortening" as a blessed device of economy and compression. The narrative, when it begins to gather the surrounding effects, or to feel the cognate pressures constantly bearing upon it, is always in danger of being overwhelmed by too much action. It needs then some built-in mechanism to absorb all these pressures without at the same time losing its intensity or form. In other words, movement is controlled with a view to producing a rendered structural block of events. Within its own framed "picture," there will yet be a kind of movement, though it will have the effect of stillness in relation to the narrative as a whole. "Foreshortening" thus amounts to converting action into "picture," narration into paraphrase or summary. This helps the novelist in "going behind" a character or a situation in such a manner that the essential unity of the story is not disturbed or violated. In the preface to Volume XVIII in the New York Edition, James refers to it in his characteristic eloquent style:

> Any real art of representation is, I make out, a controlled and guarded acceptance, in fact a perfect economic mastery, of that conflict: the general sense of the expansive, the explosive principle in one's material thoroughly noted, adroitly allowed to flush and colour and animate the disputed value, but with its other appetites and treacheries, its characteristic space-hunger and

space-cunning, kept down. The fair flower of this artful compromise is to my sense the secret of "foreshortening"—the particular economic device for which one must have a name and which has in its single blessedness and its determined pitch, I think, a higher price than twenty other clustered loosenesses; and just because full-fed statement, just because the picture of as many of the conditions as possible made and kept proportionate, just because the surface iridescent, even in the short piece, by what is beneath it and what throbs and gleams through, are things all conducive to the only compactness that has a charm, to the only spareness that has a force, to the only simplicity that has a grace—those, in each order, that produce the *rich* effect."[28]

And let James once again speak on this cherished device in the preface to *The Tragic Muse:*

To put all that is possible of one's idea into a form and compass that will contain and express it only by delicate adjustments and an exquisite chemistry, so that there will at the end be neither a drop of one's liquor left nor a hair's breadth of the rim of one's glass to spare—every artist will remember how often that sort of necessity has carried with it its particular inspiration. Therein lies the secret of the appeal, to his mind, of the successful *foreshortened* thing, where representation is arrived at, as I have already elsewhere had occasion to urge, not by the addition of items (a light that has for its attendant shadow a possible dryness) but by the art of figuring synthetically, a compactness into which the imagination may cut thick, as into the rich density of wedding-cake."[29]

"Foreshortening" is, therefore, a means of reducing the chaos of action, and of pictorializing its essence. As James observed, "picture" and "drama" are perpetually "jealous" of each other. "Foreshortening" is a way of reconciling their opposed claims. A "foreshortened" passage has necessarily a compressed and coercive charm about it. It eliminates dialogue as such, but embodies its functional and contributory values. We see it frequently employed in nearly all his important novels and tales, though in the dramatic novels of the later period the need seems more imperative than ever before. This is because the tight form requires capsuled treatment; everything that tends to cause a bulge has to be kept out. As an outstanding and extreme example of "foreshortening" James picks up the *nouvelle,* "Julia Bride," though we can see it beautifully at work in *The Tragic Muse,* "The Lesson of the Master," "The Aspern Papers," *The Reverberator,* "Graville Fane," "The Coxon Fund," and in a dozen novels and tales in the final phase.

The device of "framing" has been admirably discussed by Viola Hopkins in her essay entitled "Visual Art Devices and Parallels in the Fiction of Henry James," though the term, as she tells us, was first used by F. O. Matthiessen. This has obvious connections with painting, which remained for James a supreme art, despite his later preference for the drama. His deep interest in and knowledge of the various schools of European and American painting helped him in stylizing certain set scenes in the manner of the great masters. It is as if James were like an inspired painter using the brush to isolate figures and scenery into a unique vision of reality. Colour, *chiaroscuro,* tone, mood, atmosphere, distortion—all these are skillfully established to give the scene at once a thematic richness and an aesthetic transcendence. In the words of Viola Hopkins, "any scene or part of a scene may be considered framed if through visual imagery or description it is circumscribed and set apart from the rest of the narrative. Framing may serve various purposes: it may integrate description with action or with characterization . . . it may symbolise relationships and underline themes."[30] The examples she cites are of the scene in *Roderick Hudson* where Rowland, returning to his drawing-room after the dinner party, is "struck by the group formed by the three men," suggesting a Caravaggio; of the celebrated boating scene in *The Ambassadors* where Strether achieves his epiphany, suggesting a Renoir; of the Matcham reception in *The Golden Bowl,* suggesting a Watteau; of several such "framed" scenes in the later novels in the style of the Mannerist painters such as Bronzino, Tintoretto and Delacroix.[31]

The use of what Michael Egan calls "scenic disguise," as in *The Spoils of Poynton* for instance, is pervasive enough in the final phase when the theatre imagery and the theatre aesthetic become an overwhelming presence in James. To quote Egan, "This device involves the simple fragmentation of a single theatrical sequence, usually in dialogue form, into separate interviews divided from each other by a brief, discursive paragraph or elementary phrasing suggesting that time and locality have changed. . . . By eschewing the unity of time James achieved the unity of form."[32]

To conclude, it may be observed that James's pursuit of form was very much a priestly, if not mystic, concern. On the whole, it accounts for the wonderful sense of beauty, intensity and rotundity which are the dominant features of James's fiction. However, sometimes, this excessive concern does produce "loose and baggy monsters"[33] of form, as R. P. Blackmur avers. One wishes then, that he had followed more frequently and consistently the advice of his novelist-hero Berridge in "The Velvet Glove" (1909): "Sought and achieved consistency was but an angular, a secondary motion; compared with the air of complete freedom it might have an effect of deformity"[34]—a point reinforced by Graham in *The Ivory Tower:* "Excess of harmony might apparently work like excess of discord."[35] I repeat, however, that the later novels and tales on the whole are saved rather than ruined by "torment of form." There is a passage in *To the Lighthouse* by Virginia Woolf where we find Lily Briscoe musing over the compositional problem of the picture she is painting. To my mind, it describes exactly the quality of James's ethereal and nebulous stories held together by the discipline of form. "The whole mass of the picture," feels Lily, "was poised upon that weight. Beautiful and bright it should be on the surface, feathery and evanescent, one colour melting into another like the colours on a butterfly's wing; but beneath the fabric must be clamped together with bolts of iron."[36]

Finally, "the search for form" is almost always, at bottom, a search for a dimly perceived but acutely felt "ideal," and the quest involves a slow dawning of things, an expanding web of comprehension, and a reaching out and toward the consummation of thought and structure. The movement, particularly, in James's late novels and tales is deliberately so manipulated as to give an effect of a faint stir which, nevertheless, is portentous, even ominous at times. The slow gathering of effects is wholly in tune with the phenomenological imperatives of the situation in hand. The story, as in *The Ambassadors*, has a leisurely pace, but a brisk dynamic in terms of the incremental force of the unfolding drama. Let me quote Georges Poulet at some length in this regard.

> The Henry James novel advances . . . by a movement often almost imperceptible. . . . And in a sense as it approaches the center, it is true to say of the investigative thought, that it turns in a narrower and narrower circle. . . . But in another sense its enquiries ceaselessly grow in number, the circle containing them seems to become more and more vast; the more so as the mind is not content to perceive what is, but supposes what could be, so that the reality thus discovered is engrossed in all kinds of possibilities.[37]

5

The Point of View

Of all the techniques used by Henry James to effect the significant form in fiction, none has that kind of central importance which the celebrated "point of view" technique has. No wonder a great deal of critical attention has been paid to it, particularly since Percy Lubbock's influential essay on the subject in *The Craft of Fiction* (1921). However, much of James criticism in this behalf has been confined to the purely structural or engineering part of the problem, though, as I hope to show, the technical aspect is not only related to the Jamesian epistemology, but also receives sanction from it. Where James's "religion of consciousness" as such is discussed, the metaphysical assumptions underlying his attitude are fully aired, but it has not been widely recognized that his techniques and his metaphysics cohere to a remarkable degree. The point of view was, therefore, for him at once an artistic and a philosophical question. There is even a view that it had deep Freudian origins.[1]

James was not, of course, the first novelist to be seized of the problem. Ever since its birth in the eighteenth century, the novel had been steadily moving from the story to the drama, or from broad panorama to interior analysis, though in England and America, it remained, on the whole, a fairly promiscuous kind of exercise. On the technical side, it generally assumed the shape of a rambling department store which contained all manner of odds and ends. There was, in short, no purity of form or even purpose. Some of the time-honoured modes of narration—first person, omniscient author, disengaged narrator, confidante-recorder, etc.—were often employed simultaneously so that the structural outline was blurred. This went hand in hand with thematic confusion, for here too, all kinds of interests and attitudes, unrelated to the *donnée,* somehow got lodged in the loose, formless structure of the novel. Here and there, as in Jane Austen's *Emma,* the consciousness of the chief protagonist was fairly consistently used as a means of narration, and we watch the ironic drama of a limited or flawed heroine rendered almost in the Jamesian manner. The point of view is breached now and then, but this happens even in the most impeccable of James's novels and *nouvelles,* as we shall see presently. However, the English novel, unlike the

French, being little concerned with the integrity of form, on the whole, did not fully exploit this technique, and it was left to James to invest it with finesse and authority.

As early as 1869, when he had still to write his first novel, in a review of George Eliot's poem, *The Spanish Gypsy,* James wrote: "In every human imbroglio, be it of a comic or a tragic nature, it is good to think of an observer standing aloof, the critic, the idle commentator of it all, taking notes, we may say, in the interest of truth."[2] This seminal statement does not fully cover the shades and meanings of the point-of-view technique as he came to develop it in his later fiction, but this may well serve as a prologue to it. For here James is emphasizing his concern with it more for reasons of verisimilitude than form. Also, in his notebooks, we find an increasing distrust of the first person narrative, for, as he noted later in the preface to *The Ambassadors,* the autobiographical form was prone to "the terrible *fluidity* of self-revelation" and "foredoomed to looseness."[3] The omniscient author or narrator technique again strained the reader's credibility, and too plainly gave away the hand that manipulated the show. Thus, James was constantly in search of variations of the narrator technique whereby he could reflect the drama of life through a central or specific consciousness. This, in his view, not only ensured veracity of vision, but also a structural unity and economy. It is also possible to consider James's regard for the uninvolved, but perceptive, observer as an aspect of his romantic sensibility. A narrator reciting a tale assumes, as of old, a fairy-tale quality. He has the aura and charm of a *raconteur* out of the *Arabian Nights,* or, more frequently, the air of the traditional granny speaking to wide-eyed children at nightfall. Thus the narrator technique subsumes the folklore element, and satisfies a deep craving. Indeed, it is a measure of James's craftsmanship that in keeping the narrator tied down to the truths that fall within the line of his vision, he still manages to invest him with a wider ambience, unless, of course, he is treating him ironically.

What then really is the point of view? Technically speaking, it means simply the angle from which a tale is told, or recorded. In other words, since no story gets told or written of its own, there must be someone to do the job with the maximum of intensity and truth, and the minimum of intrusion and attenuation. In the omniscient narrator's method, the point of view is necessarily the author's; either the drift of the plot reveals it, or, as often happens, it may be voiced through a sympathetic character or a chorus or an alter-ego or a deputy. There it has little concern with the compositional aspect of the problem; the angle of vision is the primary thing. Now the author's point of view may be more comprehensive than, or even superior to, a particular character's point of view; it is not necessarily truer or more reliable. If anything, it is less so, and has the air of manipulation, if not cheerful deceit, about it. For in actual life no one person, whatever the quality of his mind or intellect, can ever have an omniscient view of things. Man experiences reality himself and alone, and the only means of doing so is his own limited consciousness. A novelist playing at "the God of Creation" is, in one sense, guilty of downright "cheek"; he is a dissembler and a mountebank vouchsafing the truth of things when, in fact, he could at best speak for himself.[4] Of course, such a show of mock-reality constitutes the raison d'etre of all art, and in challenging it on the basis of exact and literal truth, we are fatuously questioning the validity of all aesthetic experience. This throws us back to the well-known, but battered Platonic objection to poetry and art. Be that as it may, there will always be a desire in the artist to give his artifact as complete an air of reality as he can. And this, then, becomes a question of evolving a technique that can best do so. So far as the novel is concerned, James felt the maximum of effect could be achieved if the events and characters were to be viewed consistently through a *single* or selected consciousness. What it sees is what we see; no more, no less. It is the nearest approximation to reality and the closest way of apprehending it. There is a greater sense of human warmth, involvement and life-likeness when a story attaches itself to a particular pair of eyes, or to a specific intelligence. Once a reader's consciousness is hooked on the consciousness of the governing character, he is, in a manner, committed to the latter's point of view. In some of his later novels such as *The Wings of the Dove* and *The Golden Bowl,* James was to shift from the single point of view to multiple points of view but this is merely an extension of the technique, not a violation of it. If anything, it substantiates James's views regarding the relativity, incompleteness and limits of truth, a point that I have touched upon in an earlier essay. This does not amount to reverting to the omniscient author's technique wherein the novelist is generally effecting hops from consciousness to consciousness without quite relating them to a centre, compositional or otherwise. In short, the point of view or divergent points of view seemed necessary in the interests of both verisimilitude and form.

James, however, unlike Flaubert, who had employed a somewhat similar technique in *Madame Bovary,* was disinclined to use a dense "reflector" as a centre of consciousness. It is not as if half-lit consciousnesses enmeshed in vague dreams, such as Emma's is, do not in themselves present interesting insights into human nature; only they, in his view, could not adequately serve as visionary and commanding centres in view of the extremely limited qualities of their understanding. When the narrator has to take the place of the omniscient author, he must necessarily have a luminous, even if a restricted, consciousness. If he is not an "intense perceiver," what he has to tell cannot but suffer grievously in the telling. A subtle, discriminating, vibrating and watchful mind, then, is a sine qua non of the point of view technique. Since James's concern is chiefly with *interior* life, the recording mind has to have a degree of fineness that may not be violated. What is more, it is only "the conserving imagination" that can with felicity rescue significant moments from the waste and welter of life. Even here, James is careful enough to stipulate, in theory at least, that the central consciousness must not be too extraordinary to become a law unto itself, as indeed some of his own "super-subtle" narrators become in the later tales. While it has to be what James called, "conscient" as opposed to "inconscient," the narrator in each case has to be given a measured quantum of intelligence, suiting the requirements of the situation. Excessive consciousness could be as fatal as lean consciousness. The one tends to disturb the focus because of its own autonomous forays into the unknown, the other fails to form a centre because of its inability to organize patterns of experience. Occasionally, a narrator may have to be made slightly obtuse or naïve in the interests of comedy and irony as in "Four Meetings," but such "functional stupidities,"[5] as K. B. Vaid felicitously calls these limitations, are part of the scheme of things, and do not militate against the use of "conscient" reflectors as such.

It now remains to see how the point-of-view technique actually functions in James's sprawling fiction from *Roderick Hudson* to *The Ivory Tower*. Not only does James use the central consciousness in a variety of ways, he also, as he proceeds, seeks constantly to refine and extend it. In *Roderick Hudson,* it is the hero's friend and benefactor, Rowland Mallet, whose consciousness serves as a mirror and guide. A New Englander of a strong moral fibre, and a person of a cultivated sensibility, Rowland Mallet is well equipped to register faithfully and intelligently the drama of Roderick's explosive genius and stormy passions. That he should be secretly in love with Mary Garland, who in her turn has a deep and settled love for Roderick, the sculptor-hero of the novel, does add piquancy to the situation, and one could expect a certain clouding of the vision in a person thus involved, but James has invested him, as indeed he has invested Mary, with a clean, wholesome, inviolate conscience. Of course, the rigid New England conscience comes in for a good deal of criticism in some of his other works such as "Madame de Mauves," "A London Life," *The Bostonians,* etc., but here any irony, if intended, is severely toned down or dissipated in the process. That conscience can make a fool of us still, that it may unconsciously even develop into *inconscience* may not be ruled out in James's fiction, but in Rowland Mallet's case, there is little to suggest such a declension of consciousness. Or, as James says in the preface to the New York Edition of the novel: "The centre of interest throughout 'Roderick' is in Rowland Mallet's consciousness, and the drama is the very drama of that consciousness—which I had of course to make sufficiently acute in order to enable it, like a set and lighted scene, to hold the play."[6] He is certainly not the ideal, disengaged observer of truth James wants the central intelligence to be, for he is immersed in the element itself. And yet he is sufficiently objective and clear-eyed to maintain the essential truth of things; he has a kind of central sanity about him. Even the dazzling Christina Light, as she comes filtered through Rowland's consciousness, has a wing or two singed, as it were. Her ineffable charm is fully registered, even as the normative, if not neutral, eye of the observer pictorializes the drama of an imperious but fetching beauty, and an equally ruthless but irresistible genius. He is not exactly a "passive observer"[7] as J. A. Ward seems to think; the quality of his consciousness has a certain serenity about it, not passivity. Rowland indeed is a fine example of the point-of-view technique involving not the central character himself, but an engaged associate who is at once a compositional centre and a centre of vision.

In *The American,* it is the hero himself who is the primary agent, and whose consciousness is employed as a refracting medium. Christopher Newman's discovery of the self through a process of enchantment, betrayal and sacrifice is rendered almost wholly in terms of his agony and awareness. He is not telling his own story; his story is being told by James, but the reader seldom moves away from his consciousness or area of vision. In other words, there is almost an identification between the point of view of the protagonist and that of the author, though the former does not serve as a "deputy" in the usual sense of the word. What really happens is that the novelist invests the engaged sensibility with a Jamesian kind of interpretative apparatus. Each such character is thus indirectly a part of the fabulist's own interpretative field. It's what the linguistic critics call "represented discourse." A few fine ironical intimations in regard to Newman's Americanness are admitted, but, on the whole, the beauty of his moral energies and soulful exertions at once makes him a vehicle of James's world-view. Necessarily, such a technique restricts the area of experience and reality, for it is not given to any one person to absorb the totality of a situation. There is an undoubted damage to the sense of amplitude which James otherwise commends in his criticism. Its virtue, however, lies in its ability to lend full credence and coherence to the tale in hand. Also, the pernicious ethic of form which the Bellegardes finally induct into the drama could not have had that kind of thematic intensity, which it now has, if the matter had not been viewed through a *single,* mortified consciousness. Any other mode of narration would have, to some extent, diminished its psychic potential. As James says in the preface to the novel, "for the interest of everything is all that it is *his* vision, *his* conception, *his* interpretation: at the window of his wide, quite sufficiently wide, consciousness we are seated, from that admirable position we 'assist.' "[8]

Although neither *Roderick Hudson* nor *The American* is free from authorial intrusions—indeed no novel, whatever its technique, can be, in the final analysis—we see James's own intelligence and voice more subtly engaged in narrating the story of Isabel Archer through her expanding consciousness than we see in the earlier books. One may indeed aver that *The Portrait of a Lady* is a fine and revealing example of the Jamesian paradox that a technique is best honoured in the breach. Here, James had so much to convey by way of the heroine's background alone that apart from foreshortening, he was obliged to step in from the wings, and sketch the outline of the portrait before Isabel Archer, who is duly introduced in the second chapter of the novel, could take over from him the job of doing her own "portrait" in depth. Of course, once she is fully "framed," as it were, in Gardencourt, there are fewer occasions for James to dissociate the reader's mind from Isabel's engaged consciousness. Two famous instances of the departure from "the commanding centre"—Ralph Touchett's eloquent plea in behalf of his cousin which results in her uncle's magnificent legacy, and Madame Merle's sinister arrangements with Osmond in regard to Isabel's marriage—have been cited, but a closer analysis of the text will reveal several small and shy, but meaningful, "treacheries" to the point-of-view technique. Obviously, those incidents which take place behind the heroine's back cannot be rendered through her consciousness, more so, as their very secrecy or manipulation constitutes the stuff of her tragic drama. It is precisely her ignorance, or shall we say, her innocence (for here we have a poetic blend of both these traits) that has to be made dramatically viable. James apparently has no choice in the matter but to take us out of her line of vision. In the preface to "A London Life," however, he does register disappointment over the departure from Laura Wing's point of view in the interview between Lady Davenant and Wendover, and he calls it "a lapse from artistic dignity,"[9] presumably because a maturer James could have somehow conveyed the essence of the episode without infringing the governing principle of the tale. In Isabel Archer's case, the difficulty was thematic and nuclear. There are certain things which Isabel is not destined to know on her own. Ralph Touchett, who seems to be a Jamesian alter-ego, lights up for us several such areas of life in the book. Not only Isabel herself, but other characters in her drama, Madame Merle, Lord Warburton, Henrietta Stackpole, Casper Goodwood and Osmond are also at least partially realized through the subtle, evaluating consciousness of her consumptive cousin. It is not perhaps without reason that James has invested Ralph's consciousness with a luminous quality. Consumptive consciousness—Keats comes immediately to mind—seem to have a peaked awareness of reality, particularly when they are gingerly poised over the yawning abyss before them. A significant part of the novel may well be described as his disposition and vision. Towards the end, there is a convergence of his point of view and that of Isabel's, when on returning to Gardencourt from Rome, the chastened heroine of romance shares a vision of life achieved by the dying "swan," as he prepares "to ride those winds that clamour of approaching night," to recall Yeats's famous words from *Nineteen Hundred and Nineteen.*

Let me revert for a moment to the beautiful sixth chapter of Book I, and show how the author intrudes to add his own touches to the "portrait" which Isabel is supposed to be doing for herself. The title of the book perhaps is intended to convey the double meaning of that exercise; James is as much doing the "portrait" as the heroine herself.

It may be affirmed without delay that Isabel was probably very liable to the sin of self-esteem; she often surveyed with complacency the field of her own nature; she was in the habit of taking for granted, on scanty evidence that she was right; she treated herself to occasions of homage. Meanwhile her errors and delusions were frequently such as a biographer interested in preserving the dignity of his subject must shrink from specifying. Her thoughts were a tangle of vague outlines which had never been corrected by the judgement of people speaking with authority. In matters of opinion she had had her own way, and it had led her into a thousand ridiculous zigzags. . . . The girl had a certain nobleness of imagination which rendered her a good many services and played her a great many tricks. She spent half her time in thinking of beauty and bravery and magnanimity; she had a fixed determination to regard the world as a place of brightness, of free expansion, of irresistible action: she held it must be detestable to be afraid or ashamed. She had an infinite hope that she should never do anything wrong.[10]

Evidently, James in this part of the chapter is summarizing his own views and comments on Isabel Archer before he puts full wind into her sails to enable her to negotiate her stormy passage in life. These build-up touches are necessary in the interests of economy and irony. Isabel's consciousness as a medium is not fully engaged till now. There is indeed an interesting and lively discussion between Isabel and her queer aunt, Mrs. Touchett, on the subject of the "point of view."

"Now what's your point of view?" She asked of her aunt. "When you criticize everything here you should have a point of view. Yours doesn't seem to be American—you thought everything there so disagreeable. When I criticize I have mine; it's thoroughly American!"

"My dear young lady," said Mrs. Touchett, "there are as many points of view in the world as there are people of sense to make them. You may say that doesn't make them very numerous! America? Never in the world; that's shockingly narrow. My point of view, thank God, is personal!"[11]

In this comic exchange, it is our heroine who is being shown up as a stuck-up New Englander. This may well serve as a warning that though at the deeper level Isabel Archer speaks for James himself, we may not wholly identify their points of view. As a compositional centre, however, she continues to hold the book till the end, despite a few inevitable lapses or breaches. Nearly the whole of her betrayed and bruised married life is seen by the reader as a theatre of images set up in her agonized consciousness. As James wrote later in the preface: "Place the centre of the subject in the young woman's own consciousness," I said to myself, "and you get as interesting and as beautiful a difficulty as you could wish. Stick to *that*—for the centre; put the heaviest weight into *that* scale, which will be largely the scale of her relation to herself. . . . "[12]

Even as James continued to refine and expand the point-of-view technique, he kept on writing novels and tales where he does not press it into service, as, for instance, in *The Europeans, Washington Square,* and *The Bostonians.* Even in *The Princess Casamassima,* where the city of London is itself a dramatic character, it is not always Hyacinth's consciousness which can be effectively used to render the poetry of the place, for there are so many things happening all the time in that pulsating metropolis which do not, indeed, which cannot, form part of it. Thus, the breaches here in the point-of-view technique are even more significant and extended than in *The Portrait of a Lady.* Still, a great deal of this

"Dickensian" novel is enacted in the consciousness of the proletarian hero turned patrician by a tragic "turn of the screw." We see his spiritual hungers as he sees them, deeply, darkly, desperately. The "confectioner's window" complex which colours his dream life and feeds it is thus thematically linked to the technique of employing a single, bruised, baffled and expanding consciousness. Leslie A. Fiedler, in fact, goes on to find a bio-psychological basis for this pervasive Jamesian technique.

> It is this James who invents the technique of the 'center of consciousness,' i.e., a device for making the peeper the focus of a work of art, and who insists that 'art deals with what we see.' It is only in the work of art that James, like Coverdale before him, can possess symbolically what in reality he cannot touch; and of his very limitations he makes the form and substance of his fiction, which is not, as he liked to boast, 'felt life' so much as '*seen* life.'[13]

However, apart from *The Ambassadors,* the purest examples of the point-of-view technique are to be witnessed in the novels of the dramatic phase, for here consistency, economy, compression and intensity—the sought virtues—can be best achieved that way. *The Spoils of Poynton* and *What Maisie Knew,* in particular, are, technically speaking, virtuoso achievements, whatever their other faults. In the former novel, Fleda Vetch is perhaps the most teasing, involuted and extended example of a fine conscience in English fiction. This time, James uses a confidante as a centre of vision and composition. In fact, as this strange story of mother-son conflict over the ancestral objets d'art proceeds, it is not Mrs. Gereth, whose agony sparks off the action, who remains the object of our interest. It is her younger companion and trusted intimate who truly runs away with the "spoils" of the drama James is enacting. In this sense, Mrs. Gereth's dislodgement is double. She is eased out of her house by her son, and she is eased out of the story by the honest broker she has engaged in her own behalf. Mrs. Gereth, all cleverness but no intelligence, could not have served, in James's opinion, as a viable centre. With Fleda involved to the gills, so to speak, James has created a fascinating spectacle of a troubled consciousness battling its way through a mass of tangled emotions, attitudes and positions. Whether her point of view is not finally flawed or twisted as a result of her deep and settled desires is a question which raises the larger issue of James's "unreliable narrators."[14] To what extent Fleda is spared the heavier irony that hovers around Mrs. Gereth's figure is a matter of opinion, though there could be little doubt about what James thinks of inflamed and inflated consciences that must cause so much havoc in the process of vindicating themselves. One obvious defect of making the central intelligence so narrowly acute and *sui generis* is that the novelist is obliged to concentrate too pointedly and severely on its doubts and dodges, its sophistries and rationalizations. This, in the long run, reduces action to mentation or pure thought, liquefying the events and scattering the effects. This again happens in that remarkable tale, "In the Cage" (1898), where the telegraphist girl's consciousness is like a musical instrument played upon by James so long and so relentlessly that it is in danger of getting unstrung. Thus, his practice at times runs counter to his own declared view in the preface to *The Princess Casamassima* regarding "the danger of filling too full any supposed and above all any obviously limited vessel of consciousness. . . . Therefore it is that the wary reader for the most part warns the novelist against making his characters too *interpretative* of the muddle of fate, or in other words too divinely, too priggishly clever."[15]

In *What Maisie Knew* we have perhaps the most challenging use of the point-of-view technique in James, for here the novelist has to show the confused and wretched drama of gay adulteries and fornications through the bewildered, but avid, consciousness of a child. To keep the story pinned to that precarious centre meant a reduction of the complexities of the situation in such a manner as to make them intelligible and legitimate. The tangled geometry of relationships which James sets up, more, I think, to satisfy his sense of parallelism and neatness in plots than to catch the muddled and uneven truth of life, can only be but dimly comprehended by a little girl, and therefore, it has to be translated for her by the invisible author. The codes and symbols of marital intrigues and treacheries have to be gradually adjusted into the cognitive processes of "our little wonder-working agent."[16] The atmosphere of pitch and defilement in which she lives would have ordinarily coarsened her consciousness as well, but James needed a polished mirror, even if tragically limited in size. Therefore, as he says in the preface to the novel, "The small expanding consciousness would have to be saved, have to become presentable as a register of impressions."[17] One of the great problems before James must have been the problem of synchronizing the awareness of Maisie with that of the mature reader. For what are gaps and jumps and pauses, or "leaps and voids," for the child are simply the known truths of London life. That is how she becomes James's "ironic centre," and Maisie's drama is, despite its tragic overtones for her, converted into the stuff of comedy. James also notes that his "light vessel of consciousness swaying in such a draught, couldn't be with verisimilitude a rude little boy."[18] It would have to be a girl in that the female sensibility at that age is richer and more developed by contrast. This, of course, is true, though perhaps the darker reason which prompted James the *voyeur* to toy with a burgeoning erotic consciousness cannot be ruled out. That he should have classed *What Maisie Knew* with "The Pupil" in the New York Edition only shows that the repressed sexuality of James could erupt either way. Morgan Moreen, the boy in that story, is Maisie's libidinous counterpart to a considerable extent.

There is yet another interesting technical problem in *What Maisie Knew* related to the question of the central intelligence. How should the gathering impressions of a child be rendered when indeed her idiom lags far behind her perceptions? James is aware of the problem that in an average case—and Maisie is by no means a prodigy—knowledge and expression seldom go hand in hand. Often, this hiatus creates a great deal of mirth and muddlement. James is not above exploiting such situations where they serve his larger, ironic purpose, but if everything were to be told in the limited vocabulary of the child in question, verisimilitude would then be achieved at the expense of variety, range and vision. In short, the idiomatic accuracy would falsify the perceptual truth of Maisie. James also felt that an attempt to stick to a child's expression in a tale of marked complexity could not but come to grief in any case. Hence his observation: "Maisie's terms accordingly play their part—since her simpler conclusions quite depend on them; but our own commentary constantly attends and amplifies."[19] Of course, the story of a little girl could be told from her own point of view and in her own idiom quite effectively, if the technique were different. But James was not writing a stream-of-consciousness novel, which as a complete genre was a later development. His type of fiction was almost wholly dependent upon authorial analysis, reflection and comment despite the declared ideal of objectivity. F. O. Matthiessen puts it thus: "There is a vast difference between James's method and that of the novels of 'the stream of consciousness' . . . James's novels are strictly novels of intelligence rather than of full consciousness."[20] Sallie Sears says the same thing in another way. In James, we do not have consciousness "streaming," but "focused, attentive, concentrated,"[21] the process being essentially different from the Proustian method of evocation of memories.

Lately, *What Maisie Knew* has been, along with *The Sacred Fount*, subjected to a good deal of phenomenological interpretation in view of the very special *problems of seeing* and belief that this story enacts. Briefly, the phenomenological idea developed by Husserl and Merleau-Ponty is that it is possible to put aside the "natural" and habitual attitudes of perception through the operative energy of what is termed *"epoche"* or "bracketing." And such a process leads to "reduction." In other words, applied to Maisie's situation, the little girl acquires knowledge as a result of the world of phenomena. Since "wonder" is a constitutive element in a child's make-up, she is able to achieve "reduction," but even then "the natural reality" asserts and impinges on her expanding consciousness. Eventually, Maisie's drama is both a story of perception and judgement. It may be added here that *seeing* in her case is not, therefore, a purely physical phenomenon, it's also an *active* condition of the mind. As M. A. Williams puts it in a detailed study, "The Drama of Maisie's Vision," she "converts her curious situation into a unique opportunity for building creative relationships with her companions and her surroundings. And the paradox proves compelling, for out of meanness and neglect come freshness, energy and a deep sensitivity to the possibilities of experience."[22]

Another recent essay, "Narration and Nurture in *What Maisie Knew*," by Merla Wolk, traces the growth of the self in Maisie, and the "maternal" role of the narrator in guiding her perceptions. The thrust of Wolk's argument is that the narrator-author seems to separate himself only when Maisie can finally take hold of her situation en route. It may be added, however, that even then he is not "refined" out of existence, but simply structured into the gathering vision and values of the book. In other words, in Maisie's passage from innocence to experience a point comes when the compositional centre (Maisie) and the visionary centre (author-narrator) almost coalesce.[23]

And this brings me to *The Ambassadors,* where the poetry of Proust's city is rendered as a part of the climate of Strether's mind. The essences of Paris envelop it like a perfume. No other novel of James employing the central intelligence as a unifying force has so sweetly created the metropolitan aura or ambience. Roderick Hudson's, or indeed, Rowland Mallet's Rome, is charming enough in its own way, and Hyacinth's heaving London is a felt presence in every page of the book, but the means adopted by James to invoke the *spirit urbanus* in *The Ambassadors* are different. A wholly civilized city and a wholly civilized mind form a thematic or visionary unity of a rare order. One impinges upon the other to effect a profound change in the terms of reference under which the "embassy" was conceived and entrusted. Strether's consciousness is a kaleidoscope wherein all the figures and events of the drama are reflected and rotated one by one. James does not rush the pace of events, for he is not dealing with action as such, but with what G. E. Moore has called "the states of mind." The process of unfoldment is thus synchronized with the slow, ruminating processes of thought. We have our measure of everything from the point of view of Strether; we are, so to speak, tied to the tether of Strether's consciousness. A pervading irony prevents us from taking everything that comes to us through an engaged intelligence at its face value. But nothing may come to us otherwise; we are, so to speak, in the employ of Strether's imagination. It drives us along at its own sweet pace and in its own characteristic style. The whole vision of Paris, of the ineffable beauty of Madame de Vionnet, of Chad's transformation, of the ultimate epiphany in the boat scene, is distilled for us, drop by drop, by a rare and cultivated intelligence. All that is sheer accretion and waste is jettisoned; only the sweetest essences are preserved. And what we receive is not, as in *The Sacred Fount,* something cold and neutral and abstract. We do not see a blaze of emotions, but there is an unfailing *affective* glow that envelops the narrative. There is, undoubtedly, a loss of immediacy as such, and one has a feeling of things being attenuated and rarefied at times to the point of extinction, but this, in a manner, is inevitable where a writer's exclusive concern is with the life of the mind. Strether's drama, as we have seen in the preceding essay, is wholly played out in the theatre of consciousness. Events are dismantled, and then recreated as figures of thought. The physical reality, in other words, is almost wholly absorbed by the reacting consciousness, and turned into images and metaphors. This, more than anything else, makes *The Ambassadors* a truly poetic novel.

One of the most remarkable aspects of the point-of-view technique, as critics have often pointed out, following James's own assertion in the preface to *The Ambassadors,* is the creation of Mrs. Newsome's character. We never meet her in person, but she is as vividly realized for us as any other character in the book. Her felt presence is so engineered as to make her a fully involved and active figure in the drama. The covert presence of Woollett in Strether's consciousness, in fact, invokes for us not only the image of the vigilant absentee, but also the entire ethos of a provincial town in New England. By keeping everything stationed in a single consciousness, it has been possible for James to bring off this unique effect.

Another remarkable character, Maria Gostrey, conceived as a mere *ficelle,* whose function is to help extend the cognitive processes of the principal consciousness, gradually warms her way into Strether's world, and becomes its aid and ally. It is a fine example of how an auxiliary character may become a contributive agent of vision by securing a lodgement in the central consciousness. Elsewhere we have seen how a confidante can, as in *The Spoils of Poynton,* actually run away with the situation, and be the commanding centre of the book, but here, instead of becoming monarchical, she conducts herself as the hero's emissary and counsellor and listener who must in the end quietly bow out of the situation to nurse a heart grown rich in grief. Her earned effacement is entirely in keeping with the sacrificial principle of Strether's ethics. "She is," as James declares, "an enrolled, a direct, aid to lucidity; she is, in fine, to tear off her mask, the most unmitigated and abandoned of *ficelles.*"[24]

Even such a tightly structured novel is not wholly consistent in its technique, as John E. Tilford, Jr. has convincingly argued in his essay, "James the Old Intruder." "The authorial intrusion and the shifts of the view," he observes, "are sufficiently abundant"[25] to modify James's claim that what we see is entirely Strether's "sense of those things." Quite a few times the scenic method is abandoned, and James himself cites the example of the passages relating to Strether's first encounter with Chad Newsome and of those relating to Mamie Pocock's "hour of suspense in the hotel saloon" as constituting "the suffered treacheries" in the interest of representation. "The book, however, critically viewed," he observes, "is touchingly full of those disguised and repaired losses, those insidious recoveries, those intensely redemptive consistencies."[26]

There are several other *nouvelles* and stories where James uses the central consciousness as a mode of narration, though the method varies from tale to tale. In some, the involved narrator, as in "Madame de Mauves" and "Daisy Miller," rather than the central character, is the perceiving consciousness. The technique suits the latter *nouvelle* in particular in view of the peculiar nature of its *donnée.* As Wayne C. Booth has observed: "It is difficult to imagine this story as told through any other view than his, since Daisy's drama is precisely the drama of being misunderstood."[27] Thus, "a misguided observer" like Winterbourne is rightly made the instrument of our view of the American girl. "The Altar of the Dead," "The Beast in the Jungle," "The Great Good Place," "The Bench of Desolation" and "The Jolly Corner" are other outstanding examples, though in all these compositions, slight "treacheries," authorial comments and intrusions are again clearly in evidence. I share, in fact, the view of those critics who believe that no matter what a writer may do to eliminate himself, he is very much there in the text, if you know how to look for him.

Where the central intelligence is a narrator rather than the agent of the story, as in "The Aspern Papers," "The Turn of the Screw," "The Liar," "The Friends of the Friends," and *The Sacred Fount,* the problem of his veracity or reliability has raised endless controversies amongst the James critics. Undoubtedly, the best account is Professor Booth's in *The Rhetoric of Fiction,* though some of his conclusions about particular narrators and their reliability are also open to question. At any rate, it is clear that James was not able to solve completely the problem of "the unreliable narrator." A tale told through a narrator's consciousness has hazards which may not be avoided even by as watchful and scrupulous an artist as James. From a mere observer, a narrator begins to grow into an interfering and interloping intelligence, thus drawing a whole cloud of doubt across the narrative he has recorded. However, there is a way of viewing the matter differently. In making a narrator-consciousness a strictly limited affair, James may well be suggesting the idea that the truth cannot be wholly realized in human affairs, and that this very limitation may serve as a spur to a more intensified and varied effort. This is how Walter Wright seems to see the issue. "Precisely in the limitations of the narrator's consciousness," he remarks, "is the creative value of the story as a search for truth. The truth comes to us the more completely as we see it transcending the very consciousness which reports it to us."[28]

Though James uses the technique of the multiple points of view in earlier novels also to a limited extent, Ralph Touchett's case in *The Portrait of a Lady* being one instance, it is in *The Wings of the Dove* and *The Golden Bowl* that it is contemplated as a full-blown compositional principle. That is to say, more than one consciousness is employed to render or dramatize the *donnée.* We watch events successively through the eyes of the chief protagonists, and are left to collate our impressions and draw our conclusions. This has the merit of extending the area of interest, and of breaking the monopoly of vision. The technique, as J. A. Ward points out, singularly suits the type of novel which relies on multiplying relationships. "The novel of relations," he adds, "logically requires the technique of multiple points of view; the technique not only supports the subject, it is the subject."[29] Thus, where a novel is conceived as a single-character show, all other figures being subordinated to its interests, as in *The American* and *The Portrait of a Lady* and *The Ambassadors,* the single point of view technique alone can lend sufficient intensity and saturation to the tale, but where two or more principal characters are, more or less, of equal force and magnificence, and where the poetry of tension is released as a result of that polarity, the multiple points of view technique can best ensure the complex vision of the book.

Take *The Wings of the Dove,* for instance. Here, James has fixed three "centres"—Kate Croy, Merton Densher and Milly Theale—in addition to one "reflector," Mrs. Stringham, whose point of view may be seen at work intermittently in several sections of the novel. Of course, she does not become at any stage a visionary centre also, and the tragic and harrowing drama of love, complicity and betrayed trust is processed individually through the three involved consciousnesses and the supplementary mirror. As James tells us in the preface, being free from the tyranny of serialization, he had the necessary freedom to "go behind" and start as far back as possible before introducing us to the central figure. Thus Milly's "superficial" absence from Book First is a part of the design of the book which is conceived in terms of structural "blocks." To begin with, therefore, we see things as Kate Croy sees them; her world of love, thwarted by circumstance, is fully worked out in terms of her creature needs and the importunate promptings of the heart. There is a desperate beauty, if not holiness, about her passion for Densher, and we cannot but salute its vigour and daring. Thus, to reach the central centre—Milly Theale—it was necessary for James's purpose that the reader pass through Kate's consciousness, which is to serve as one of the "successive centres." As James puts it: "If one had seen that her stricken state was but half her case, the correlative half being the state of others as affected by her (they too should have a "case," bless them, quite as much as she!) then, I was free to choose, as it were, the half with which I should begin."[30] Again, since Densher's point of view at this stage coincides with that of Kate, James "through the associated consciousness" of his "two prime young persons" has consented "under stress, to a practical *fusion* of consciousness."[31] Thus a sly shift from one to the other consciousness constitutes in his view no essential departure from the principle of keeping things tied to one centre.

It is in Book Fifth that we begin to see the "single throbbing consciousness" of Milly in full play. The drama that was being played behind her back now shifts to the theatre of her mind, and in a brilliant shadow-world lit-up cunningly by Jamesian rhetoric, issues are isolated and framed afresh. It is a movement from the work-a-day *without* to the significant *within*. When after a lapse in Book Sixth, where we are obliged to move out of the range of her vision, we return to her agonized consciousness in the end, it is already a consciousness too crowded to bear the full burden of her "ordeal." Structurally speaking, as James has recognized, the severely foreshortened latter half of the novel is a failure, with its "misplaced pivot."[32] Milly's consciousness as a medium is not as fully used, as, for instance, Kate Croy's in the opening section.

With Milly having "turned her face to the wall," we are left with the lacerated consciousness of Densher seeking its own salvation and transcendence. There is a tragic irony of fate in that he himself becomes a victim, stretched infinitely on the rack of a roused conscience. The spoils of Milly's millions and the spoils of passion will not somehow cohere to form a unified pattern of happiness. His conscience is his "scourge and minister," and we see him through his own consciousness struggling for release.

The Golden Bowl is another fine dramatic novel of interlocking relationships, involving four characters in mutual, intersecting destinies, struggling to tease out the puzzle of marriage, stitch by stitch. Here James fixes two primary centres of consciousness—Amerigo and Maggie Verver—and the book is divided structurally into two paralleling halves, showing a tight organizational economy and finish. The issues framed in one consciousness are tested in the other. A kind of stereoscopic view is thus established, giving the reader a rounder view of things. In fact, the first half, which deals with the Prince's view of Maggie and Adam Verver and Charlotte Stant has an exact counterpart in the second half, which deals with the Princess's view of the same persons, situations and entanglements. Not that there are no fresh events or developments; only the basic imbroglio, which sets up a whole humming school of doubts and falsities for both the wronged and the wrongers, now begins to unwind itself in the light of later events. "It is the Prince," writes James, "who opens the door to half our light upon Maggie, just as it is she, who opens it to half our light upon himself; the rest of our impression, in either case, coming straight from the very motion with which that act is performed."[33] In this, Mrs. Assingham and her husband—a kind of ironic chorus in the book—perform their allotted roles within the bounds of their ill-lit consciousnesses.

Of course, things filtering through the consciousness of Maggie have far more intensity and poetry compared with the reverberations emanating from her husband's consciousness. Obviously, a bruised female psyche painfully waking up to the dangers ahead and the darknesses behind has for James, the analyst and the moralist, infinite depths to be sounded. The phantasmagoria of harrowing images staged in her consciousness has a piercing and haunting quality about it. It is "as if a magic lantern threw the nerves in patterns on a screen," to use T. S. Eliot's vivid line. As compared with the consciousness of the protagonists in the earlier novels, that of Maggie has a vertiginous, swollen, aggressive aspect that is truly stupendous. But the final beauty of it all lies in the slow, chemical change that is taking place in her point of view. The crack in her marriage, like the crack in "the golden bowl," at last brings her to recognize the fact that the form of things is as necessary as the spirit, in adultery as in life, that the appearances are as necessary as the essences. Maggie, the "little trapezist girl," has earned her salvation in the end by stretching her consciousness to the limits of the balancing exercise. Perhaps it's not too much to infer from Amerigo's complete surrender that Maggie's Pyrrhic victory at least unites two erring consciousnesses in a common vision of the darknesses waiting to spring upon life like "the beast in the jungle." They converge, so to speak, on this side of the horror and the abyss.

From these brief illustrations, it should be clear that for James, the point-of-view technique was something more than a purely artistic question or a problem of form. As we have seen, the sovereignty of consciousness is emphasized with a view to establishing the sum of earned insights and values, of moral beauties and felicities. A consciousness in travail is a conscience in the making. Its own moral and spiritual energies are fully roused and engaged only in moments of crises, or in extreme situations. It has to have, in other words, a full assault of life before it gives off its finest sounds. It grows rich in pain and suffering; it develops moral muscles in combat and conflict. Thus, consciousness *qua* consciousness was for James a smithy of the spirit.

This worship of consciousness, so to speak, stems on the one hand, from James's belief in the Cartesian doctrine of "I think, therefore I exist," and in the Lockian view of individual consciousness as the primary mode of cognition, and on the other from the Transcendentalist reverence for its spontaneity, freedom and capacity for transcendence. In a manner, he has absorbed, without much conscious ado, the philosophical ideas of his brother William, and of his Swedenborgian father. A little careful analysis will show that Henry James Senior's type of Transcendentalism subsumes William James's type of Pragmatism, with its roots in the eighteenth-century philosophy of Locke and Spinoza. James was never sold on the one or the other, though these metaphysical positions are assuredly reflected in his works in various ways. In short, though the high value he attached to making a central consciousness the fulcrum of his fiction was primarily for the purposes of compositional beauty, precision, economy and elegance, his faith in the poetry and reach of consciousness gave the technique in question a philosophical stance. That's why indeed we talk of the compositional centre and of the visionary centre in his more fully realized novels and tales. In a novel like *The Ambassadors,* for instance, the two centres gradually close in upon each other to form a unified, coherent and organic whole.

Undoubtedly, the point-of-view technique has some built-in weaknesses and insufficiencies. For instance, when things are seen through a single, restricted consciousness, the great bustle or hum of life around it does not cease to exist, only because it does not directly fall within its experience. In fact, it keeps impinging upon it all the time in the form of the time-spirit. A consciousness preoccupied almost wholly with its own special concerns is, historically speaking, an atomized consciousness. Again, though the physical and human reality is fundamentally reached via an individual consciousness, it does not, for that reason, become essentially subjective. Not the reality, which is objective and social, but the manner of apprehending it is subjective. Indeed, it is this confusion in thought which led to the romantic faith in the sovereignty of consciousness. Consciousness is sovereign insofar as it is individual, private and unique; it is not sovereign in the sense of owing no allegiance to social reality. This, in fact, drives us back to the well-known Marxist view that it is not the consciousness of men which determines their being, it is their social being which determines their consciousness. Thus, when a single consciousness becomes a law unto itself, it soon descends into rank solipsism. Apart from these philosophical inadequacies, there are a few serious compositional difficulties also in the point-of-view technique. Since a Newman's or a Strether's consciousness alone connects us with other characters in the novel, since through his eyes *alone* we see and evaluate others, how are we really to know exactly what is passing in their minds? The omniscient author having abdicated, except in the case of the central consciousness character himself, who is to guide us into the inner chambers of their psyches, which must necessarily remain costumed, if not opaque, to the eye of the central viewer? He can at best see them from the outside, for he cannot dart in and out of others' consciousnesses in the manner of the omniscient creator. Again, in reducing action to thought in the mind of a hyper-sensitive character, James reduces the feeling of life's flow or fluidity. This happens again and again in some of the later "monsters" of Henry James. And, finally, there remains the unsolved question of the "the unreliable narrator" in the tales where the central intelligence is not the agent of the drama, but a mere "register" or a "mirror." However, the technique served James excellently on the whole, and lent his fiction a philosophy of form. Above all, it cohered with his world-view. Elitism of some kind becomes inevitable when one views reality as an exclusive, special and private concern. Also, no other technique could so well embody James's idea of the relativity of truth and the ambiguous nature of reality.

6

The International Theme

The sustained presence of the international theme in Henry James's fiction has many an interesting and revealing aspect. Considering the fact that it continued to engage his mind throughout his creative career, and that it is associated with some of his most powerful and involved works, one is apt to seek in it a clue to the energies that informed his art. Did he, perchance, land upon it early in *Roderick Hudson* and then, following the phenomenal success of *Daisy Miller* a few years later, go on to make it a professional concern? Or, did he have from the start a vision of life and art which could be best rendered in terms of what he called the international "situation," "proposition" or "prospect"? From his letters and notebooks and prefaces, it is clear that though he would have loved to play upon the American-European syndrome, if that could ensure fame and fortune, he was obviously much more possessed by the theme than would appear at first sight. There are deeper and unconscious urges which assuredly sparked off James's interest, though as he grew richer in experience and art it became a conscious and comprehensive metaphor for him. In other words, the international theme became ultimately his most favoured operational area wherein he could work out, not only his world-view, but also his complex strategies and techniques. Somehow, it suited his situation, his genius and his art. His imagination, so to speak, appropriated it out of a welter of competing themes, and made it a unique emotive concern in the same way that Conrad, for instance, made the sea, or Hemingway the bull ring, a *condition* of his theme, vision and craft. Or perhaps it may be truer to suggest that James's epistemological, ethical and aesthetic concerns—the ambiguity of truth, the nature of evil, the rationale of form, the experience of art, etc.—which in themselves constitute his leading themes otherwise, found their objective correlative in the international "situation" as envisaged by him.

James's own stray comments on the subject are to be found in several of his prefaces though he states his position more fully in the prefaces to Volume XIII and Volume XIV in the New York Edition. He is aware of the fact that so many international tales in the collected corpus of his work could not but attract critical attention in relation to the variations on this theme. "I have already had occasion," he writes, "to say that the 'international' light lay thick, from period to period, on the general scene of my observation—a truth the reasons and bearings of which will require in due course to be intelligibly stated. . . . "[1] He even gives the impression of being too much confined to "the patchless desert of a single and of a not specially rich or fruitful aspect." Though he knows, for the sake of the truth of experience, he must make the maximum of his "appointed thematic doom."[2]

Since his view of the European-American problem underwent a chemical change in the period between *Roderick Hudson* and *The Golden Bowl*, it is not surprising to see critics fasten on some aspect of the question in preference to other related and, perhaps, equally valid aspects. The accent falls somewhat differently in different novels and tales, even though in each case the crisis is reached as a result of the international situation. Broadly speaking, then, there are three ways of viewing the international theme: to regard it as a compulsive expression of a deracinated psyche; to treat it as a rich ground for dramatizing the broad comedy of life and manners; and to consider it as a sustained exercise of the cosmopolitan imagination. These different approaches are not mutually exclusive, and indeed no international tale of James may be wholly explained in terms of any single aspect. For instance, the international setting or background of the later novels has a different order of relevance to the themes, and could be properly understood only in relation to that variation. However, the novelist's imagination of fusion some-how made it possible in the end to view the whole thing in the round.

The simplest fact to grasp about James's involvement in the international theme is the fact of his experience. For him the intercontinental straddle was as much of a reality as London was for Dickens, or Wessex was for Hardy. His "region," so to speak, extended from New England to Western Europe; he became an "interpreter on both sides of the sea,"[3] simply because his condition warranted such a role. From his earliest days, as he ruefully acknowledges in his autobio-graphical and other writings, he had become a "hotel" child, moving from country to country, somewhat in the manner of Morgan in "The Pupil," except that the Jameses had nothing of the American vagrancy and vulgarity of the Moreens. Thus, having been reared in that element, he could not but turn his youthful impressions of the American-European imbroglio to account from the start. It was, let it be understood, not a sought condition in the first instance, though as he lapped up more and more of the European reality, his appetite for it grew sharper and sharper till in the end it became as much of a vice as a felicity. The marked ambivalence of the final phase testifies to this peculiar dilemma of his "complex fate." The seeds of this dichotomy lay in the act and manner of his initiation. As he wrote in the preface to *The Reverberator:* "The nostalgic cup had been applied to my lips even before I was conscious of it—I had been hurried off to London and Paris immediately after my birth, and then and there, I was ever afterwards strangely to feel, that poison had entered my veins—. The unnatural precocity which I had in fine 'taken' to Europe was to be revealed to me later on . . . an interval during which I supposed my young life to have been made bitter, under whatever appearances of smug accommodation, by too prompt a mouthful—recklessly administered to one's helplessness by responsible hands—of the fruit of the tree of knowledge."[4] The imagery of poison and sin would undoubtedly suggest the damage done to a fine and receptive psyche at a tender age, but it would be a mistake to think that James turned away wholly from Europe towards the end. There is enough to suggest in *The Ambassadors* and other tales of the later period that Europe, despite its depleted charm, continued to be "a sacred fount" in so many ways. In fact, it may well be summed up thus that while his imagination was ensnared by Europe, his "resinous" heart continued to feed on the American fantasy and dream.

This peculiar love-hate attitude towards America persisted in James till the end. There are several statements scattered in his writings to prove that though American provincialism, vulgarity and strident morality distressed him a great deal, he was fully aware of the beauty and innocence and poetry of America. Europe too was a courtesan full of finesse and charm. Even as she administered to one's aesthetic sense, she exacted a fearful price. James was never to forswear one or the other; the way his genius had been saturated left him no choice but to turn to the international situation. Towards the end, in fact, he began to view the Anglo-American reality as an extension and a continuum. Thus the Jamesian choice of the international theme stemmed from the facts of his situation in the first instance. It was as natural as the London fog or the Italian sun. He didn't quite select it, so to speak; it got selected of its own. "The great truth in the whole connexion," he observes, "however, is, I think, that one never really chooses one's general range of vision. . . . The subject thus pressed upon the artist is the necessity of his case and the fruit of his consciousness. The artist—for it is of this strange brood we speak—has but to have his honest sense of life to find it fed at every pore even as the birds of the air are fed. . . . "[5] James is indeed sceptical about the labours of the critics who love to "go behind," and search for reasons, when indeed the truth of the matter is as plain as plateglass. However, the whole affair is not as simple as James seems to suggest, and there are certain aspects, not reasons, which do need going into in view of the long history of his international fiction.

The American "fixation" on Europe is a complex psychological problem, and this is no place to consider it. It involves the interaction of several urges and myths and fantasies. One of the most thorough and penetrating analyses of the subject, incidentally, is to be found in Leslie A. Fiedler's *Love and Death in the American Novel*. Suffice it to say here that the need of the New World to connect with the Old was so deep and pervasive that the younger culture, never quite secure and viable, constantly sought authentication or vindication in more settled attitudes and stances, in more proven and achieved forms. The backward glance was not quite a wholesome affair, and in some cases, created a whole continent of gratuitous suffering as a result of this distorted vision. James's own story, "Europe," is a fine ironic example of such a spiritual displacement. However, James himself is not free from this "complex," and one recalls in this context his famous lament (in his book on Hawthorne) on the absence of cultural graces and civilized institutions and appurtenances in America, which has

> no State, in the European sense of the word, and indeed barely a specific national name. No sovereign, no court, no personal loyalty, no aristocracy, no church, no clergy, no army, no diplomatic service, no country gentlemen, no palaces, no castles, nor manors, nor old country houses, nor parsonages, nor thatched cottages, nor ivied ruins; no cathedrals, nor abbeys, nor little Norman churches, no great universities nor public schools—no Oxford, nor Eton, nor Harrow, no literature, no novels, no museums, no pictures, no Epsom nor Ascot! . . . The American knows that a great deal remains; what it is that remains—that is his secret, his joke, as one may say. . . . [6]

There is again a somewhat similar cry in that early story "The Madonna of the Future" (1873) where an American painter settled in Italy bemoans his American origin.

> "We're the disinherited of Art! We're condemned to be superficial! We're excluded from the magic circle! The soil of American perception is a poor little barren artificial deposit! Yes, we're wedded to imperfection! An American, to excel, has first ten times as much to learn as a European! We lack the deeper sense! We have neither taste nor tact nor force! How *should* we have them? Our crude and garish climate, our silent past, our deafening present, the constant pressures about us of unlovely conditions, are as void of all that nourishes and prompts and inspires the artist as my sad heart is void of bitterness in saying so! We poor aspirants must live in perpetual exile."[7]

Again, in "A Passionate Pilgrim" (1871), the earliest of the international tales which James regards, along with its two companion pieces, "Madame de Mauves" and "The Madonna of the Future," as "sops instinctively thrown to the international Cerberus,"[8] Clement Searle, the American "pilgrim," a somewhat importunate Jamesian alter-ego, represents allegorically the perpetual quest of the American psyche for distant and dark forbears. Thus, a journey to England or to the Continent was at once a journey into the past and the interior, a voyage into "the Collective Unconscious." The quest, of course, was also at the same time a romantic adventure comparable in reverse to the quest of Columbus. And indeed there is in the unfinished novel, *The Sense of the Past,* a significant reference to the Columbian spirit of the hero, Ralph Pendrel, another Jamesian deputy. "He had sniffed the elder world from afar, very much as Columbus had caught on *his* immortal approach the spices of the Western Isles."[9] Ironical overtones, however, are not altogether missing even in these stories of the questing self, and doubts are raised at times regarding the rationale of these passionate gropings and strivings in the void, but, on the whole, there is reason to believe that James was, for the most part, voicing deep-seated, archetypal desires of the American psyche.

Perhaps the key to the Jamesian attitude in this respect lies, as I have hinted earlier, in his ingrained ambivalence. If the passages quoted above regarding James's distrust and disparagement of American civilization are not to be entirely misunderstood, it would be but proper to set down in juxtaposition some of his well-known statements and observations of roughly the same period affirming his faith in American moorings and values. In a letter written at the age of twenty-four, he congratulates himself on having been born in America, and goes on to pay a handsome tribute to the American spirit—"our moral consciousness, our unprecedented spiritual lightness and vigour."[10] Again, elsewhere he talks of the American sufficiencies and affirmations. "Our salvation," writes one of his American characters, Marcellus Cockerel, "is here, if we have eyes to see it, and the salvation of Europe, into the bargain. . . . "[11] What, then, is one to make of these contradictory statements and attitudes except to say that there was a double pull at the Jamesian heart-strings and imagination. It was a dialectic of polarities, and his fiction garnered a great deal of poetry from it.

This is a conclusion which will not find favour with those who subscribe to the theory of James's deracination and consequent erosion. There is, of course, always a loss when an artist moves away from his native soil; a certain kind of warmth and immediacy and spontaneity goes with it. It is also true he needs a known and felt framework of references if his work is to achieve typicality. But in the case of James the damage was not as severe as is made out by such critics as Brooks, Parrington, Geismar and others. And this for the simple reason that he was truly as much a native of America as of Europe. One is only deracinated when, as W. H. Auden has pointed out, one settles in an entirely different cultural milieu. That is, more or less, what L. B. Holland says: "Natives and foreigners become aliens only by virtue of residence *in* a society whose structure renders them alien."[12] James, if I may say so, was a "European," as to "the manner born." The differences in culture and values were not so grievously wide as to land him in a total vacuum, though they were acute enough to provide him powder for humour and irony. Rebecca West clinched the issue thus: "For the essential thing about Mr. James was that he was an American; that meant, for his type and generation, that he could never feel at home until he was in exile."[13] Similarly, Pelham Edgar observed that James's expatriation was not as disastrous as some critics would have us believe, and added that James "at the age of thirty had absorbed all the American impressions his nature was capable of receiving."[14] Edna Kenton goes on to challenge the whole theory of expatriation and opines that not expatriation but "dispatriation" (James's own word), "disattachment from any single measure of values"[15] really describes James's true position. His letter to John Hay about Howell's "dismal fate of trying to live in two countries—in two worlds—at once,"[16] and his famous advice to Edith Wharton that "she *must* be tethered in native pastures even if it reduces her to a backyard in New York,"[17] along with the moral of his biography of the American painter, Story, and the meaning of his enigmatic parable, "The Jolly Corner," would certainly suggest a peculiar restiveness in James, and his painful awareness of the expense of spirit involved in it. However, I am inclined to believe that in James's own case a great deal more was achieved than lost in his attempt to live simultaneously in two worlds. Eventually, he carved out a country of the mind and the imagination, and it is there that he truly belongs. Viewed thus, the international theme also represents a facet of the search for the "Great Good Place."

It is not commonly realized that even if James had never left the American shores, his basic themes and the manner of treatment would not have been essentially different. That the international situation somehow became an inescapable condition of his art and vision only goes to prove the essential truth of his experience. For, he was, like Jane Austen, keenly interested in the drama of contrasts, and if he had perchance remained confined to New England, he would have found enough comedy in the cultural shades that divide town from country, the Brahminical East from the pragmatic West, and the liberal North from the conservative South. *The Bostonians* is a novel sufficiently representative of James's true genius. Thus, it should not be difficult to see that "the interest of contrasted things . . . the opposition of aspects from country to country"[18] to which he refers in the opening lines of the preface to Volume XIV in the New York Edition is at bottom an engagement of the dramatic imagination which revels anytime anywhere in climactic situations and in characters caught in clash and contrast. From this point of view, the American-European scene offered a far richer field for operative ironies than the native one. National prides and prejudices, forms and styles, postures and positions presented necessarily a more varied and heightened picture, particularly as the impasse of communication was more acute and intractable. And it may be added that one of the important Jamesian themes otherwise is the bedevilment of human relations as a result of tragic misunderstanding and lack of communication. Thus, James's interest in the international "proposition" was fundamentally an extension of his interest in the drama of character contrasts, ambiguity and confusion. Such a drama could take a tragic turn, as it does in *The American* and "Madame de Mauves," or a comic one as in *The Europeans,* or have shades of the both as in "Daisy Miller" and *The Reverberator*. Essentially, everything serves as grist to his dramatic mill. Perhaps the best explanation of the international novel is offered by Oscar Cargill. "It is," he writes, "the novelist's equivalent of providing a special medium in a laboratory for studying the behavior of the organism, only here it is a device for the revelation of character. James appears to have been the first to realise the potentialities of the type to bring it to full development."[19]

Though *Roderick Hudson* dramatizes the tragic tale of the American sculptor's wasting and destructive passions against the Italian and Swiss backdrop, James is not primarily interested in the confrontation of two cultures or ways of life. His real object is the eternal clash between art and passion, and in another way, the eternal tragedy of explosive and unrequited genius. The Italian aspect lends colour and piquancy to the situation in that Italy has been traditionally the home and temple of art, but Hudson's drama could well have been staged in his native New England. It is not essential for James's thematic purpose that he transfer his hero's interests to Europe. That he does so is quite another thing. Nevertheless, there are in *Roderick Hudson* nearly all the important aspects of the international question, though they appear here in subsidiary and contributive measures. The European world of leisure, art and ceremony is contrasted with the American world of innocence, moral energy and material enterprise. In fact, the principal characters—Roderick Hudson, Rowland Mallet and Christina Light—are the archetypes of the international characters in James's fiction. Roderick and Rowland, "two sides of the same medal" as Leon Edel calls them, together make up Christopher Newman, while Christina, "the achieved woman of a corrupt society," will "in a later transformation become Madame Merle in *Portrait* and Kate Croy in *Wings*."[20] It is also interesting to note that from the start, James opposes his American "innocents" not as much to pure Europeans as to the Europeanized Americans. This pattern is significantly repeated in later books, and one is tempted to add that in the Jamesian interlock, the final showdown is between Americans and ex-Americans,[21] or between two competing halves of the same psyche. In "Madame de Mauves" and *The American,* and, to an extent, in *The Ambassadors,* the clash is, of course, between the purely French and the purely American values, but this is not a very frequent phenomenon in James. In these fictions also, the shades of the expatriated Americans lie heavy and thick even otherwise. In two of his most pointed international novels, *The Europeans* and *The Reverberator,* the opposing characters once again are New Englanders and de-racinated Americans. As for the international tales involving English life and manners, such as "An International Episode," "The Siege of London," "Lady Barbarina," "A London Life," etc., the stolid and serried English aristocracy with its delightful country houses is pitted against the footloose American tribe of incurable innocents and "flaming vulgarians," though even in some of the stories the American expatriates or ex-Americans somehow queer the pitch of the international drama.

In the "Parisian" fictions, the American-European modes of thought and behaviour, on the whole, are more fully contrasted and explored than in the London-based tales. Perhaps in James's view, the Gallic temperament roused or baited the American innocence and moral pride more than the phlegmatic English character, and was, therefore, more likely to yield a richer drama in terms of scenes and crises. Although the balance of sympathy nearly always tilts in favour of the American "victims," except in *The Ambassadors,* we are never allowed to forget American lapses, eccentricities and frigidities. In fact, James is careful enough to present a rounded picture of both American and French virtues and vices. The Americans' innocence, freshness, spontaneity, energy, enterprise and freedom which, in sum, make up their moral beauty, are set off against their ignorance, brashness, provincialism, philistinism, puritanism and commercialism—some of the traits that characterize "the ugly American" image abroad. Even their reputed innocence is in later novels sometimes viewed as predatory and rapacious—Milly Theale and Maggie Verver being fine examples. Similarly, the French-European love of art and form, their cultivated tastes and institutions, their delicate gestures and graces which add up to the settled serenities of life beloved of James, are undermined by their ingrained deceit and cunning, their moral laxity and expediency, their opportunism and inhumanity. Both F. R. Leavis and Marius Bewley are therefore justified in believing that James did not in particular fancy one set of values as against the others, but I doubt if he was consciously engineering "a dialectic of nations."[22] I rather tend to agree with J. A. Ward that in the end he could not resolve the conflict between European manners and American morals, and that he was simply content to dramatize the issue in all its ramifications. His ambivalence abides.

Perhaps the entire conflict could be described as a question of form and spirit. In Ferner Nehn's memorable words, "Europe is form without spirit, America is spirit without form."[23] Whilst James's aesthetic sensibility demanded form as much in life as in fiction, his moral sensibility was perpetually engaged in behalf of spirit. It was, in a manner, a clash of opposing categories in James himself, and, to that extent, the international issue was, strictly speaking, a personal and subjective affair. The conflict between manners and morals was at bottom an aspect of the dialectical clash between style and content, between restraint and expansion. Alternatively, it could be described as a confrontation between the twilight region of European experience and the noonday glare of American reality. The two categories or principles are described by Lionel Trilling as "radical" and "conservative." He observes:

> They may be thought of as energy and inertia; or spirit and matter; or spirit and letter; or force and form; or creation and possession; or Libido and Thanatos. In their simpler manifestations in the first term of the grandiose duality is generally regarded with unqualified sympathy and is identified with the ideality of youth, or with truth or with art, or with America; the second term is regarded with hostility and represented as being one with age, or convention, or philistinism, or decadent Europe. But James's mind is nothing if not "dialectical"—the values assigned to each of the two opposing principles are not permitted to be fixed and constant.[24]

This is well put, except that James, on the whole, tended to associate "art" with Europe and "philistinism" with America. One recalls in this connection James's own statement that "the flower of art blooms only where the soil is deep."[25] Again, "form" as opposed to "force" is not viewed with as much "hostility" as Professor Trilling thinks, though when it becomes an institutionalized and massed tyranny as in *The American* and *The Reverberator,* it certainly rouses James's ire. In fact, the rule of his fiction, that the form can best be preserved in its violation, is equally applicable where form in society and life is concerned. The diabolical to-do about family honour in the name of form and appearances which the Bellegardes and the Proberts enact to thwart the free flow of love is naturally viewed askance. The sheer inhumanity and chicanery of pure form, such as we later notice in Gilbert Osmond also, is something wholly distasteful to James. When the innocent Dossons are visibly pleased with the outcome of the Probert visit at the start, it is Gaston who is worried about the misunderstanding which a mere show of correct form and manners could cause. For, "he noticed how a manner might be a very misleading symbol, might cover pitfalls and bottomless gulfs when it had reached that perfection and corresponded so little to fact."[26]

Ultimately, I think, James is troubled about the French or European marital and sexual ethics, though he is by no means wholly opposed to its saving form. "Madame de Mauves" is one of the earliest examples of the cynical, but pragmatic, European code which recognized tacitly the existence, and even desirability, of lovers in married life. Euphemia's horror at her husband's proposal that she too take a lover—in this case, her American compatriot, Longmore—is understandable, for even though "the young American unmarried girl," to quote Tocqueville, "is less constrained than elsewhere, the wife is subjected to stricter obligation."[27] The pleated duplicity of the French aristocracy, which cheerfully combines "religion with immorality," as Edith Wharton tells us in her celebrated "Madame de Treymes," cannot but be taken as an unpardonable affront to one's dignity by the American psyche. Their muted and murky ethics was naturally anathema to those who had been reared in "that clear American air where there are no obscurities, no mysteries."[28] In short, an ethic of convenience and expediency was nothing but an outrage upon decency where the New Englanders were concerned. It is significant, however, to note that in his later international novels such as *The Ambassadors* and *The Golden Bowl,* the question of adultery and marital lapses is viewed far more tolerantly and humanely than in the earlier tales. The necessity of form and appearances in civilized life is recognized, and an ethic of compassion and understanding is clearly endorsed.

In fact, as I have suggested earlier, the American rigidities are also opposed from the start. To James's cultivated sensibility, there was something clearly unnatural and unwholesome about a conscience that exulted in inflicting pain upon itself and upon others. These masochistic and sadistic aspects are to be seen in most of the American heroines from Euphemia to Maggie Verver. The long line of St. Theresas is surely not without a moral. Longmore, a chastened and humanized American, baffled and tormented by Euphemia's unbending attitude, is constrained to remark: "You're killing yourself with stoicism—that's what is the matter with you."[29] And later, when her husband is obliged to blow out his brains in the face of her aggressive and menacing morality, she is spared no tears. "She was stone, she was ice, she was outraged virtue."[30] One is reminded of Yeats's famous line from "Easter 1916": "Too long a sacrifice can make a stone of the heart." Lest I be misunderstood, let me make it clear that in the balance, James admired the clarity, consistency and beauty of the American conscience—the conscience of a Christopher Newman, of an Isabel Archer, of a Francie Dosson, of a Milly Theale, of a Strether—what he dreaded was the spectacle of a conscience that would admit no spark of pity, mercy or understanding. In the end, for him a disengaged conscience was as grievous a bar to happiness as an "indurated conscience." Similarly, an overworked and stretched conscience such as Laura Wing's in "A London Life" is viewed with a great deal of irony and even mirth.

This brings me to "Daisy Miller" and *The Europeans,* two of James's most celebrated international fictions whose *leitmotif* is not pain and pathos, but irony and humour. "Daisy Miller," of course, has not the clear sun-lit quality of *The Europeans,* and the drama of the American *belle* in Rome resulting in her death by cold has undoubtedly a graver aspect, but the emphasis, on the whole, is on the sum of comic misunderstandings, born of cultural differences and divisions. For, as often as not, misunderstanding in life can be a source of high fun and drama. The story of Daisy Miller is essentially light, and James in his preface speaks of "an object scant and superficially vulgar—from which, however, a sufficiently brooding tenderness might eventually extract a shy incongruous charm."[31] The young woman, "a child of nature and of freedom,"[32] brings with her to Rome all her native innocence and insouciance, spirit and sangfroid, little knowing that in the sophisticated but soiled world of continental love, her very virtues will be seen as vices, that her natural, inborn joie de vivre or spiritedness will unleash a comedy of errors, and eventually, a needless tragedy. Winterbourne's misunderstanding—and it is through his eyes that we watch this drama of American ebullience—under the circumstances is unavoidable. How innocence, unbesmirched but compromised, may come to grief in an alien land is the theme of "Daisy Miller." Back home in the United States, the American girl would have carried the world before her without raising as much as an eyebrow. She is killed less by the Roman weather than by the absurdity of her situation. And indeed, her death, in a manner, is an example of the absurd.

In *The Europeans,* James, writing a collateral novel to *The American,* reverses not the formula of the international theme but the locale and the manner of conducting it. It is the Europeans, or preferably, the deracinated Americans, who are, so to speak, let loose amongst a school of guileless Americans on their home ground. In this comedy of confrontation, innocence is almost subverted in its Edenic atmosphere. The visiting "Europeans"—Felix and his sister, Eugenia—are by no means "serpents"; if anything, they are finally the agents of James's vision of tolerance and accommodation. Felix's idea that the Wentworths took "a painful view of life," and his quip about Mr. Wentworth's perpetual "martyrdom, not by fire, but by freezing"[33] are undoubtedly to be seen as James's deep distrust of strangulating New England conventions and attitudes. The Baroness, on the other hand, is put out by American provincialism and moral myopia. No wonder she calls America at the outset "this dreadful country," while Felix's phrase for it is "this comical country, this delightful country!"[34] In fact, James takes pains to emphasize Felix's spontaneity and warmth against the moral chill of New England, thereby transferring a part of American charm to this gay European, making a song and a lark of life. And there is a lot to be said for the insightful observation of J. A. Ward that the suggestion of the Europeans being "more archetypically American than the New Englanders is recurrent"[35] in the novel. Felix also succeeds in touching the European vein in his American cousin, Gertrude, who according to her sister Charlotte and her suitor, Mr. Brand (mark the name!), has been turned away from the natural current of American methods. "Oh, Felix, Felix!" she cried, "what have you done to her?" To which he replies, "I think she was asleep, I have waked her up!"[36] In this light drama of contrasts and reversals, of expectations and disappointments, James appears to be making another point, and that is that happiness is at once a condition of money and the mind. The Europeans of the novel have talent, sophistication and charm, but no money; the Americans have fortunes and estates and innocence, but no pedigree, no cultivation, no taste for high life. Together, Felix and Gertrude complete the circle, though Eugenia must return to the old European pastures. There is no doubt at all that James's kindly irony scarcely hurts the Baroness, whose European morality comes in for a few well-merited swipes. She is in some ways a prefiguration of a much more charming and soulful European woman, Madame de Vionnet. Again, this is not to say that the Americans are not given their due. Despite their faux pas and the heavier irony to which they are continually subjected, James does not let their essential moral beauty come under a cloud. In fact, it breaks through again and again, and surprises us with its perennial power. Even Mr. Wentworth is not an abandoned soul at all; on the contrary, there is a gentle, shy charm about this Puritan worthy.

> Over these young people—a vague report of their existence had come to his ears—Mr. Wentworth had not, in the course of years, allowed his imagination to hover. It had plenty of occupation nearer home, and, though he had many cares upon his conscience, the idea that he had been an unnatural uncle was very properly never among the number. Now that his nephew and niece had come before him, he perceived that they were the fruit of influences and circumstances very different from those under which his own familiar progeny had reached a vaguely-qualified maturity. He felt no provocation to say that these influences had been exerted for evil; but he was sometimes afraid that he should not be able to like his distinguished, delicate, lady-like niece. He was paralysed and bewildered by her foreignness. She spoke, somehow, a different language. There was something strange in her words. He had a feeling that another man, in his place, would accommodate himself to her tone; would ask her questions and joke with her, reply to those pleasantries of her own which sometimes seemed startling as addressed to an uncle. But Mr. Wentworth could not do these things. He could not even bring himself to attempt to measure her position in the world. She was the wife of a foreign nobleman who desired to repudiate her. This had a singular sound, but the old man felt himself destitute of the materials for a judgment. It seemed to him that he ought to find them in his own experience, as a man of the world and an almost public character; but they were not there, and he was ashamed to confess to himself—much more to reveal to Eugenia by interrogations possibly too innocent—the unfurnished condition of his repository. . . . [37]

If this is not a portrait of love, it is certainly not a portrait of contempt.

Although the tragic comedy of cultural contrasts and clashing values continues to occupy James till the end in one form or another, the international novels and tales of the later phase record a subtle shift in his perspective. This is first felt significantly in *The Portrait of a Lady,* though the full impact of the change is not seen till the turn of the century. In *The Portrait,* the comedy of confrontation largely veers round subsidiary characters like Henrietta, Mrs. Touchett, Mrs. Gemini, and though the principal protagonists—Isabel Archer, Osmond and Madame Merle—too are not spared a spray of irony, where their cultural obtusenesses and deficiencies are concerned, James is obviously much less concerned with the cultural contrasts here than with the fundamental questions of innocence and experience, appearance and reality, silence and communication. In part, these questions present themselves in *The American* also, but James's epistemological interests are not as yet fully roused. James himself was fully aware of the subsidiary significance of the international theme in his later novels. As he wrote in the preface to Volume XIV of the New York Edition:

> Yet there are cases in which, however obvious and however contributive, its office for the particular demonstration has been quite secondary, and in which the work is by no means merely addressed to the illustration of it. These things have had in the latter case their proper subject: as, for instance, the subject of 'The Wings of the Dove,' or that of 'The Golden Bowl,' has not been the exhibited behaviour of certain Americans as Americans, of certain English persons as English, of certain Romans as Romans. Americans, Englishmen, Romans are, in the whole matter, agents or victims, but this is in virtue of an association nowadays so developed, so easily to be taken for granted, to have created a new scale of relations altogether, as a state of things from which *emphasised* internationalism has either quite dropped or is well on its way to drop."[38]

In the later novels, Europe becomes for the American protagonists a test of moral values, and a ground for proving the truths of the heart and the imagination. It emerges as a symbol of "the extreme situation." In this respect, James's later work is a prefiguration of the work of such modern novelists as Conrad, Greene, Camus and Malraux who place their protagonists in physical situations of such intensity and complexity as to force moral choices upon them. A Malaysian settlement in the back of beyond, an African lepers' colony, a stricken Algerian town, a Chinese city in the throes of a revolutionary upsurge—all these and similar locales in their fiction are meant primarily to bring out the best and the worst in human nature. We find that James's moral imagination also is most fully engaged only when his characters find themselves in situations of extreme spiritual travail. Gradually, the road to be taken becomes so narrow and straight that they cannot but choose, and in so doing, must affirm themselves to the uttermost. It's not that they will always come out into the warm open sun from a condition of moral fog and bafflement, but we shall see them heroically struggling to stop inner erosion, and to seek some kind of commitment, if not transcendence, as in the case of Milly Theale. For

James, then, Europe served largely as a huge spider that held the American "innocents" captive, and forced them to make moral and spiritual exertions to free themselves. Even European affirmations and felicities such as we find in Strether's Paris are to be seen in the light of a moral vision earned by the hero as a result of such exertions. If confrontation with death and the irrational brought a Lord Jim or a Dr. Rieux to a state of moral boil, confrontation with spiritual death put an Isabel Archer and a Maggie Verver at their fighting best. James needed not the wildernesses of the sea, the jungle and the desert to test the moral fibre or mettle of his American protagonists; the Old World was powder enough for the spirit to be ignited.

Viewed slightly differently, the European-American complex could be taken as James's extension of his abiding interest in the themes of appearance and reality, innocence and experience, good and evil. These are perennial and archetypal questions again.[39] Each artist has to work out his own schemata for the purpose, and James found the Continent exemplifying to a rare degree the clash between these existential antinomies. A ready and handy framework of opposed attitudes was available, thanks to his American origin and long European stay, and he saw in it a valuable syndrome for dramatizing these eternal verities of life. Tony Tanner, for instance, regards James's international tales as primarily concerned with the basic issues confronting man. London was to the novelist, then, "a metaphor for a dense conglomeration of sensations and values . . . the biggest aggregation of human life—the most complex compendium of the world."[40] It may perhaps be more pertinent to suggest the Rome-Paris-London axis as James's massed metaphor representing a structured, but ambivalent human reality. The New England assault only helped realize this in a vivid and pointed manner.

And finally, there is the view that the international novels and tales prove James's increasing and awakened interest in cosmopolitanism. Leon Edel, in particular, emphasizes this point in some of his later writings on James. He regards the maturer work of the novelist as a sustained exercise in international understanding and amity. In his inaugural address "Henry James and the Cosmopolitan Imagination" delivered in 1967 at New York University, he cites well-known passages from James's letters and works to prove that his cosmopolitanism was a deep-seated, ingrained quality, and that it fertilized his muse from the start. "Within his work," says Professor Edel, "we find not merely a superficial chronicle of comedies of tourism, but great cosmopolitan feeling, that act of life which resides in observation and notation, in sympathetic comprehension and acceptance of international differences—manners, customs, traditions, the fabric of social history which is the fabric of the art of fiction."[41] J. A. Ward discussing the "structural irony" of James's "Madame de Mauves" observes that the theme of this earlier story "has to do not with the significance but with the insignificance of national differences."[42] Some critics have even gone on to invest James with something of an international halo. Indeed, the rise of the James tide has almost been attributed to the spirit of the United Nations founded around that time. I confess, much as I admire James's catholicity of mind, I cannot visualize him in the role of a visionary Wendell Wilkie selling the ideal of "One World" across the globe. There is no doubt at all about James's distrust of all types of provincialisms and parochialisms. "There comes a time," he writes in 1878, "when one set of customs wherever it may be found, grows to seem about as provincial as another."[43] But this, as I view it, is more an aesthetic than a humanist dimension in his work. That there is a moral edge to it in his later fiction may not be denied, and yet the James who rued the decline of British Imperialism,[44] and who had a Napoleonic vision of power and glory on his death-bed[45] could not be, in all fairness, seen as a culture hero of the post-war period. He simply did not have a larger historical perspective. His cosmopolitanism is essentially a matter of form, style and manners—a movement away from the shabbiness, clumsiness and squalor of life. Its idealistic potential is severely limited. As compared with him, H. G. Wells, for instance, was far more committed to international ideals, and was ideologically much more alive. In short, James was not as *weltoffen*, i.e., conscious of the undercurrents of history and thought, as some critics would have us believe. He himself wrote, when young: "To be a cosmopolite is not, I think, an ideal, the ideal should be to be a concentrated patriot. Being a cosmopolite is an accident, but one must make the best of it. . . . The consequence of the cosmopolite spirit is to initiate you into the merits of all peoples, to convince you that national virtues are numerous, though they may be very different and to make downright preference really very hard."[46]

In short, James's cosmopolitanism, though an achieved insight, is not really integral and nuclear in character. Leon Edel is, of course, right when elsewhere he shows the novelist viewing the international question in the end "as a big Anglo-Saxon total."[47] F. R. Leavis too refers to the international dialectic, and to James's search for a positive ideal, through "a critical interplay between different traditions."[48] Assuredly, towards the end of his life, James had gained a peep into the "swan soul" of Europe, and of America. He saw the energies that agitated the two Worlds, and though he was somewhat frightened by the lengthening shadow of baronial capitalism, as in *The Ivory Tower,* he still made an honest and desperate effort to discover a spiritual identity between Europe and America. His Francie Dosson, when baffled by French manners and ethics, could in all sincerity utter: "We are terribly different"; to which the later James could well have added: "We are *terribly identical*—at a deeper level!"

A Vision of the American Woman

When critics talk of Henry James's Shakespearian qualities, it is generally under-stood that they mean the qualities of poetry in his fiction—felicity and inevitability of idiom, sensuous apprehension of thought, sweep of the imagination, the elements of myth and drama, icons and symbols, evocation and ambience. And undoubtedly, these qualities are to be found in his work from the beginning, though it is in the involved or "mystic" novels and tales of the final phase that we see James's poetry in full tide. There is, however, yet another Shakespearian dimension to his great gifts, and that is his genius for divining and rendering the poetry of the female psyche. There are, to be sure, a few tragic gaps in his treatment of young women, particularly in relation to their passional or sexual experiences, but few novelists in the English language have shown a better understanding of their tender and dreaming hearts than James. Only Jane Austen and George Eliot among women, and Sir Walter Scott, George Meredith and Thomas Hardy among his predecessors and contemporaries have shown any-thing like the reach and grasp seen in his fiction. Perhaps George Eliot's heroines—Dorothea Brooke and Gwendolen Harleth, in particular—are the nearest approximations to James's own, for we know the young American novelist was deeply affected by their spiritual charm and moral beauty. Reviewing *Middlemarch,* he wrote about Dorothea: "She exhales a sort of aroma of spiritual sweetness."[1] It may not, therefore, be too much to suggest that James had a truly feminine sensibility. In other words, his work at the deepest level is inspired by emotion and intuition rather than by intelligence and intellect. It is the richness of consciousness or interior life which engages his imagination at its best. James's type of novel, thus, is not primarily the athletic novel of action and decision, but the aesthetic novel of reaction and deliberation. Of course, he has some very moving and fine portraits of heroes—Roderick Hudson, Christopher Newman, Hyacinth Robinson, Lambert Strether—but they too are, by and large, examples of the supremacy of the life of the imagination and the mind. Their characteristic actions are still, in the end, actions of poetic souls in travail. It is, therefore, to James's great American heroines—Catherine Sloper, Daisy Miller, Isabel Archer,

Francie Dosson, Milly Theale and Maggie Verver, above all—that we must turn for the ultimate meaning of his books. Their English counterparts—Fleda Vetch and Nanda Brookenham, amongst others—are the products of the same "loving" imagination, though in spiritual grandeur they do not measure up to James's American women. And it is not because the English heroines are subjected to a heavier irony—there is irony enough in the treatment of the American heroine's aggressive innocence and tragic ignorance—but because, for certain deep, psychological reasons, the young American woman evoked the strongest spiritual response in James till the end. As for his European or Europeanized heroines—Christina Light, Eugenia and Madame de Vionnet—they represent a different order and style of charm. Their appeal is that of the "achieved" woman. Madame Merle, Kate Croy and Charlotte Stant too belong here, except that they are cast too pointedly in the role of the "wicked" woman. Whereas the American heroine is invested with a vestal aura, the European woman, usually older and more experienced, is given a deep, sexual attraction à la Cleopatra. Her fatal fascination is one of the ineluctable mysteries of life. Leslie A. Fiedler's percep-tive account of "the Dark Lady and the Fair Girl archetype"[2] both in Hawthorne and James suggests the presence of "the sentimental heresy" in the American mind, and this is plausibly argued, but I doubt if "the snow maidens" of James are all ultimately an expression of the "necrophiliac" imagination, as he thinks. There are, of course, in James a number of *thanatos*-oriented stories, the most celebrated being "The Altar of the Dead," and there are in the climactic gestures of his three celebrated heroines, Isabel Archer, Milly Theale and Maggie Verver, symbolic overtures to death—Isabel's controversial return from Gardencourt to "the house of death and suffocation," Milly's turning of the face to the wall, Maggie's masochistic movements in the end—but it would be a mistake to regard the typical Jamesian heroine as a symbol of cold death. For renunciation could at once be interpreted as death of the spirit and as heroic existence at a higher altitude. The ambivalence of James does leave us mystified. It could be argued with equal force that the Jamesian heroine, in fact, represents the principle of health, sanity and sunshine. This high-souled, tight-lipped, crucified woman who seeks to graduate to a beatific vision remains a redeeming agent in this sorry and dusty world of contaminating and compulsive evil.

The Jamesian heroine is, of course, nearly always an idealized figure, though not untypical or unauthentic for that reason. Her ethereal quality would, at first sight, appear to make her a sort of Pre-Raphaelite figure of nebulous and drowsy charm, but if we learn to live in her presence for a while, we are struck by the force of her will and soul. There is an awesome magnificence about this delicate and fragile creature. It must not be forgotten that the person we are alluding to is the young American woman of the last century—the woman in whom the pristine dream was not yet spent. She not only still nursed the Puritan conscience, but also the voyaging spirit of her *Mayflower* ancestors. Perhaps more than the American male, she embodied visions of the good and sufficient life. Daughter of the Bible and the Edenic soil of New England, unbroken to the ways of the world and, therefore, more vulnerable, she carried the New World burden on her slender but heroic shoulders. That in the business and traffic of life she would be bruised and despoiled only went to prove that the price of idealism was always and everywhere dark and long and deep suffering. And if she were also slightly sullied en route, it would only show that living soiled even a saint. The pilgrim soul had to take "full in the face the whole assault of life,"[3] and yet remain inviolate to the greatest extent possible. It is as if her puritan forbears were almost always an invisible presence with her, and would permit no subversion. Lest I be misunderstood, let me make it clear that I do not regard Isabel Archer and her younger compatriots as puritan in any theological or doctrinal sense. This puritanism is, in fact, in more liberal and awakened sensibilities, another name for a soul-force that resists evil in all its forms, and gives it battle ineluctably and unsleepingly. In the Jamesian heroine, then, the traditional harshness and sadism of male puritanism is purified, as if filtered through a fine sieve. Here and there, some stern, unbending daughter of Calvinistic descent may survive—Euphemia of "Madame de Mauves," for instance, but she is not James's ideal of the American woman. She is, on the contrary, an extreme example of ingrown virtue amounting to inhumanity. The heroine who solicits his imagination is the young woman who carries her puritanism lightly and unobtrusively. She has imbibed it, so to speak, with her mother's milk. In her, it has become a settled stance, an attitude of life. Of course, "the Collective Unconscious" will still govern her personality, and will, at times, break out on the surface, but there is, on the whole, a fine adjustment between what Freud calls "the pleasure principle" and "the reality principle." Part of the spiritual serenity we associate with the Jamesian heroine stems from this unconscious force, this automatic balancing of the instinct of freedom with the dictates of the moral law.

That James intends to make his heroine the agent of his moral vision is clear from our first view of her, which is nearly always soulful. More than the eye, it is the mind which leaps up at the extraordinary beauty and fineness of the figure before us. Obviously, the poetry that is pressed into service is intended to invest her, from the start, with an aura of mystic charm. Sometimes, the physical background of the scene helps place her in that poetic perspective. Take, for instance, the celebrated opening scene of *The Portrait of a Lady*. Undoubtedly, the serene beauty of that English country-house, Gardencourt, invades the reader's senses, as James goes on adding meaningful little strokes to the impressionistic picture he is painting. A high summer afternoon on the wane, the tea ceremony, the invalid master of the house in a wicker chair with a collie dog nestling at his feet, a pair of animated young men strolling about on neat, lush, expansive lawns, the stately mansion in the background with its patches of ivy and creepers and festooned windows redolent of history—all these little details give the scene the quality of a Constable or a Whistler landscape. And though we are charmed by it for its own sake too, I think, the restful beauty of the place is primarily intended to serve us an apt background to Isabel Archer's "aristocratic" compulsions and her "garden-like" qualities which are emphasized throughout the book. Her sudden arrival amidst these sylvan surroundings has the effect of a pleasing breeze in the face. The young American lady steps like a princess into the enchanted place. There is almost a feeling that she has stepped into a framed picture. After James has sketched the Albany hinterland, and we have seen her disporting herself at Gardencourt, there is a straight miniature "portrait" offered us in chapter 11. The beautiful young "egoist" with "a flame-like spirit" and a vivacity and magnanimity of imagination has, despite her fault of "self-esteem," an ineffable floral charm, a fragrance of character that envelops her person. That is how James describes it:

> She was always planning out her development, desiring her perfection, observing her progress. Her nature had, in her conceit, a certain garden-like quality, a suggestion of perfume and murmuring boughs, of shady bowers and lengthening vistas, which made her feel that introspection was, after all, an exercise in the open air, and that a visit to the recesses of one's spirit was harmless when one returned from it with a lapful of roses.[4]

> Her uncle's house seemed a picture made real; no refinement of the agreeable was lost upon Isabel; the rich perfection of Gardencourt at once revealed a world and gratified a need. The large, low rooms, with brown ceilings and dusky corners, the deep embrasures and curious casements, the quiet light on dark, polished panels, the deep greenness outside, that seemed always peeping in, the sense of well-ordered privacy in the centre of a "property"—a place where sounds were felicitously accidental, where the tread was muffled by the earth itself and in the thick mild air all friction dropped out of contact and all shrillness out of talk—these things were much to the taste of our young lady, whose taste played a considerable part in her emotions.[5]

> The old man was full of kindness for her; it was a long time, as he said, since they had had any young life in the house; and our rustling, quickly-moving, clear-voiced heroine was as agreeable to his sense as the sound of flowing water. He wanted to do something for her and wished she would ask it of him. She would ask nothing but questions; it is true that of these she asked a quantity.[6]

The effect of Isabel's presence upon her old and dying uncle is like "a touch of June in November," and recalls to mind Galsworthy's famous interlude, "The Indian Summer of a Forsyte," where Irene brings into old Jolyon's wintry days a feeling of the sun and the fireside. Youthful female beauty at its purest has a transcendent aspect, and James's fiction is full of this feeling.

Another heroine of this period, Francie Dosson of *The Reverberator*, is a fine example of American innocence and loveliness, except that while Isabel Archer is done in oil, the portrait of the younger lady is done in water-colour. She is like James's other Americans "almost incredibly *unaware of life*—as the European order expressed life."[7] While she herself is "as straight as a wand and as true as a gem," her millionaire father is described as "a character as cipherable as a sum of two figures."[8] Father and daughter, like Adam Verver and Maggie in *The Golden Bowl,* almost constitute a wry order of saints. When Waterlow, an American painter settled in Paris, tells Gaston that Francie is "the softest finest material that breathes,"[9] he is undoubtedly voicing James's sentiment. These motherless[10] American girls are indeed the stuff men's dreams are made on. In the preface to *The Reverberator,* James talks of these "unprecedented creatures"—"the Francie Dossons, the Daisy Millers, the Bessie Aldens and the Pandora Days" of "thirty or forty years ago" who, unmindful of their "deficiencies and dangers," romped through Europe "so that the grace of youth and innocence and freshness aiding, their negatives were converted, and became in certain relations lively positives and values."[11]

The European pilgrimage of the Jamesian heroine, as we have seen in the preceding essay, has many an involved aspect. The international tales were at once an expression of the clash of cultural values and of existential verities. Thus, for dramatizing such a confrontation between opposed modes of thought and patterns of conduct on the one hand, and between innocence and experience, between appearance and reality on the other, James was obliged to ship off his heroine to Europe. The continent was not merely "the great American sedative"[12] or "a gilded holiday toy,"[13] but also a testing laboratory for determining the potency of the ultimate American values. This was at once a nostalgic regression in behalf of more settled and sophisticated postures, and a provocative challenge in behalf of new possibilities. Today, the distance between American innocence and European venality is nearly bridged, and a contemporary Henry James may well reverse the traffic, though that will prove nothing except the equality of Occidental morality. This is not being facetious, for in our own time, to explore the "heart of darkness," Graham Greene, who shares with James a sustained interest in evil, sin and redemption, had to take his "quiet" American to the Far East to provide an extreme situation such as both Europe and America did not offer today. Back home, sin had lost its attraction; it had almost been domesticated. It no longer had its exotic and primeval appeal. As Lionel Trilling observes in another context: "The extreme has become the commonplace of today."[14] In James's time, Europe still had the attraction of "the forbidden fruit," and the American female in particular was irresistibly drawn to it. Thus, the Jamesian heroine needs must seek fulfillment in the experience-fields of Europe. It is an urgent requirement of her expanding psyche. One may go even so far as to say that the European contact is a kind of therapeutic orgasm which, in proving or vindicating her, also liberates her from her romantic illusions and fantasies. Perhaps, there is in the American woman a deep and dark wish to be violated by the European male. Her downy, dove-like innocence seeks ravishment much in the same way as Yeats's Muses do.[15] She grows rich in pain and suffering for the experience, and is the more magnificent for that. A moral beauty is born out of sheer laceration. That is the meaning of Milly Theale's "crucifixion," or of Maggie Verver's "martyrdom."

Apart from the Continental dream, which is perhaps her strongest single compulsion, there is a whole complex of urges and evocations, hungers and desires to be found in the Jamesian heroine. One of these is the desire to remove cumbersome reality and exist as spirit. In his essay on Howells in *The Opposing Self,* Lionel Trilling devotes a couple of insightful pages to this generic American trait. The American love of things and artifacts and machines is, at bottom, he observes, an effort to transcend physical reality. The good things of life—health, education, material comforts, etc.—are all there to feed the spirit, as it were. "Somewhere in our mental constitution," he writes, "is the demand for life as pure spirit."[16] Obviously, Professor Trilling resists the Marxist idea that the preoccupation with things per se cannot but turn to commodity fetishism in the end, and therefore, to the death of the spirit. He seems to believe that beneath all the materialistic gloss of American life, there is still a strong and visible undercurrent of the voyaging spirit or of the questing self. All the materialistic distortions and aberrations are, if anything, a proof of the wrenchings and travail of that spirit. It is an attractive thesis, and does seem to offer a clue to the peculiar American dilemma. Whether this is true of the present-day American reality or not, it certainly does offer a most helpful and revealing peep into the psychology of the Jamesian heroine. This is a point which James clearly understood. He felt that while the American male at his finest, as in the case of Christopher Newman, could preserve the beauty of spirit even when condemned to manufacturing bath-tubs, the young American woman did so as a matter of course. There was a sense of spiritual ease about her. Somehow the grossness and vulgarity associated with the pursuit of lucre did not seem to touch her. One is reminded of George Eliot's words about these queens of the spirit quoted by James in the preface to *The Portrait of a Lady:* "In these frail vessels is borne onward through the ages the treasure of human affection."[17] Obviously, for James, the young American woman became a mystic carrier of the pure ancestral dream. This was also the belief of James's father who regarded woman as an instrument of destiny and salvation. She was for him and for other American writers "the priestess of the American heritage, untainted by commercialism, committed to the future, representative of widening possibilities,"[18] in the words of Quentin Anderson.

It could be argued with some force that this "heiress of all the ages"[19] was simply a Jamesian myth that hid the awful facts of the economic situation. You do not soil your hands so long as someone else handles the pitch for you. The spirit is free to indulge itself meanwhile, if you please. It would, however, be uncharitable, in my view, to regard the Isabel Archers and the Milly Theales in that light. James rightly saw in them a soul-force that in the end was not wholly conditioned by their millions. None of them has what you call a low, grasping money-grubbing spirit. On the other hand, magnanimity of spirit was a condition of their being. Even a heroine of such limited means and beauty as Miss Spencer of "Four Meetings" whose "eager and tender imagination"[20] is exploited by an unscrupulous cousin during her visit to Europe disarms us with the utter beauty and simplicity of her conduct. The urge to live as spirit is perhaps another way of acknowledging the need of the American psyche for freedom at all levels of being and existence. For several historical and psychological reasons, there is nothing that brings it so soon into a state of combat as any overt threat to undermine its sovereignty. No wonder the Statue of Liberty has assumed the dimensions of a national totem. It is, however, characteristic of advanced industrialized societies to nurse all types of constitutional and academic freedoms in proportion as existential freedom is more and more covertly subverted in the process of mechanization and authoritarianism. Thus, freedom tends to become something of an abstraction and a fetish even as it is being eroded from within. That the Jamesian heroine too, like James himself, does not understand the dialectics of freedom, as Arnold Kettle[21] argues, is correct, though this does not diminish the value of her effort to preserve it at all costs. There is indeed something both pathetic and heroic about her sustained struggle in behalf of a noble but shadowy ideal. What matters in the end is the quality of her defiance. And in that we see the vindication of her spirit. She will be "contesting every inch of the road."[22] This is best illustrated in Isabel Archer's case, though other Jamesian heroines like Milly Theale and Maggie Verver too are equally mistaken about the nature of freedom, and equally magnificent in their struggle to maintain the integrity of their souls. Isabel starts her sojourn at the spacious and enchanting Gardencourt with two disarming statements: "I'm not a candidate for adoption"[23] and "I like my liberty too much."[24] So far, everything is all right, and we admire our heroine for her playful assertion of spirit. We are prepared even to admire a view of life and happiness which extends over "a swift carriage of a dark night, rattling with four horses over roads that one cannot see."[25] The youth may well be granted the courage of their extravagant dreams. But in rejecting two honourable offers of marriage, and in accepting Osmond, who symbolizes the sterility and cruelty of pure aestheticism, Isabel has only been faithful to the illusions of freedom and felicity she has nourished all along her adult life. Nor does she recognize, till it is too late, the corroding, soiling and subverting power of unearned money in a society sold on hedonism. The wind which Ralph Touchett wants to put in her sails, as he ruefully acknowledges later, is precisely the element that rocks her boat and nearly sinks it. Whether she is in the end really liberated from her romantic illusions and twisted visions, as Tony Tanner[26] claims, is a question that has never been satisfactorily answered. Perhaps, one of the deepest illusions of life is to believe that one is at last free from illusions. There is, in any case, a teasing ambiguity about her controversial return to Rome. One thing, however, may be asserted with confidence. Isabel Archer has never surrendered her right to act in full freedom, as she understands it. Till the end, she keeps her options and choices open. If she has married, as she asserts, in full view of the world, she returns to her unregenerated husband in full view of her disabilities and her strengths. Perhaps that is the beginning, and not the end, of her spiritual pilgrimage. She may yet walk out on Osmond in the full beauty of her tragic destiny, should her symbolic gesture of reconciliation fail to sensitize his ossified moral sensibility.

A view strongly persists, however, that Isabel's return from light to darkness, from freedom to a hermetic, tortured life inside "a cage" is a typical example of psychological suicide, as Dennis O'Connor makes it out in a recent article,[27] but I would still suggest a more moral meaning of her action—a definitive act of the personality in combat with circumstance and reality. Undoubtedly, the return carries a hint of nunlike chillness, as also a wash of the romantic agony, but it also indicates strongly a toughening of the spirit, and a making of the moral being. That is how, I trust, James tends to see his American woman, a figure of moral beauty and spiritual sweetness. Her freedom is now *interiorized,* her illusions and insufficiencies notwithstanding.

Similarly, Milly Theale's rhapsodic desire "to enjoy boundless freedom, the freedom of the wind in the desert"[28] is academically a highly laudable sentiment. Only she too, proud soul, will learn in the end that all her millions were simply arid promises in a world peopled by smooth and covetous adventurers. Just when the dream of her heart lies broken in the dust, and the riches of life all spilt, she, by a superhuman act of the will, converts her defeat into a triumph of the spirit. It is as pure flame that she exists in the finest hour of her life before her extinction, and it is as pure spirit that she exists in the memory of those whose faces had been brushed by the luminous "wings of the dove." James's tender references in his letters to the dead Minny Temple abiding as "a pure eloquent vision" long after her death perfectly dovetail with the meaning of Milly Theale's incorporeal existence after her exit from the book. The Jamesian heroine, when pressed to the wall, will live as spirit, or not live at all.

Maggie Verver's case is different in degree only. She is in the end more vulnerable, and, therefore, more human. But she too has learnt to forgive, if not forget. She has finally recovered the Prince not only physically, but also morally and spiritually. It is, I grant, a sort of inverted triumph, when looking at her husband's face with "pity and dread," she "buried her own in his breast,"[29] but it is also a gesture of her own endearing surrender without which there can never be any real understanding or restored harmony. The golden bowl, a work of exquisite workmanship, probably of Indian origin, was to be a symbol of conjugal sufficiency, felicity and preciousness, and now she would have to pick up the formless fragments to create an order of beauty out of them. And when she tells Mrs. Assingham about her father, and Charlotte: "For they're the ones who are saved, we're the ones who are lost,"[30] I think she might duly be reminded of Ralph Touchett's remark to Isabel Archer: "I don't think such a mistake as yours can hurt you for more than a little."[31] Her mistake had been to have taken appearance for reality, and then to have tried to shape reality into appearance. If she commits the sin of manipulating other peoples' lives, and if she betrays unmistakable signs of incestuous and destructive impulses, as some critics have persuasively argued, it should in fairness be also emphasized that Maggie's essential humanity remains uncompromised, that her mistakes are the mistakes of her position and of generosity, not of cold calculation. James himself refers to Maggie's "beautiful generosity." A soul in mortal travail—and there is no other heroine of James who suffers so much at different levels of her being—may pardonably be guilty of striking out for any type of shore. The point we may not be allowed to forget is that even this flawed little saint has a magnificence of spirit that shines through her frail frame. In a manner, she shows a greater soul-force than Milly Theale who may strike us as almost non-human as a person, more properly envisioned as a spirit than a body. For all her human weaknesses, Maggie shows how the spirit may yet prevail and hoist the flag amidst a prospect of ruins and defeats. This is to snatch a victory in the teeth of guile and ugliness and absurdity.

In the context of the Jamesian heroine's urge to live as spirit, and to live in utter freedom, I may, in passing, refer to the multiplying and pervading imagery of freedom in the three novels I have briefly touched upon—*The Portrait of a Lady, The Wings of the Dove* and *The Golden Bowl*. On the one hand, we have the free and open images of wings, plumage and flight; on the other, we have the claustrophobic images of darkened and shut-in mansions, cages, prisons and tunnels. Obviously, the poetic images imply the American heroine's overwhelming desire for freedom from worldly accommodations. The spirit will not be confined, nor compromised in the effort to negotiate life.

The question of freedom for the Jamesian heroine is also umbilically connected with yet another compulsion—the question of *persona* and mask, of style and stance. Almost always, the American *jeune fille* is an open-minded, warm-hearted, clear-eyed person who responds richly to the music and fragrance of life. Attuned to the deeper rhythms of nature, she accepts the world around her on its face value, and is prepared to stretch her faith to the point of pitiful and tragic artlessness. Uninhibited and unconditioned, she is open to fresh views and vistas. Morally inflammable, she carries a clean, fine and wholesome conscience which will brook no insult, casuistry and temporization. Armed thus with nothing better than her splendid innocence, insouciance and integrity, she comes to Europe on a pilgrimage of self-discovery. She has always a defined style of life, and a moral stance which she guards most jealously. Even when she is not initially rich, as is the case with Isabel Archer, she has an unmistakable aristocracy of the mind and a royalty of the soul. She is rich in the sense Ralph Touchett defines affluence: "I call people rich when they're able to meet the requirements of their imagination."[32] She doesn't have to marry a prince as Maggie Verver does, to be called princess. Milly Theale, without a formal title, is invariably referred to as such by her loving companion, Mrs. Stringham. In short, she is like a gold sovereign (a favourite Jamesian image) issued and presented on a velvet platter. However, her virginal freshness and extreme spontaneity are the very qualities which mark her out as a victim. She does not realize that the world is not tailored to order in consonance with her delicate sensibility. Like the lady in the limerick, she rides the European tiger with a smile on her face, but before long the smile is transferred to the face of the cunning cat. Europe has indeed an enormous appetite for American "chicks" and "doves." She is thus a sitting target for the Continental sharp-shooters. No wonder, when the first traumatic shock is received by her, she reacts to it violently, even though, for the most part, she "must fight soundlessly, and in the dark,"[33] as Austin Warren says apropos of Maggie Verver. Though she often shows remarkable reservoirs of spiritual energy in meeting the affront to her ego or psyche, she cannot but withdraw into the fastnesses of her mind and heart. This leads to the hardening of the stance, and to the solidifying of the mask. Under no circumstances henceforth will she permit any intruder a peep into the privacies and sacred sufferings of her life. On the contrary, she will develop a mystique of martyrdom, and continue to wear a crown of thorns in the manner of a latter-day St. Theresa even when she has discovered her error. Isabel Archer will not "publish" her "mistake," but will enter, in the words of R. P. Blackmur, "a convent of her own making."[34] Milly Theale, whose "ferocity of modesty" and "intensity of pride" suggest a hidden violence, will develop a pathological dread of pity. Even an earlier heroine like Catherine Sloper of *Washington Square,* when crushed by her lover's perfidy and by her father's cruelty, would not permit her comic aunt, Mrs. Penniman, the luxury of pity. This plain, mute and awkward girl acquires in her suffering a beauty and an eloquence and an ease undreamt of before. Maggie Verver will herself affirm this when talking to her father on Charlotte Stant's earlier failure in love. "What happens at least is that where there's a great deal of pride, there's a great deal of silence."[35] Or, as she tells Mrs. Assingham later when her own life is an utter shambles: "And if I'm both helpless and tormented I stuff my pocket-handkerchief into my mouth, I keep it there, for the most part, night and day, so as not to be heard too indecently moaning."[36] And Mrs. Assingham is consolingly right when she says: "But the precious little innermost, say this time little, golden, personal nature of you. . . . I'm not sure you've ever consentingly shown it to anyone."[37] It may indeed be affirmed that in this respect the Jamesian heroine shared her creator's intense regard for the sanctity and beauty and privacy of grief. Nothing, in fact, distressed James more than an open or overt indelicacy in life. Even a grievous hurt was not to be aired in the full, vulgar light of the day. It had to be suggested, distilled and purified.

In short, the Jamesian heroine who engineers her suffering chiefly out of the magnanimity of spirit will in the end wear pain like a russet mantle over her head, and hide tears in smiles that are very nearly wrung out of a breaking heart. She will look queenly in suffering, and mint a philosophy of fortitude out of it. And that is why perhaps she is a truly tragic figure in the sense Reinhold Niebuhr views the matter of tragic magnificence in *Beyond Tragedy.*[38]

Perhaps the reason why the Jamesian heroine suffers so terribly in life is that her very virtues have a tendency to turn into vices. A surfeit of innocence and imagination, of refinement and sophistication may not save even the bravest spirit from a certain kind of crippling unreality, and even hardness of heart. James was fully aware of the peculiar vulnerability of his heroines, and that is why poetry and irony go hand in hand, with the honours clearly in favour of the poetry in the end. It did not perhaps occur to him though that his own world-view and style were, considered thus, equally vulnerable, and that his heroines were the victims of his own unconscious scruples and cunning.

And there is finally the question of the Jamesian heroine's sexual frigidity. There is no doubt that James's own repressed sexuality, which breaks out in his later fiction in the form of "the Lolita complex,"[39] is chiefly responsible for her emotional shrinking and diffidence in the presence of roused sexuality. The colour of love in the end is not grey, but red, though James tends to become peculiarly queasy, mannered and involved when it comes to painting the passional scenes. The sexual passion receiving a cerebral bath loses its urgency and immediacy and vitality, even though it gains in refinement and formal grace.

Isabel Archer's case is often cited as a typical example of sexual fear and frigidity. Perhaps deep down in her puritan psyche, there is still the idea of the essential ugliness and bestiality of sex—an idea which somehow is not wholly dissipated, for all her cultural enlightenment. In fact, her very refinement of spirit compounds her error, and adds to such distortions in her vision. Her rejection of Caspar Goodwood, in particular, appears to be a rejection of male sexuality roused to a desperate pitch. Somehow her spirit quailed at the thought of her body's violation by so insistent a lover. That is how James describes her feelings:

> Caspar Goodwood expressed for her an energy—and she had already felt it as a power—that was of his very nature. It was in no degree a matter of his "advantages"—it was a matter of the spirit that sat in his clear-burning eyes like some tireless watcher at a window. She might like it or not, but he insisted, ever, with his whole weight and force: even in one's usual contact with him one had to reckon with that. . . . Sometimes Caspar Goodwood had seemed to range himself on the side of her destiny, to be the stubbornest fact, she knew.[40]

That she should have later escaped headlong from his arms and "the lightning kiss," even as she felt dissolved in that ecstasy of impassioned love, shows as much her deep distrust of phallic love, as her fear of the danger of surrender she has felt like a flash in her half-yielding body. One is reminded of the climactic moment in Yeats's "Leda and the Swan." In fact, a deep and deadly irony seems to attend her choice of the effete, modish and depleted Osmond. It is a choice not made by the whole of Isabel's self, but by a frozen part thereof. It's almost like the cold calling unto the cold. However, whereas Isabel's "freeze" is partly the result of her New England sensibility, that of Osmond has something of the Alpine snow-abstraction about it. James's references to Diana, the cold and white goddess of chastity, in relation to Isabel help reinforce the images of frigidity. In F. O. Matthiessen's view, she "remained essentially virginal despite her marriage."[41] Dorothea Krook recognizes in Isabel "a tendency to withdraw," but she doesn't consider this a matter of sexual frigidity. It is Isabel's fine and sensitive nature which comes up against the challenges of full surrender demanded by marriage. Her seeming coldness is a protective armour. However, Dorothea Krook admits "that James shared his heroine's fear of, and even revulsion from, the sexual passion in its more violent, importunate forms, and for reasons *mutatis mutandis* essentially similar to hers."[42] The later James, she acknowledges, saw things very differently, and, in fact, came to regard passion as "the sacred fount of all creative endeavour."[43] This is correct to a large extent, though in Milly Theale, a consumptive heroine, the sexual pulse hardly ever seems to throb. In fact, James seems to find her sexual situation peculiarly uncomfortable, if not unclean. Maggie Verver is, of course, more natural, though it is more than likely that Amerigo does not draw that deep and dark sexual satisfaction from her which he seems to do from the more passionate and potent Charlotte Stant. The American woman somehow remains inhospitable to vigorous and athletic passion. For the satisfaction of dark carnal desires, and indeed for the restorative powers of sexuality, James in the end turns to his European women—to Madame de Vionnet and those "other women" like Kate Croy who had, as he puts it, a "direct talent for life."[44]

The American heroine of James, however, remains an attractive riddle till the end. Her mysteriousness, though, is the mysteriousness of a vestal virgin, not that of a Mona Lisa; that enigmatic quality belongs to James's European heroines like Christina Light and Madame de Vionnet. The old French lady, grandmother of Euphemia's husband in "Madame de Mauves," addressing the American daughter-in-law says: "I don't know whether you're better, but you seem to me to have been wound up by some key that isn't kept by your governess or your confessor or even your mother."[45] It is a key that James came very near to fashioning and possessing in the end. Even then, all the chambers of the mysterious mansion, he knew, could not be unlocked!

8

The Sense of Evil

All great writers have, sooner or later, to acknowledge the reality and mystery of evil. It is an inescapable challenge to their powers of comprehending the facts and imponderables of life. Any effort to gloss over, sidetrack, minimize, or relegate it will somehow affect the quality of their writing. And by this I mean not the techniques of a book, but its ontological and visionary centre. In fact, it may well be asserted that it is only when a writer confronts the massed power of evil in its various forms and aspects, and knows that the time has come for him to grapple with these monsters to the utmost of his spiritual and mental powers that he may be said to have attained the age of understanding. It is not necessary that his work be a sustained and relentless inquiry into the genesis and meaning of evil as Melville's, Dostoievsky's or Kafka's is. The mere presence in him of "the sense of evil"[1] is enough to lend authenticity and sincerity to the picture he is painting. Since evil, like the insidious fog, creeps in through all kinds of nooks and crannies, he can best deal with it when he is equipped with certain insights into the nature of this ubiquitous and disquieting phenomenon. The history of every major writer in the English language—Shakespeare, Milton, Blake, Keats, Dickens, George Eliot, Hardy, Yeats, T. S. Eliot, Hawthorne, Melville, Poe, to quote a few examples, shows that the visionary breakthrough was attained only when the nature of evil in man, in society and in nature dawned upon him. The dialectic of growth was related to the understanding of the dialectic of evil. This is not to suggest that a vision of evil become an ultimate value. On the contrary, greatness is vouchsafed only when the power of evil is not only understood, but also subjected to a vision of transcendence.

Therefore, when Henry James referred to the lack of the sense of evil in Howells and in Emerson—two American writers he admired otherwise—he was obviously inferring that their work somehow remained incomplete, if not flawed, since their spirit had had no brush with evil in any significant form. If one never descended into the depths, one never ultimately attained the heights. No moral vision whose ladders did not start from the pit was likely to stand the abrasive test of reality. Now, the sense of evil is not a quality that can be cultivated or acquired.

Some persons are by a happy coincidence never destined to know evil in its profoundest form; others are precluded by the bent of their temperament or character. Such, for instance, is James's own heroine, Maggie Verver, "to whom a wrong thing could least be communicated."[2] Captain Delano of Melville's little masterpiece, "Benito Cereno," is another such person. His bafflement on the stricken ship, "San Dominick," is primarily the result of a trusting, loving, unsuspecting and cheerful disposition. He is the archetypal American innocent abroad who, unable to distinguish between appearance and reality, is intrigued by the inexplicable nature of human reality, and nearly comes to grief. Not to know evil, Melville seems to suggest, is in itself a kind of evil. It is, at any rate, a crippling disadvantage. One should be able to recognize "the mark of the beast," if a hold on reality is to be purchased. Pure whiteness too is the colour of corruption and evil. James, thus, felt intensely with Melville, Poe and Hawthorne, amongst other American writers, what Melville styled as "power of blackness." It is a power that "derives its force from its appeal to that Calvinistic sense of Innate Depravity and Original Sin, from whose visitations, in some shape or other, no deeply thinking mind is always and wholly free."[3] In this respect, James was more deeply American than is commonly granted. As Harry Levin has brilliantly shown in *The Power of Blackness,* the archetypal American imagination was from the very beginning primeval and metaphysical. It was forever concerned with the dark imponderables of life. "The issue," he writes, "is as old as the black snow of Anaxagorus, and as enigmatic as Rilke's image of black milk."[4]

Although James's own vision of "the abyss" becomes somewhat Melvillean only towards the end of his literary career, there is an unmistakable sense of sin and evil present in his earliest stories such as "Poor Richard" (1867), "The Romance of Certain Old Clothes" (1868) and in his first novel, *Watch and Ward* (1871). However, there, the tone being academic and melodramatic, the evil does not bite into the mind in the manner it does in such later tales and novels as "The Turn of the Screw," *The Other House* and *What Maisie Knew,* etc. One of the earliest examples of evil felt on the pulse and felt down the spine is to be seen in *Washington Square* (1880). Dr. Sloper's sadistic impulses coupled with the biblical sin of pride and cynicism are our first significant peep into the "heart of darkness." That scene in the Alps where Catherine feels overwhelmed by atavistic evil in the figure of her father is something in the nature of a dark epiphany. We are taken very close to the edge of the yawning and deep abyss, and left gingerly poised over it.

> The Doctor looked around him too. "Should you like to be left in such a place as this to starve?"
> "What do you mean?" cried the girl.
> "That will be your fate—that's how he will leave you."
> He would not touch her, but he had touched Morris.
> The strangest part of it was that he had said he was not a good man; Catherine wondered a good deal about what he had meant by that. . . . [5]

Quite obviously, the rich and cultured New York physician has dropped his guard for a moment, and let his child see a heart of ice in that snow-bound mountain.

Dr. Sloper's type of evil, however, assumes another form in the societal context—the sin of manipulation. Parental authority becomes ugly and grasping and wicked when it would bend or break an innocent and beautiful, but brave, spirit in the name of expediency and conformity. In *Washington Square,* the assault on a tender psyche is so naked as to resemble aggression rather than manipulation. Dr. Sloper apparently wanted to manipulate his daughter's life and happiness; in actual fact, he was at the deeper, unconscious level, violating her virgin soul. He was guilty of deflowering his daughter spiritually, and maiming her in the spirit. It was a case of spiritual "incest." Evil does not have to show the proverbial horns and hoofs; it may as well sport a stethoscope and a pince-nez.

The evil of manipulation from now onwards becomes a major motif in James's fiction. Whenever or wherever a person seeks to dominate, control, twist or mould another psyche, James sees in it a threat not only to individual freedom, but also to society and to civilized existence. The instinct of aggrandizement is basically a bio-psychological necessity; it is, in other words, part of the subterranean evil in man. However, in the tortured and complex relationships that have arisen as a result of the pressure generated by the industrial society, it assumes a sociological aspect. In the next two novels, *The Portrait of a Lady* and *The Bostonians,* this form of evil is particularly active and ravaging.

That James's finest heroine, Isabel Archer, should have been made a victim of deep deception and manipulation shows how the novelist viewed this kind of evil in particular. Apparently, as Isabel herself asserts, she was nobody's tool or instrument or scapegoat; all her actions, including her disastrous marriage, had been perfectly open and free acts of the will. In this respect, she is a far freer agent than Catherine Sloper. However, it is precisely the obscure and muffled nature of her unfreedom which makes her tragedy more ironic, and also more terrible. For the type of deception practised by Madame Merle and Osmond is so subtle and treacherous that the victim may not only not guess the real nature of her disabilities, she may even, thanks to the generosity of her impulses, begin to develop a bad conscience, a distrust of her own self. Such a manipulation is all the more difficult to perceive in that social appearances and forms are scrupulously maintained. It is only some time after her marriage that Isabel begins to see clearly the outlines of the evil pressing in upon her in "the house of darkness, the house of dumbness, the house of suffocation."[6] That its nature strikes us as primeval and sinful is supported by the biblical imagery James employs here in describing the subtle subversion of Isabel's soul by her fiendish husband: "Under all his culture, his cleverness, his amenity, under his good-nature, his facility, his knowledge of life, his egotism lay hidden like a serpent in a bank of flowers."[7]

However, her husband's covert and genteel aggression against her style of life does not fully develop into a vision of terror till her climactic confrontation with the prime, but pressed, agent of evil, Madame Merle, in chapter 49.

> "Who are you—what are you?" Isabel murmured.
> "What have you to do with my husband?" It was strange that for a moment she drew as near to him as if she had loved him.
> "Ah then. You take it heroically. I'm very sorry. Don't think, however, that I shall do so."
> "What have you to do with me?" Isabel went on. Madame Merle slowly got up, stroking her muff, but not removing her eyes from Isabel's face. "Everything," she answered. Isabel sat there looking up at her, without rising; her face was almost a prayer to be enlightened. But the light of this woman's eyes seemed only a darkness. "Oh misery!" she murmured at last; and she fell back, covering her face with her hands. It had come over her like a high-surging wave that Mrs. Touchett was right. Madame Merle had married her. Before she uncovered her face again that lady had left the room.[8]

And it is in chapter 52 during their second and ultimate confrontation, which Isabel, now knowing the truth of her hideous position, turns into a mute but massive accusation, that we realize the full nature of the injury and affront done to her life. She had been made a convenience of, something that she considered depraved and unclean. It amounted to doing dirt on her spirit—an unpardonable sin in James.

> She saw, in the crude light of that revelation which had already become a part of experience and to which the very frailty of the vessel in which it had been offered her only gave an intrinsic price, the dry staring fact that she had been an applied handled hung-up tool, as senseless and convenient as mere shaped wood and iron. All the bitterness of this knowledge surged into her soul again; it was as if she felt on her lips the taste of dishonour. There was a moment during which, if she had turned and spoken, she would have said something that would hiss like a lash. But she closed her eyes, and then the hideous vision dropped. What remained was the cleverest woman in the world standing there within a few feet of her and knowing as little what to think as the meanest. . . . [9]

In *The Bostonians,* the evil of manipulation is indeed one of the principal themes, and James dramatizes it in all its unmasked hideousness and lurking brutality. The story of the troubled and tortured relationship between the militant and flaming suffragette, Olive Chancellor, and her beautiful, but bemused protégée, Verena Terrant, is ultimately less a story about the political rights of women than a story about the psychic invasion and subversion of personality. True, James appears concerned with and concerned about petticoat politics, but it would be noticed that in rendering the same in a comic and satirical vein, he is obviously playing up its priggish and Messianic aspects with a view to deflating them. As the story progresses, the larger issues of the feminist movement begin to recede, and the smaller, but more inflammable, issue of the violation of human psyche takes on an obsessive form. For the struggle for the body and soul of

Verena between two equally committed and consecrated fanatics, Olive and Basil Ransom, eventually is a clash at the elemental level of personality. I therefore think Daniel Lerner and Oscar Cargill to be essentially correct when they declare that in *"The Bostonians,* the subject is a struggle of personalities instead of a conflict of characters; not ethical justification for human behavior, but human motivation as the source of behavior, is what we are invited to consider."[10] However, it may be added that the sexual aspect of the struggle—Olive's Lesbianism being never in doubt—has been effectively subsumed under the ideological clash that ostensibly occupies the centre of the stage in the first half of the book. James, it appears to me, sees the two kinds of aggressions—sexual and ideological—as fundamentally identical. In either case, there is a strong, unconscious desire to possess and aggrandize, to bring a resisting personality to utter subservience. In one case, it is a rape of the body, in the other, a rape of the mind. Thus Olive Chancellor's twisted and malignant sexuality finds a perfect correlative in the politics of possession and manipulation. From the beginning, she strikes us as a gloomy bird of prey, balancing its wings in the air to swoop on innocent birds of the skies. That is how in a striking predatory image, James describes Olive's swift conquest of Verena: "Olive had taken her in the literal sense of the phrase, like a bird of the air, had spread an extraordinary pair of wings, and carried her through the dizzying void of space."[11]

Thus the evil in *The Bostonians* is primarily rooted in the sin of manipulation. Commenting on this aspect of the novel, Irving Howe compares James with Hawthorne. "Both are," he observes, "obsessed by the problem of integrity; how, they repeatedly ask, can a human being, involved as he must be in limiting and treacherous social relationships, yet maintain something of the personal uniqueness? The great sin in Hawthorne's novels, which is the presumption of taking into one's hands the destiny of another person, is also the great sin in James's novels."[12]

Though Basil Ransom is somewhat spared the sharper and more biting edge of James's satire, and the irony is less evenly distributed, it is quite clearly James's intention to underscore the point that innocent and malleable Verena stood almost as much in danger of being violated in personality from the Southerner who pursues her from town to town and from meeting to meeting as from the "St. Theresa of Beacon Hill,"[13] who has initially succeeded in turning the genuine current of her sympathetic impulses, and in shaping her almost into a pair of "angry bellows," to recall a Yeatsian phrase. Even as Verena and Ransom are about to celebrate their nuptials, James is unwilling to let that consummation stand as a vision of happiness. He is not sure that the evil, humbled in the shape of Olive Chancellor, is wholly dissipated, that it will not, as in the case of Osmond, assume a subtle, serpentine aspect, once the physical conquest has been completed. The concluding sentence of the novel does strike an ominous note. "It is to be feared that with the union, so far from brilliant, into which she was about to enter, these [tears] will not be the last she was destined to shed."[14] The sin of manipulation, though proceeding from varied and complex motives, is finally an aspect of moral evil. Though its force seems somewhat to decrease in the face of other more menacing and inexplicable forms of evil to be seen at work in James's later fiction, it continues to exist in one form or another till the end. Mrs. Wix of *What Maisie Knew*, for instance, represents, though to a lesser extent, this type of evil. She is a somewhat ineffective manipulator, symbolizing the misery and poverty of suppressed sex, and of loud and aggrieved morality. Maggie Verver's case, however, stands on a different footing. Her unconscious urge to manipulate the life of her father and Charlotte Stant, seen as sin and evil by some critics, is not to be confused with the evil of Dr. Sloper, of Madame Merle, of Osmond or of Olive Chancellor. There is a qualitative difference in the two types of manipulation. One, whatever its harmful effects, proceeds from a vision of love; the other is inevitably the product of a vision of power. *The Golden Bowl* does have a large quantum of "evil seated all at its ease,"[15] but its primal agent certainly is not our heroine.

With the darkening of James's vision around the mid-nineties, we find the novelist pitching headlong into the pit of damnation to scoop up as much of muck as may fill the dramatic moulds of his fancy. He appears impelled by "the power of blackness." Something in his soul drives him almost demoniacally toward the abyss. Evil now erupts in his work in the form of sexual violence and tyranny. He begins to see the maggot and the worm at the core of sexual love. How one's appetites may obliterate one's moral insights and cause chaos in life is the subject of several novels and tales. The compulsive nature of this evil seems to bring him face to face with the idea of original sin. James has by no means a theological imagination, though he feels, more than ever, the power of the fiend beneath "the girdle" and the stench issuing from "the sulphurous pit." James's sexual imagination, of course, does not attain the piercing quality of Lear's epiphany on the heath, but it is, if I may say so, a fecund force in all his work after the *Guy Domville* episode, which, as we have seen earlier, had the nature of a sexual trauma.

It is not surprising that James's libidinous fantasies and urges assume a compulsive quality after he has turned fifty. A lifelong abstinence is beginning to tell. The starved body has at last its sweet revenge. James's displaced eroticism is manifestly seen in such later novels and tales as *What Maisie Knew, The Awkward Age, The Sacred Fount,* "The Turn of the Screw," "In the Cage," "The Great Good Place," "The Pupil," "Crapy Cornelia," etc. We find here nearly all types of Freudian complexes and aberrations, typical of middle-aged spinsters, breaking out in the form of a rash—sexual repression and vicarious, ersatz satisfactions, voyeurism or "peep-hole psychology," "the Lolita complex" or the fixation on "nymphets" and nubile girls, homosexuality and sexual freemasonry. And since sex appears here in its forbidden, tortured, twisted and manipulated forms, the idea of evil sexuality is clearly at work. This is, in fact, an aspect of James's suppressed puritanism. For all his boast of the Calvinistic heritage "as a danger after all escaped,"[16] he continues to remain at bottom an uneasy cousin of Hawthorne.

It appears indeed that James's long stay in London had brought him face to face with the jungle and the pit of upper bourgeois life. Though a thorough "insider," sharing its values and visions, he nevertheless has the freedom and integrity of the imagination to portray in art the uglier side of genteel society. Behind the splendid facade of their mansions, of their stiff and starched shirts, of their liveried servants, there lurks the odour of underhand sex. It is a world of gay fornications and jolly adulteries, held together by a clandestine code. Sex has become an abstract "game of chess," inhuman and life-denying. If London is not exactly an open sewer or an analogue of stinking sex, it is, in any case, a symbol of scented and sophisticated vulgarity, such as Mrs. Brookenham and women of her ilk represent. "A London Life" and several other similar tales and novels reveal James's penetrating understanding of the sickness of this society, though his analysis seldom amounts to a full indictment. In such a society, sexual evil is revealed as a subtle, insidious force, entrenched and unconcerned. It is difficult to dislodge, not only because it is covert and surreptitious, but also because it has been institutionalized and invested with charm. Its horrors are the horrors of domestication and domicile.

Though the London-based stories do suggest again and again the idea of evil sexuality, it would be a mistake to think that James regarded all sex as something essentially depraved and sinful. On the contrary, some of the later stories and novels like "The Lesson of the Master," "The Beast in the Jungle," *The Ambassadors* and "Mona Montravers" deal almost lyrically with the beauty and felicity of sex, "the sacred fount" of being. In all these tales, the theme of the missed intensities and ecstasies of youth is emphasized with a view to affirming the place of passion in life. Thus it would appear that for James, sex was at once something tainted and sacred, ugly and soulful. Such an attitude forms part of his innate ambivalence in relation to human reality.

The ambiguity of evil in James's later fiction such as "The Turn of the Screw" and *The Other House* has led critics to the view that the novelist's vision of life was essentially Manichean. That is to say, he regarded evil as eternal and infinite, a dark, fecund force coextensive with good, an ineluctable part of the human condition. And indeed some of the stories tend to create such an impression. There is a claustrophobic feeling of a nameless hideous terror lying in wait to spring upon you. We are indeed reminded of James's vision of "the awful agent, creature or presence,"[17] of the paralysing nightmarish and malignant figure seen by his brother, William, and of the damned shape emitting "a fetid influence"[18] seen by his father—all visions of pure evil. In his well-known essay, "Henry James the Melodramatist," Jacques Barzun sees traces of Manicheanism in both William and

Henry, and goes on to describe the novelist's account of the fire-fighting incident at Lamb House in Rye as "symbolic of the Manichean fight."[19] Similarly, Graham Greene in his essay on James called "The Private Universe" regards the entire James family as stricken and impelled by darkness. In the novelist he finds "the sense of the abyss always lurking beneath the fragile surface." "If ever a man's imagination," he adds, "was clouded by the Pit, it was James's."[20] And this he tends to see as a variety of "spiritual evil." And, finally, we have James's own striking observation in a late letter to A. C. Benson: "But I have the imagination of disaster—and see life as ferocious and sinister."[21] All this appears weighty enough to give James's sense of evil an atavistic and Manichean aspect. However, in view of the pervading spirit of humour and irony in his earlier work, of ambivalence in the later, it is difficult to consider James a Jansenist, as Graham Greene would have us believe. The intensity of the idiom does not necessarily show James's dread and *angst* as religious. Unlike his father and brother, he seldom pondered deeply the religious mystery of life, for, by temperament, he was precluded from such strenuous gropings and searchings, strivings and reachings. His gloom in the later years of his life has psychological, moral and sociological, rather than religious or spiritual, genesis. Again, despite his occasional use of the biblical imagery of the garden and the serpent, as for instance in relation to Osmond in *The Portrait of a Lady,* he does not insist upon the presence of evil in the lapsed man as part of his spiritual inheritance. In short, his puritanism is more a moral than a theological influence. The concept of the fallen man would suggest a pattern and a design and direction; whereas evil in the later novels of James appears loose, formless, incoherent and inexplicable.

At times, James's sense of evil suggests affinities with Conrad's or even Kafka's sense of evil. That is to say, evil erupts in the form of the wanton, the irrational and the absurd. There is an undercurrent of anxiety in regard to the contingent, indeterminate, inchoate and brittle structure of man's being. In short, James's attitude has metaphysical and existential overtones. Though such a view could be sustained, it appears to me we would do well to regard the question of evil in *The Wings of the Dove, The Golden Bowl* and *The Ivory Tower* as essentially moral and social rather than cosmic or metaphysical. James's forays into the underworld of the human heart are, as a rule, initiated by his ethical concerns; the metaphysical echoes do not assume a compulsive character.

That the seat of evil in James is the human heart or the human psyche may be illustrated from any one of his major works. Such an evil as Mrs. Gereth and Mrs. Wix represent is necessarily rooted in individual consciousness, as is the evil represented by Madame Merle, Kate Croy and Charlotte Stant, though, as J. A. Ward, supporting such a view in his perceptive and wide-ranging book on the subject, *The Imagination of Disaster,* adds: "Evil partakes of the forms of civilization"[22] in James's fiction. Mrs. Brookenham, Amerigo, even Mrs. Gereth are the products of a grasping world in which appetite and ego have been given forms of respectability. Evil has sought refuge in the very citadel or sanctuary of society. It has assumed an aspect of social necessity.

Strange as it may appear, in James's fiction the first hint of evil frequently issues from woman rather than man. Madame Merle, Olive Chancellor, Mrs. Gereth, Rose Armiger, Kate Croy, Charlotte Stant—all these women are, in a manner, primary agents of evil, setting into motion dark and uncontrollable forces of destruction. Nuclear evil seems thus to be peculiarly associated with women in James. If this suggests the biblical idea of the fallen Eve, as it well may, it is, I think, more a matter of chance or coincidence than of purpose or design. Or, if it is James's intention to show that the hand which launches the vessels of evil and burns the temples and towers of man is inevitably the hand of some driven Helen, it has no overtly theological or doctrinal echoes. All that we may conclude from such a position is that in James the passional crime or sin is more likely to stem from some woman, if only because woman's passion has a desperate beauty and poetry and single-mindedness about it. Also, since the victim too is nearly always a woman in James's later fiction, there may well be a hint of cosmic irony in it. The Osmonds and Denshers and Amerigos of the novels are but contributory agents who, so to speak, take over the complex mechanism of evil with something of a skipper's aplomb and dexterity. We do not have an Iago in James. A Dr. Sloper or an Osmond, despite his darknesses, will simply not do. He does not have the genius of evil on the grandest scale. His evil is measurable, and within the ken of human limitations and understanding. In Dr. Sloper's case, it is even inspired by warped parental love. The nearest James comes to enacting a Greek drama of pure evil is in *The Other House,* though even Rose Armiger is more of a Lady Macbeth impelled by an overwhelming human passion than a female Iago whose demented soul is ridden by an imp from hell. And when Rose, asked by Tony as to how she could see Mrs. Beever with her back turned toward her, replies: "It's with my back turned that I see most";[23] or, when to Dennis Vidal's question, "Will you have lights?" she says, "No lights, thanks," "It's the thing I am—what that is—I now count on you to stand by,"[24] we have shades of Shakespearian poetry in an otherwise contrived and melodramatic plot. In any case, evil as a monolithic column with its roots reaching down to prehistoric depths, and taking all that comes before it in its inexorable march, is not a typically Jamesian phenomenon. Shakespearian evil has altogether a magnitude and a magnificence which we find missing in James. And when Professor Ward avers that the novelist's sense of evil is nearer to Shakespeare's and Milton's than to Zola's or Dreiser's, he is right only to the extent that "James's view of evil is more absolutist than the modern mind allows for."[25] It may perhaps be better to suggest that both in Shakespeare and James, moral evil is more pervasive and pernicious than environmental evil. Where the question of existential and atavistic evil is concerned, James is far less Shakespearian than it would appear on the surface. In fact, even absolutes of morality are in the end viewed with suspicion by him.

James, it appears, does feel pity for his Kate Croys, and Charlotte Stants, the wrongdoers, and, assuredly, a great deal of lovely compassion and concern for his Madame de Vionnets, the beautiful sinners, because he cannot but salute the poetry and holiness of passion, and accept, to an extent, the truth of the heart's imperatives and irrational reasons. In *Roderick Hudson,* passion is simply seen as wasteful and destructive, but in *The Ambassadors* and other later tales there is a marked tendency to treat it as beautiful and ennobling. And, as for understanding and pity and charity, it's best we learned not only to live within the limits of our crippling and agonizing experience of human reality, but also to live by the truths proved on our pulse and sweated out by our system. For a long and searching peep into the wastes and the wells of the human heart may never be endured. Thus, if James has "the imagination of disaster" or of "terror,"[26] he has also the imagination of compassion. Even adultery, a sin for which he had great revulsion, is, in the end, humanized, and rescued from a vision of brimstone and hell. For, if it is ugly because of its deceit, it is bearable because of its passion. I cannot, therefore, endorse the view of Dupee that James is a stricter puritan than Hawthorne, for whom adultery had "the color of life-blood and of roses."[27] In the final analysis, treachery in human relationships is the ultimate Jamesian sin, whether such a sin is committed by a spouse or a friend. However, the treachery of passion has a compulsive and saving quality which the treachery of ambition or cupidity does not have.

The question of evil in children presented in varying aspects in "The Turn of the Screw," *What Maisie Knew* and "The Pupil" is too significant to be set aside. Certainly, the later James saw some of these children as potential cynics, liars and manipulators. Some of the evil of their betters and elders did rub off on them in the process of growing up. However, I am unable to accept the view that Flora and Miles in "The Screw" are utterly given over to the devil. "The patter of Satan's feet"[28] which Eli Siegel, for instance, hears is at least not audible to one reader, though Miles, sure enough, had been sent down from the school for some sexual misdemeanour. What these stories show is the insidious and malignant nature of evil which can violate the very sanctuary of innocence.[29]

Again, Professor Ward's observation that "the evil character in James is almost never reflective"[30] seems to connect with the Jamesian view of the primacy of thought in life. That is to say, those prone to evil are persons of action and dynamism rather than of thought or reflection. A Strether in whom the gross reality of life has been distilled into essence, and absorbed in consciousness, is incapable of any real evil. He has achieved what the Cambridge philosopher, G. E. Moore, called "good states of mind." On the other hand, pure will and action, as in Rose Armiger, cannot but result in darkness and destruction. There is something to be said for this point of view, though James, it appears to me, is not entirely unconscious of the evil that proceeds from passivity and inaction. Osmond, for instance, represents the type of evil that is associated with abstract aestheticism.

At another level, the narrator of *The Sacred Fount* symbolizes the inhumanity of pure mentation or cerebration—a trap James himself frequently falls into in some of his later works. Action, even when evil, must spend itself, and thus generate a fresh condition of life, but unanchored and monarchical thought wallowing in the void cannot but lead to a closed-in world, and to moral anarchy. Thus, the dynamism of action is to be preferred to the stasis of thought. Of course, the ideal would be to have a living and dialectical relationship between thought and action, a thing rarely achieved in James's fiction.

There is finally one aspect of James's sense of evil which is not seen in the novelist till he is about to lay down his pen. I am referring to the question of the evil first dimly apprehended in his great book of travel, *The American Scene,* and later suggested obliquely in the unfinished novel, *The Ivory Tower.* And that is the evil of dark baronial finance erupting in the life of Gray Fielder. That James did not have a politico-historical imagination acute enough to penetrate the subterranean vaults of Wall Street is clear enough. His bourgeois upbringing and world-view would seem to leave him ill-equipped for any such vision. Nevertheless, the unfinished book and his "Notes for the Ivory Tower" raise interesting possibilities of a breakthrough. In one manner, money has nearly always been a major source of evil in James's fiction, Isabel Archer and Milly Theale being its exquisite victims, but in the earlier books, there is seldom a hint or suggestion of its tainted origin. In fact, his innocent tycoons and millionaires—Christopher Newman, Mr. Dosson and Adam Verver—are all naïve examples of American capitalism. There is no real understanding of its rationale or genius on the part of Henry James. If anything, there is admiration for the energy and enterprise behind these immense fortunes. A peculiar innocence or shyness bordering on unconcern with wealth is to be seen at work in these captains of industry. It never occurs to him that no fortune as large as Mr. Dosson's or Mr. Adam's could be gathered in one generation without the forces of rapacious economy coming into full play. In *The Princess Casamassima,* the idea of ill-gotten wealth, as the revolutionaries see it, is a poignant presence, but James is not concerned with the anatomy of money as such. In fact, the presence of large unearned fortunes is not only taken for granted, it is the inevitable and inescapable framework of Jamesian stories. Or, as F. W. Dupee puts it, "James's fascination with a baronial state of society was a very condition of his literary existence."[31] It is only after his American visit in 1905 that he begins to show signs of uneasiness in regard to the monster forces impinging upon the lives of ordinary men and women. The evil of class, of culture and of country is encountered in the international novels and tales; what he now appears to be groping towards in *The Ivory Tower* is the massed evil of dark finance, casting its huge shadow over man. The millions of Mr. Gaw or of Mr. Betterman suggest no felicity, beauty or poetry. If anything, their octopus nature is hinted at. As Rosanna Gaw puts it, Mr. Betterman is "dying of twenty millions" and adds: "Having to do with it consists, you know, of the things you do *for* it—which are mostly very awful. . . . The effect has been to dry up his life. There's nothing at last left to pay with."[32] Again, in the "Notes," Rosanna's own inherited millions are shown as "so dishonoured and blackened at their very roots, that it seems to her that they carry their curse with them. . . ."[33] Perhaps it is still the old James occupied with the moral aspect of things and persons, though the stirrings of a sociological imagination, troubled and questing, may not be altogether ruled out. Evil has very nearly shifted its habitat, and assumed a new aspect and menacing proportions. Its monster shape is perhaps beginning to "trouble" James's "eyesight"!

9

The Overarching Irony

The world of human and social reality is so bewilderingly complex, so treacherously beguiling that no effort at reducing it to entirely intelligible or even communicable dimensions can ever hope to succeed. Something of this reality will not only remain opaque and intractable, it will indeed return us, bemused and perplexed, to our faded truths with increased scepticism and doubt. Beyond a point, we find our labours mocked at, our quest unrewarding. Even rhetoric stops short in the tracks, unable to bear the full weight and agony of enigmatic experience.[1] And when it does appear equal to the task as in paradox, how may we be sure that in appropriating the imponderables of life, it has not itself turned into a decoy and a trap? In short, a mind in search of certitudes or absolutes cannot but gather a dust of doubt in the process. The very business or traffic of life raises clouds of queries and uncertainties.

This is so because the human reality is an eternal continuum of contradictions and contraries, of antinomies and polarities, a truth known to us in terms of philosophy from the earliest days of both Greek and Hindu thought. However, the bafflement of each connecting psyche is so acute in the face of this challenging duality that no dialectics may fully span the gulf of ambiguity. Indeed, it may well be asserted with modern Existentialists that all human truths are sweated out in the process of being and becoming, that there are no a priori truths. Man makes his truths as he negotiates the turns and twists of life, and these are always of a moving and circular nature. In fact, Karl Jaspers's metaphor for the process is "the Encompassing." At each given moment, our truth has the quality of the encompassing horizon, and yet its completeness is but illusory. The horizon moves with us, and we keep recreating our truths. Truth lies in chasing the truth. The archetypal Ulysses, as Margaret L. Wiley tells us in *Creative Sceptic,* "would continually be touching the hem of the retreating garment of the Encompassing."[2]

In dealing with Henry James's irony and ambivalence, it is necessary that we understand, so far as it is possible, the nature of the metaphysical assumptions underlying his view of human reality. I do not think he consciously followed the Transcendentalist-Swedenborgian thought of his father, as Quentin Anderson seeks to prove in *The American Henry James*. On the contrary, its cloudy integument or lineaments and its lyrical profusion often distressed him. But by an entirely different dialectic, he does seem to have arrived in the end at some of the Emersonian positions in regard to the shifting, receding and emerging vistas of reality, without, at the same time, getting involved in transcendental visions of the Oversoul, etc. The "mystic" James of the later phase is a critical extravagance, but the "doubting" James is an indisputable reality.

At the start of his literary career, James's irony is already a settled stance, though it shades off more into humour and satire than vision or dialectic. Its operative nature, on the whole, is verbal, and there is an impression of ease and urbanity. It has, at times, even a meretricious quality, as if the young novelist were hitting out in a spirit of gay abandon and effect. Its sources lie not in doubt, but in debate. Irony here is then a hand-maiden to comedy and is, therefore, less biting and abrasive. However, as early as *Roderick Hudson,* it begins to have a thematic significance. The entire international "imbroglio," as we have seen, is viewed by James as an ironic exercise, and its limits appear to have been reached in *Daisy Miller*. Rowland Mallet, for instance, though acting as a normative consciousness, by and large, is not altogether himself free from ironic treatment. He at once serves as a corrective measure to Hudson's romantic fantasies and as an object of mild satire and fun in relation to the hard and fixed code of puritan ethics. There is also "the ironic effect of his having fallen in love with the girl who is herself in love with Roderick,"[3] as James puts it. Such an irony is at once the irony of circumstance and of character. A Calvinistic conscience will not let the heart turn its miseries to advantage even though at a deeper level, it is not free from temptation and fantasy.[4] Similarly, Christina Light's relations with her mother have ironic overtones, and James uses the infinite resources of verbal irony to buttress his view of this relationship. And the irony here tends heavily toward comedy. Here is Christina's ambitious but absurd mother, Mrs. Light, complaining to Rowland about her daughter's conduct:

> "If ever a woman was desperate, frantic, heart-broken, I am that woman. I can't begin to tell you. To have nourished a serpent, sir, all these years! To have lavished one's self upon a viper that turns and stings her own poor mother! To have toiled and prayed, to have pushed and struggled, to have eaten the bread of bitterness, and all the rest of it, sir—and at the end of all things to find myself at this pass. It can't be, it's too cruel, such things don't happen, the Lord don't allow it. I'm a religious woman, sir, and the Lord knows all about me. With his own hand he had given me this reward! I would have lain down in the dust and let her walk over me; I would have given her the eyes out of my head, if she had taken fancy to them. No, she's a cruel, wicked, heartless, unnatural girl."[5]

As Richard Poirier observes, "the obvious parodies of Biblical language"[6] here are all too plain to need any ironic comment. The inflated and mock rhetoric carries its own irony.

Similarly, in *Washington Square* we have that famous comic character, Mrs. Penniman, whose romantic fantasies and schoolgirl penchant for elopements and concealments and drama are subjected to a great deal of wit and verbal irony. Not only is she given a taste of Dr. Sloper's vitriol again and again, she is also made to look delightfully foolish in her daily doings and fanciful flights: "Mrs. Penniman delighted of all things in a drama, and she flattered herself that a drama would now be enacted. Combining as she did the zeal of the prompter with the impatience of a spectator she had too long since done her utmost to pull up the curtain."[7]

Here the theatre imagery has the same ironic import as the biblical imagery in the passage from *Roderick Hudson*. However, it must be added that the irony, chiefly confined to language, has a traditional Dickensian air. It is almost indistinguishable from pure humour. And that's why it has nothing disturbing or chilling about it. Within the ironic structure of the novel itself, verbal irony spends itself, and suggests no cosmic significance. The idea of the ironic structure would posit an ironic vision, but as yet James is more concerned with balancing blocks or paralleling panels for their architectural competence than with a dialectic of ambiguity as such. The dialogues, for instance, depend heavily for their effect on reversal or inversion of ideas—a stylistic trick James will never quite get over till the end.

Instances of verbal, structural and thematic irony could again be seen to advantage in those two companion novels, *The American* and *The Europeans*. In the latter, there is a perfect blend of humour and irony, and each is enriched by the presence of the other. In these earlier volumes, then, irony is frequently a question of idiomatic adroitness, of the play of the mind and the imagination, of neat, antithetical halves. The international theme does admit of the possibility of an ironical vision which will not endorse either the American "innocence" or the European "form," or which views almost with equal concern the question of American evil and of European evil, but the graver doubts regarding the very structure of human reality are not yet entertained in any serious manner. Even *The Portrait of a Lady* and *The Bostonians*, for all their ironic characters and situations and endings, do not embody James's fecund scepticism of the final phase. Isabel Archer is administered a dash of irony, and Basil Ransom a much heavier dose, but they still retain their author's fundamental love and respect. The two extreme examples in *The Bostonians*—Olive Chancellor and Miss Birdseye, one tending to cruel mockery, and the other to genial fun—are again within the compass of the arching irony. They do not however suggest knots and depths and deceptions. The irony that dissolves into indivisible and inexplicable ambiguity is not yet fully at work.

The Jamesian irony that perplexes the reader and teases him into wildernesses of thought is the one that arrives with the darkening of the vision. The gnomic quality of the muse and the gnarled, knotted quality of the style seem to herald the birth of a new restiveness and a new mode of understanding and meeting the assault of reality. In actual fact, this is not a qualitative leap, but an intensification of a mode of thought inherent in James. This mode, as we have seen, is basically the mode of dramatic contrasts, parallels and correspondences—a mode that had an aesthetic appeal for him. However, with evil becoming more and more subtle and ambiguous in his later fiction, his irony too assumes a darker aspect. Now, even more than before, almost every aspect of life and every institution of man seems open to doubt and derision. Uncertainty grips the mind, and "the imagination of alternatives"[8] coincides with "the imagination of disaster." Even "the strength of applied irony" which rests for James in "the sincerities, the lucidities, the utilities that stand behind it"[9] now appears undermined by a gathering gloom in the mind. Reuben Arthur Brower who uses this quotation in his perceptive note on irony in *The Fields of Light* observes that behind any piece of sustained irony, there are "positive allegiances" and meaningful "continuities," and that it is the business of criticism to relate the same to its "ironic design." And he remarks that "in Swift and in James himself the relationship is so subtle as to defy satisfactory analysis."[10] Could this difficulty in the later James be imputed to the manner and style, or to a change in vision, or to both? For "the figure in the carpet" may turn out to be an illusion of the eye or the mind, and the quest for it yet another "turn of the screw." In short, the "lucidities" and the "continuities" themselves now begin to look suspect, making it almost impossible to swear by any one set of "allegiances." Irony, in the final analysis, itself becomes subject to irony, throwing everything into confusion. We are reminded of Yeats's "mockers mocked." Is this a sign of an Olympian or lordly view of reality, or a sign of a deep dichotomy in the mind? Has James achieved a visionary breakthrough, or has he descended into the fields of doubt and darkness? In his book, *The Compass of Irony*, D. C. Muecke discussing "the poetics of irony" observes that irony "like beauty, is in the eye of the beholder, and is not a quality inherent in any remark, event or situation."[11] In other words, irony is allied to relativity, and defies comprehension in terms of fixed truths. Mr. Muecke, who does not mention Henry James as one of the great ironists in literature, and has but a couple of passing references to the novelist in his volume, has provided here a clue to the Jamesian irony. More importantly, what he has to say on the objectivity and detachment of the ironist has a great deal of relevance to James's use of the narrators, observers and reflectors in his later tales. "The ironist's awareness of himself as the unobserved observer," he writes, "tends to enhance his feeling of freedom and induce a mood perhaps of serenity, or joyfulness, or even exultation. His awareness of the victim's unawareness invites him to see the victim as committed where he feels disengaged; bound or trapped where he feels free. . . . "[12] And to buttress this view, he quotes Thomas Mann when he speaks of irony "as an all embracing crystal clear and serene glance, which is the very glance of art itself, that is to say, a glance of the utmost freedom and calm and of an objectivity untroubled by any moralism."[13] Could such a view of irony and of the ironist be deduced from James's work? I do not think so. Not only is there little of the feeling of "calm," "repose" and "serenity" in the troubled James of the final phase, there is, in fact, a dark streak of doubt to be seen in relation to his own detached observers and narrators. Do they indeed tell all that they see? Do they remain really uninvolved? And finally, does not the tale change in the telling in that the language itself, though our sole vehicle of communication, has built-in insufficiencies? This brings us inevitably to a discussion of what Wayne C. Booth calls "unreliable narrators,"[14] and to the uses and abuses of irony as a technique.

James criticism, of late, has particularly fastened on such novels and *nouvelles* as *The Spoils of Poynton* and *The Sacred Fount* and "The Turn of the Screw," for these compositions in particular admit of not only different, but almost wholly opposed interpretations. The Jamesian irony at times comes home to roost. Fleda Vetch of *The Spoils* is an interesting and intriguing example of how a character may be read at several levels of understanding in the light of a laminated irony. While for most of the readers she is one of James's finest *ficelles,* carrying a clear, wholesome and beautiful conscience, quite a few critics such as Oscar Cargill, Robert Marks and John A. Clair see her as morally compromised, affirming James's ironic treatment of her character. Charles Hoffman, however, sees irony not in the treatment of her character, but in her situation. "She lost her chance for happiness," he opines, "but she retained her dignity and integrity."[15] For Laurence B. Holland, Fleda helps engineer a "vision of love." In the end, he adds: "The ironies which characterize the crisis illuminate its dialectical nature, for they inhere in the fact that the process of salvage and transformation engages all the antagonists whose conflict helps bring it about."[16] Fleda's fruitful ambiguity which creates "the double possibility of success and failure, moral triumph and culpability"[17] is conceded by Professor Holland, though she is finally made the redemptive agent of the complex drama. As I see the matter, Fleda is intended by James as an extreme example of a *nice* conscience strangulating the natural urges of the heart. The irony perhaps lies in the paradox of a conscience turning silly in the effort to maintain its stretched integrity. Indeed, James may well be suggesting that Fleda's kind of "sacrifice" or renunciation is at once heroic and absurd, beautiful and exasperating. In short, the ironic vision which informs the structure of the novel permeates the delineation of Fleda's character. She retains her integrity at the cost of a gratuitous, and possibly questionable, sacrifice. Too much of a conscience may make fools of us all! That appears to be at least one of the plausible conclusions.

The narrator of *The Sacred Fount* is another character who has divided James criticism from end to end. He has the dubious distinction of starting as many critical hares as perhaps Hamlet, without having the brilliance and genius of the prince of Denmark. He is, in fact, a monster of curiosity who, armed with a fantastic theory of libidinous energy, is perhaps chasing in the proverbial dark room the black cat that is not there. And he has led the critics many a merry dance.[18] The novel has been interpreted as a tongue-in-cheek parody by James of his own late style (Follett), as an extended exercise in epistemology (Dupee), as a sustained enquiry into the mock-world of art (Edel), as a variant of the vampire legend (Van Wyck Brooks), as a fable about the imagination (Edmund Wilson), as the story of emotional cannibalism (Putt), as a solemn quest after "the insanity of art" (Tony Tanner), and as a plunge into the universe of rhetoric (Sallie Sears). Similarly, the narrator himself has been roundly called a spiritual Paul Pry, a Nosey Parker, a metaphysical detective, an epistemological sadist, an all-seeing modern Tiresias, an obsessed clown and a death's head at a banquet, a visionary in search of the ultimate truth, a Jamesian alter-ego and so on. And finally, in a whole volume devoted to the subject, *Jamesian Ambiguity and The Sacred Fount,* Jean Frantz Blackall, discussing most of the prominent and controversial views, more or less, reaches the conclusion that behind all the artifice and embroidery of invention, James is simply enacting a comedy of the "palace of thought"[19] in a highly ironic vein. The narrator is a deceitful observer, an "unreliable" reflector. And she observes: "My own belief is that in this instance the impulse toward comedy ran away with a potentially serious subject."[20] Now, whatever the meaning of this erotic "game of chess" James has constructed within the closed world of fantasy, one thing is quite clear; the story and the narrator draw too many red herrings across the trail to let the reader form any definite view at all. Eventually, one could in this guessing game come to grief as much through critical sophistication as through critical naivete. Perhaps James, for once, treats himself to an elaborate and massive private joke, daring us into a fantasia of fun at our own risk. Could, therefore, all this ambiguity be viewed, not *resolved,* in the light of a private and pleated irony? Would it be possible to say that for James sex is at once a fount of renewal and a well of depletion, that the world of art is at once an illusion and a reality, that the imagination is at once a beloved and a siren, that rhetoric is at once a bridge and a trap? In short, like a true ironist, James is keeping his fingers crossed. The smiling sphinx will vouchsafe no answer. The riddle abides. As a novel, *The Sacred Fount* is almost a dead kitten, suffocated by the lack of fresh, natural air, or killed by its own monstrous cunning. It is a pale, unhealthy thing, and has the compelling attraction of a cadaver.

If the narrator of *The Sacred Fount* is a critical enigma, the governess of "The Turn of the Screw" is no less. Neglected by her employer on whom she appears to have had a terrible crush, she has taken a posthumous literary revenge on us. And no discussion of James may indeed leave her out; she has become an analogue of ambiguity. There have, however, always been "straight" readers and critics for whom James's own comments on this "amusette,"[21] and on the perfect reliability of the governess, with all her implied imperfections, are evidence enough, if evidence indeed were needed, of the general meaning of this ghost story told with uncommon cunning. The impressive list includes such critics as Joseph Warren Beach, F. O. Matthiessen, F. R. Leavis, Philip Rahv, Robert B. Heilman, J. A.

Ward, Wayne C. Booth and Eli Siegel, though even among themselves, they offer clashing reasons for the governess's rectitude, and conflicting views on the phenomenon of evil, etc. Meanwhile, the Freudian school, best represented by Edmund Wilson and Edna Kenton, and supported in various ways by Leon Edel, Oscar Cargill and others, tends to see the sexually starved and fixated young governess as guilty of morbid fantasies and fabrications. A neurotic, ingrown spinster invents the ghosts, and tends to involve innocent children in an orgy of evil that is of her own making. Discounting James's own view to the contrary, Edmund Wilson remarks: "One is led to conclude that, in "The Turn of the Screw," not merely is the governess self-deceived, but that James is self-deceived about her," though in a postscript of 1959, he adds: "Since writing the above, I have been convinced that James knew exactly what he was doing and that he intended the governess to be suffering from delusions."[22] As evidence, he cites Marius Bewley's interpretation of "The Liar," a story significantly appearing next to "The Turn of the Screw" in the New York Edition. The moral, says Professor Edel, is that the children are "direct and guileless," and that "it is indeed the governess who has become the devil."[23] And now to add to this critical confusion, we also have the theory, held by John A. Clair, among others, that makes Mrs. Grose, and not the governess, the villain of the piece. The operative irony lies in our seeing Mrs. Grose's lies, a fact which he seeks to establish by examining her "jumbled chronology."[24]

What then, are we to make of the endless ambiguity of this tale whose very title suggests both sexual and structural problems? If James was indeed fully conscious of all the dark and desperate meanings we now find embedded in it, how may we reconcile obvious contradictions in the story except through a resort to the spirit of irony in James? Perhaps, the "turns" he goes on giving to the "screw" may also mean the twists applied to the reader's tail with a view to beguiling him along with the bemused governess into a wild goose chase. A mystery is created where indeed there is no mystery. There is no joke like a straight joke, if only because its transparency is also its shield. In which case, the irony here partakes of the nature of a huge leg-pull, as it possibly does in *The Sacred Fount*. Again, it could suggest the ambiguous nature of evil—evil residing ironically in the least probable of places: children! Innocence, James seems to be saying, may not rest till it has been violated and soiled. Or, evil may not feel safe till it finds itself ensconced in the very sanctuary of innocence! That is the paradox of human experience. It may well be, as R. B. Heilman thinks, that the apparent ambiguity of the story is simply "a by-product of James's method,"[25] a method that, of necessity, envelops things in a cloud of uncertainty; but the idea of nuclear ambiguity which is allied here to the ironic vision of evil cannot be ruled out. The governess may not be "an ironic center of narration,"[26] as K. B. Vaid insists—and indeed it does appear to me that she is not a "Freudian" witch, but a harassed Victorian young woman pitched suddenly into a world of doubt and darkness—but this does not eliminate operative irony, which, disengaged from the narrator, attaches itself to the theme and the structure of the story. The levels of irony are too many to be ignored in any fair reading of the tale. James's preface suggests nothing beyond a deliberate mystification in the interest of "effect." The imagination was to play the game "off its own bat," as it were. And even evil was to be more "portentous" than plausible, more suggestive than demonstrable. Did the tale exceed its brief? Not likely. A planned work of prose, even when it partakes of the genius of poetry, does not carry dark, unresolved elements that may undermine its intended meaning. And James, in any case, was much too careful and meticulous an artist to let a tale run away with the situation. Even in his most monstrous fantasies he manages to keep a cold, steady eye on the proceedings.

Similarly, in *What Maisie Knew,* a novel saturated with compelling and competing ironies, the little heroine is an "ironic centre,"[27] as James tells us in his preface, not in the sense of herself being turned into the opposite of what she stands for in the process of working out and balancing the twisted geometry of adulterous relationships, but in the sense of being the compositional centre which subsumes and promotes various ironies, and to which they must go back "homing," if we are to enjoy the comedy as intended by the author. Recalling the original impulse of the story, James tells us how the idea struck him as one capable of carrying "some deeper depth of irony," and its charm "lurked in the crude postulate like a buried scent." Elaborating, he remarks: "I was in presence of the red dramatic spark that glowed at the core of my vision and that, as I gently blew upon it, burned higher, and clearer. This precious particle was the *full* ironic truth—the most interesting item to be read into the child's *situation*"[28] (italics mine). Obviously, then, Maisie's hapless and awkward position rather than her character or person is to be seen as the object of irony. However, critics have, not without some semblance of truth, raised doubts in regard to Maisie's own innocence. As her burgeoning sexual consciousness is subjected to the multiplying assaults and temptations, the cunning little agent of the drama, it is believed, appears to be silently converting all the situations to her own advantage with a finesse beyond her years! She, it would appear, has ceased to be a victim of her parents' guile, and has instead begun to enjoy herself tremendously in the role allotted to her. Knowledge, in short, has soiled her as well, and she has almost developed a taste for "the game of chess" in which her elders and superiors are involved. The irony, then, would appear to be in the reversal of her role, in the besmirching of innocence by evil. Her virginity is offered to Sir Claude as a bait in the end, when at the beginning all that she offers is a beautiful and tender friendship. Indeed, in the novel itself, there are loaded hints in this direction, and the figurative and ironic prose may well lead a reader to the conclusion that in "flattening her nose upon the hard windowpane of the sweetshop of knowledge,"[29] like Hyacinth Robinson in *The Princess Casamassima,* Maisie too is executing a pattern of experience that has ironic overtones. She is seen as a potential candidate for the spoils of passion. Oscar

Cargill, for instance, quotes Carl Van Doren and Harris W. Wilson to support the view that Maisie is tainted, that she is "the refuge-catching vortex about whom a current of dissolute life pulses and whirls."[30] Again, Sallie Sears says apropos of Maisie: "Her innocence is in fact called into the service not of a moral vision but of an ironic one."[31] For Maxwell Geismar, she is a "voyeur glass,"[32] so to speak, for the obliquely reflected sexual antics of her elders. However, most critics maintain that Maisie not only retains her essential innocence and purity, but, in fact, acts as a regenerative agent of moral beauty. This is what F. R. Leavis refers to when he talks of "the incorruptible innocence of Maisie; innocence that not merely preserves itself in what have seemed to be irresistibly corrupting circumstances, but can even generate decency out of the egotistic squalors of adult personal relations."[33] Similarly, James W. Gargano maintains that like Nanda of *The Awkward Age,* Maisie is not simply "a sort of drain-pipe with everything flowing through." She keeps not only her innocence "unsmirched in the immediate proximity of pitch,"[34] but also achieves a moral effect. My own reading of the novel in the context of James's preface is that Maisie's innocence is not compromised in terms of morality; it is compromised in terms of experience. And since in James morals are finally won out of and proved in experience, the child poised on the discovery of sex is like a sailor freshly broken to the boat, eager and authentic, but already lured by the call of the dark sea. If experience means the loss of innocence, the despoiling process also creates compensatory values. It is not that remaining in the element of pitch she cannot escape defilement; it is that the very process of cognition and growth requires a pragmatic approach to reality. Maisie's verbal faux pas in an adult world of sin and venality are apt not only to cause mirth, but also to create a misleading impression. She certainly learns to live and breathe in that foul atmosphere, and even extract a wry amusement in the midst of bewilderment, but her "diplomacy" is a question of her survival, not of her depravity. All the resources of her limited vocabulary are not enough to bridge the gaps in her rapid initiation, and though, toward the end, the distance appears to be narrowing, she is not really in complete command of the situation. A great deal of irony, thus, inheres in Maisie's half-knowledge and incomplete equations. In one of the best essays on the subject, Tony Tanner rightly emphasizes the cognitive aspect of the story. For him, Maisie remains "unspoiled by knowledge, and none of the surrounding badness rubs off onto her." And he adds, "she is the recipient of innumerable impressions: but she lacks any coordinating key."[35] And from this he proceeds to develop the idea of the limits of vision in Henry James—the question of his "epistemological scepticism" and his belief in the "relativity of all knowledge."[36] In short, in *What Maisie Knew* we are up against not only the situational and incidental ironies of life, but also against the fundamental irony of vision and of cognition.

In fact, if we are looking for the irony of character in *What Maisie Knew,* we had better turn to that comic creature of inflated rectitude, Mrs. Wix, whose

morality runs away with her. Her concern for the wretched ward stems as much
from a puritanical ethics as from her suppressed sexuality. For James leaves little
doubt in our minds in regard to her own obscure crush on Sir Claude. Her mixed
motives make her at once a comic and a pathetic creature. James's gathering irony
completely envelops her in the end. That "extraordinary warmth of pity for both
Maisie and Mrs. Wix"[37] which S. Gorley Putt finds welling up in the novel is, at
least in respect of the governess, a wholly misunderstood sentiment. A certain
compassion for all victims of passion is a characteristic feature of the later James,
but this does not put Mrs. Wix in the same class as Pinnie of *The Princess
Casamassima,* or Miss Birdseye of *The Bostonians,* or Mrs. Stringham of *The
Wings of the Dove*. Whereas the other ladies enjoy the warmth of Jamesian irony,
Mrs. Wix gets its chilly edge only. In a final, desperate bid to storm Sir Claude's
moral consciousness, after she has failed to rouse Maisie to her "duty," she is
almost reduced to the vulgarity of loud pathos: *"Take me, take me. . . .* Here I
am, I know what I am and what I ain't; but I say boldly to the face of you both that
I'll do better for you, far, than ever she'll try to" (italics mine).[38] Unless I am
entirely mistaken, I see a Jamesian chuckle in the insistent "take me, take me," in
this unconscious eruption of sexual hysteria in Mrs. Wix's idiom.

Though irony encompasses nearly every major novel or tale in the end, James
criticism has particularly unearthed several levels of conscious and unconscious
irony in such later works as "The Aspern Papers," "The Liar," "A London Life,"
"The Pupil," "The Lesson of the Master," "The Chaperon," "The Figure in the
Carpet" and "The Jolly Corner." Whether the narrator of "The Aspern Papers," the
painter Lyon, Laura Wing, Mr. Pamberton, Rose Tramore and Alice Staverton are
all "liars" instead of being "straight" characters is a question that cannot be settled
in a paragraph or two.[39] One thing, however, is clear enough; it is dangerous to
accept a Jamesian character or narrative at its face value. Nearly always, there is
either a sting in the tail, or a rent in the garment, that is showing. All these tales,
then, raise the eternal question of James's ambiguity. The deceptive mask of irony
or the protective shield of irony, as the case may be, is an inescapable presence in
James. It is as often a dramatic device as the instrument of a vision of reality.

That the three great novels of the major phase should carry intersecting
ironies, refined to the point of abstraction, is not therefore surprising. The entire
drift of James's thought now reveals a preoccupation with the uncertainties,
treacheries and abysses of life. Some of the earlier attitudes and certitudes are
being silently questioned, if not repudiated. At any rate, viewing reality in the
round is now a settled practice. The very form or structure of these novels, as we
have seen in an earlier essay, rests upon the principles of polarity and parallelism,
of contradiction and contrast. The style becomes indirect, elliptical and
"mannered." Thus, the various ironies, structural, thematic and verbal, are now
part of the ironic vision which lies at the heart of these books.

The Ambassadors, in particular, is a fine example of the operative irony
subsuming subsidiary ironies. The pattern of the plot itself and an altered view of

life cohere to suggest such a conclusion. The entire drama turns round the "embassy" of Strether—the ironic centre of the novel—who finds his terms of reference and engagement falsified as he grows rich in Parisian experience. In view of his age and scholarship and culture, he is thought best suited to salvage the lost Chad, but things turn out to be wholly different from what Woollett has imagined. Strether's "embassy" goes sour on him; and he appears won over to the enemy camp. In a manner, the novel echoes the ironic pattern of Anatole France's *Thais*. The roles are reversed; it's Strether who is "lost," and Chad who has "won," so far as Woollett is concerned. But this too really does not fully complete the circle of irony for James. The finest twist comes with the return of Strether to Woollett—a tragic return that mocks his "embassy," but authenticates his moral vision. Strether is a "renegade" who is the more magnificent for his sacrificial return, while Chad, the "prodigal" come home, is shown a cad for all his Parisian experience. And not only Strether, but also Mamie Pocock and her husband, the new "ambassadors," are a "sell" from the point of view of Woollett, though the irony attending upon them has only comic overtones.

That Strether himself is also subjected to a gentle and sympathetic irony by James is clear enough. His academic flirtation with Maria Gostrey, and his shy passion for Madame de Vionnet do lend a certain ponderous air to the story, and James, himself a prude, cannot help but cast an ironic glance over the evasive and distilled proceedings. And there may well be an ironic hint in "the return of the native" to the New England pastures, a return which is also, in a way, a retreat and a regression. The sacrifice of Maria in behalf of a "woolly" ideal is to show the covert influence of Woollett after all! But if an irony is implied, it is of the gentlest kind, suggesting that no sacrifice in the world may be effected without at the same time springing a leak through which the essence may flow out. I am unable to accept the thesis of Robert E. Garis that for Strether, "there has been no education at all,"[40] and that in this lies the ironic intent of the novel. Nor is U. C. Knoepflamacher's essay, "O Rare for Strether!: *Antony and Cleopatra* and *The Ambassadors*," though well argued in terms of its given premise, a correct measure of James's own diplomacy. The irony does not lie in the defeat of Strether's "romantic imagination,"[41] with a deflated Cleopatra crying like a "kitchen-maid" before him, but in the pragmatic truth that in the affairs of the heart, queens and maids are all ruled ultimately by the same imperatives.

Again, in *The Wings of the Dove,* James's irony, which in the beginning hovers round such conventional characters as Mrs. Lowder, that massive image of "Britannia" at the Lancaster Gate house, and Mrs. Stringham, that romantic busybody tailoring a fantasy of love for her "Princess," is diffused, and partakes of the tragic vision which informs the book. As the story gathers the weight of related complexities, and the drama of mixed motives begins to unfold itself, the inherent ambiguities of the situation come into full play. The tenuous, insinuating dialogues, coiling and uncoiling, create an air of tension, foreboding and uncertainty. In short, the thematic irony of the novel is matched by a corresponding verbal irony. As Densher is drawn deeper and deeper into the silken web woven by Kate, he develops a playful irony which has in fact a "portentous" aspect. Here, he is talking to Kate about Milly:

> Still he just brooded, "She takes things from you exactly as I do?"
> "Exactly as you do."
> "She's just such another victim?"
> "Just such another. You're a pair."
> "Then if anything happens," said Densher, "we can console each other?"
> "Ah, something, *may* indeed happen," she exclaimed, "if you'll only go straight."
> He watched the others an instant through the window. "What do you mean by going straight?"
> "Not worrying. Doing as you like. Try, as I've told you before, and you'll see. You'll have me perfectly, always to refer to."[42]

The greatest irony, of course, lies in the dramatic reversal of not only hopes or expectations, but also of roles. Who, in the end, is indeed the "victim," and who the victimizer? In the final analysis, the cruellest blow is reserved for Kate who must lose either love or money, or perhaps both. She has engineered a desolate fate, hoist, so to speak, with her own petard. Even as we salute her "stupendous" beauty and courage, we are appalled by "the awesome irony"[43] of her career! The terrible finality of her concluding words: "We shall never be again as we were!" leaves open a wide chasm of doubt and speculation in regard to their future.

I do not share the view that Milly's great act of beauty in her fabulous bequest to Densher is also in a subtle, oblique way the revenge of an injured psyche, an act almost of what Sartre would call "bad faith." To talk about the "dove" and "dirt," in the end, is to misunderstand the symbolic meaning of her sacrifice. The magnanimity of her soul not only remains untarnished; it positively reaches with this act a new level of spiritual significance. It is now a question of the eternal holiness of the heart's affections, and of the spirit's magnanimities. Of course, the shadow of her violated soul would forever continue to fall athwart the blighted lives of her violators, but this is an aspect of the dramatic irony on which the novel rests. And the irony is of James's making, not of Milly's. And if we were to grant for a moment the thesis of "bad faith," what then are we to make of the regeneration or redemption of Densher, whose innermost being has been ineffably touched by the spirit of the dead woman? The triumph of spirit over circumstance and contingency and matter could not have been more dramatically emphasized than in the ironic paradox of Milly dead being a more shattering and moving force than Milly alive!

The irony of *The Golden Bowl* is again to be seen in the ambiguous and teasing form or structure of the story, and it dovetails with the irony underlying the theme of the book. It is, James appears to say, the paradox of marriage that it could best survive under tension, stretch and accommodation. The injury done to the form in the end ensures its health; a crack in the bowl is but a wry acknowledgement of the inadequacies of any institution, whatever its other graces and felicities.

Whether Maggie Verver's victory in the end is Pyrrhic as suggested by some critics, or truly magnificent in its moral beauty, is a matter of opinion. One thing, however, is difficult to accept—the idea of Maggie's "aggression" and Charlotte Stant's "innocence," a view offered by F. R. Leavis, among others. True, Maggie is no saint—indeed, she is too human in her weaknesses, and in her energetic assertion of her rights—but it would be a grievous error to think that James's irony in the end converts a wholly innocent and lovable person into a monster of outraged virtue. She is not the only one to be viewed with an indulgent irony—nearly every Jamesian heroine, as we have seen earlier, has the hose turned in her direction for a mild spray—only in her case, the irony appears more trenchant in view of her unconscious oedipal impulses. The darker side of James's irony in *The Golden Bowl* is to be seen at work not in relation to Maggie, but to the smooth and surreptitious nature of the evil of which she is a victim.

What, then, are our conclusions in regard to the nature of irony in James? Is it essentially detached, philosophic or Olympian? Is it pure, luminous and serene? Or, is it troubled, dark and portentous? Does it show a coherent, consistent and viable pattern? I think one thing is clear enough: James did not have a philosophic mind capable of rendering metaphysical subtleties and knots. Nearly all the wire-drawn subtleties of the later phase are those of manner, style and form rather than of ideas per se. As T. S. Eliot put it, he had a mind that preyed "not upon ideas but upon living beings."[44] Thus, the Jamesian irony is less ideational than structural or thematic, though themes include ideas, and to that extent have, at least in the later novels and tales, a theoretic aspect. Nor is the all-seeing eye unclouded and clear, directing things from a lofty perch. If anything, the mind has developed a trick of thought. It cannot see things squarely without casting a shy glance at the possible chinks and crevices in them, or at the abysses underneath them. No systematic irony, as Dupee observes,[45] may be seen in James, unless of course the habit of distrusting reality in the end constituted some kind of a system. James may well have held with Paul Tillich that the only thing we know for certain is that we know nothing for certain. James, however, did not have Tillich's trust in "the dynamics of faith," and he remains in Margaret L. Wiley's view an "incomplete sceptic."[46]

Of the "four phases of the sceptic process" listed by Professor Wiley, "nescience, dualism, paradox, and knowing by doing,"[47] James is principally concerned with the middle two: dualism and paradox. The concept of nescience posits a premise that the human truth, or any truth for that matter, is essentially unknowable. There is no strong evidence of such a belief in James, though in his later fiction, he comes very close to questioning the rationale of almost everything. As for dualism, we have noticed the constant opposition and interplay of antinomies and polarities in his work. Even the metaphors and symbols, such as those of the tiger and the lamb, of the snake and the dove, of the pit and the garden, are organized on this principle. What is more, the principle extends to his architectonics. Irony, thus, is firmly allied to the concept of dualism. As Reuben

Arthur Brower believes, to experience the nature of irony, "we must entertain both of the clashing possibilities."[48] Similarly, the paradoxical mode of expression is habitual to James in his later phase—an index of the operative irony. Sometimes, the paradox inheres in the theme or in a character. At least one critic, Sallie Sears, emphasizes the paradox of "the tiger in the lamb," of the fusion of "predator and victim"[49] in Maggie Verver. However, I am unable to share Professor Wiley's view that James moves on even to the fourth stage of the ironic process, "to the language of action." True, for him, "stasis, arrest and fixity are evil,"[50] but there is no real stir or movement in his thought; we have only an agitated rhetoric. J. A. Ward, as we have seen earlier, in fact, tends to associate action with evil in James, and reflection or states of mind with achieved good. This is a mistake James made, as most aesthetes do, but its presence in his work is not to be denied.

The really teasing thing about the late novels and tales is that there are ironies within ironies, as in a Chinese box, and it's seldom clear which irony can be called *operative* and *visionary,* and which *subversive.* For the irony that undercuts other collateral ironies itself at times begins to show fatigue and unease. Usually, for some time James is able to maintain the line and control of the operative irony, but the superstructure in the end becomes so heavy and so drawn-out as to confuse even a vigilant reader. There is also a danger of the "super-subtle" reader becoming a rival to James. He may, then, begin to put his own imagination into "the game," as it were, and in this strange author-reader relationship (explored by the linguistic critics in their kind of aesthetic), one is tempted to see the predator-victim idea and the "vampire" theory at work. Pursued further, it may even mean that where the writer is "aged" and depleted, the reader is "young," providing "the sacred fount" of inspiration and energy. In short, as the aged Master's fable grows in power, it correspondingly diminishes the more imaginatively alive reader's own responses. A fanciful extension of the Jamesian *donnée,* if you like!

The truth of irony is refreshing on the whole, and helps clear cobwebs of sentimentalism and runaway romance. However, its indiscriminate use can make it self-defeating and destructive. It then becomes a counterpart of sentimentalism. When it hardens into an attitude, it begins to lose the colour and warmth of life. It becomes, in short, a protective armour, covering the writer's own inner failings or weaknesses. "The author," writes Wayne C. Booth, "who maintains his invulnerability by suggesting irony at all points but never holding himself responsible for definition of its limits can be as irresponsible as the writer of best-sellers based on naïve identification."[51] In James, though the darker side of irony is more dominant and pervasive in the end, there is nearly always some saving grace. Thus, we have in him at once "the negative imagination" and "the imagination of loving." The two do not cancel out each other. On the contrary, they are supplementary, and make up the totality of James's universe. Somehow, "the imagination of disaster" is prevented from taking an irretrievable plunge into the world of chaos. The irony is not permitted to spill over and waste away its energies and beauties.

10

The Quest of Art

Henry James's concern with art *qua* art is so intense and abiding that it has led critics either to damn him as a sterile and pompous aesthete, or to cry him up as a mystic visionary in search of "the holy grail." Each of these interpretations, I think, is based on a misconception about the meaning of art and its operative energy in the work of James. No doubt, he never quite succeeds in shedding his innate Pateresque aestheticism; no doubt, he has the poetic and passionate quality of an involved visionary when in labour, but these things do not add up to either of the two pictures presented to us. The confusion arises from the fact that James does offer striking and contradictory evidence, and no critic is quite safe against indulgence. My aim in this essay, then, is simply to show that his quest of art, though seeming to shade off into a mystic pursuit, remains, nevertheless, till the end a purely aesthetic and mundane concern. What's more, the feeling of the numinous in his later fiction, supported by the imagery of transcendence and salvation, as in *The Wings of the Dove*, is not to be equated with religious emotion. The only religion he has is "a religion of art,"[1] as Leon Edel puts it.

In the first instance, to talk of the visionary and mystic quest of a writer whose public image is that of a prim and faintly snobbish prude dining in stately and spacious English country houses, is to beg the question. However, as I proceed, I hope to show that despite the fact that he is almost emptied by his excessive scruples, and smothered by his own delicate draperies, James is unique among the great novelists of the world in regard to the integrity and purity of his search for values via art—a search that spans nearly half a century of unsleeping and uncompromising commitment, and makes him "a priest of the eternal imagination," to use a Joycean expression. Which is not to say that all the values he cared for were necessarily correct or even viable. In fact, his world-view today strikes us as curiously queasy and ingrown. Some splendid affirmations and epiphanies have been encrusted with frostings that are too plainly showing. What, therefore, makes James a visionary is not the quality of his dream, but the quality of his pursuit. In short, it is the mechanics of the quest rather than its spiritual or mystic potential that really mattered for him. The idea here is not of the reach being greater than the grasp; as we shall see, James, on the whole, had no importunate gropings and strivings and reachings, no vistas or visitations of the beatific and the ineffable. Even, the "play of the portentous" was for him a purely fictional device, and the supernatural apprehension of reality, which some critics see in him, was, in fact, the intensity of an illumined consciousness that finally became a law unto itself. There was no white light of eternity here, no quest after the grail. No, James was not a "possessed" writer in the sense Dostoievsky was, or Kafka, unless, of course, his passion for art—Arnold Bennett wondered if James "ever felt a passion except for literature"[2]—could be taken as a mystic compulsion of some sort. For this is how his awe and reverence and piety in the presence of art could perhaps be understood.

If his father's Swedenborgian dreams had any significant effect on James's sensibility as Quentin Anderson argues, surely this was seldom a conscious cultivation. The mocking, ironical and pragmatic son had little sympathy with those vague and expansive fantasies of the soul. He gazed so long and so intensely at the ordeals of engaged consciousnesses that the kind of abstraction associated with mysticism could almost be felt by the reader. When, therefore, Orage suggests that "James was in love with the next world, or the next state of consciousness, the borderland between the conscious and the unconscious,"[3] it would be wrong to assume that this was a truly mystic state of mind. Perhaps T. S. Eliot was nearer the mark when he said that despite his indifference to religious doctrine or dogma, James had "an exceptional awareness of spiritual reality."[4] This reality, it may be reiterated, has little to do with mystic transcendence or immortality, etc. This "spiritual reality" is simply James's recognition of the hungers and felicities of the human soul. In terms of art and experience, it signified his nostalgia for the poetry of facts, and for the poetry behind facts. F. W. Dupee's happy description of James as "a visionary of the small act"[5] is, I think, wholly relevant. Or, as Hana Wirth-Nesher in her essay on the artist tales observes, in James there was a need for the apotheosis of art as a replacement for Christianity, though art must remain "a secular salvation."[6]

As I have said elsewhere in this volume, James's apotheosis of art could well be a form of gratification sought by a lean life. The energy and opulence of art appeared to make up for the intensities of felt experience. This vicarious experience is at once a compensation and a displacement, and accounts, to an extent, for the peculiar turns and twists of the Jamesian "screw." What indeed should have gone into the making of life has gone finally into the making of art. The body has not burnt to the wick to produce the truth; instead the mind has appropriated experience as an act of the imagination. That James was well aware of such a lack may best be seen in his treatment of the theme of life's unappeased hungers in his later fiction.

Since, from the beginning of his literary career, James was fully aware of the need to discipline his muse in the employ of art, he began to ponder the mystery of the aesthetic process, and the vocation of the artist. And this sustained interest found expression not only in his earlier reviews, letters, critical essays and prefaces, etc., but also in a number of novels and tales concerning the artist, his craft and his destiny. Some of these are no more than fictional essays on the subject, their human or emotional potential being severely limited. Others are thinly veiled autobiographical sketches voicing his ironic bafflement and pique. And yet it is amazing how he has turned the mechanics of his craft or the sinews of his art to art itself. Together, these variations, however, do not present a comprehensive and consistent philosophy of art, and once again, we are intrigued by his characteristic ambiguity. Nevertheless, a few general strains can be traced, even if they cannot be fully defended. The problems which appear to have both fascinated and baffled him in this regard principally were blandishments of art in opposition to life, art and artifice, art and ethics, art as salvation, and finally the validity of art itself. Naturally where the entire rationale of art and its practice are being examined, the question of the artist's life, labour and sacrifice inevitably will receive pointed attention. Art and artist in the end are, like Yeats's dance and dancer, indivisible.

As early as "The Madonna of the Future" James begins to explore the ambivalent nature of art. There is at once something divine and something ridiculous about this monkish pursuit. The American painter, Theobald, has for years been cooling his heels in Florence to produce his masterpiece, rhapsodizing over the mystic beauty of art, and waiting to receive the green signal from beyond—his moment of illumination and fulfillment, a signal which, as in Samuel Beckett's *Waiting for Godot,* never comes! His long and suffering wait mocks his protracted labour, and his wakening in the end is a measure of the distance he has travelled since his first meeting with the narrator. Although his inflated aestheticism is clearly held up to ridicule, there is, at the same time, a feeling of reverence for a passion so pure and abiding, so flame-like in its ascetic energy. That in Theobald's case the bonfire of the imagination produces no conflagration only reveals the irony of his fate. Where an aesthetic ideal is divorced from talent and practice, the result will inevitably be a "dawdling" and drooling lover slobbering over a slut whom his pawned imagination has taken for a rare beauty! James may also be saying in this fable that though the idea of an "inglorious Milton" or a mute genius is irrelevant—a view incidentally aired by Sartre also—there is at least something to be said for the beauty of so pure a pursuit as Theobald's. In the end, perhaps, one thing that really mattered for the health of the artist was, to use an Indian expression, *sadhana,* i.e., self-effacing and sacrificial labour in the service of an ideal. Here the narrator is talking about the painter's devotion to the goddess of art:

> If my friend was not a genius, he was certainly a natural rhapsodist, or even a harmless madman; and I found the play of his temper, his humour, and his candid and unworldly character as quaint as if he had been a creature from another planet. He seemed indeed to know very little of this one, and lived and moved altogether in his boundless province of art. A creature more

unsullied by the accidents of life it's impossible to conceive, and I *sometimes questioned the reality of an artistic virtue, an esthetic purity, on which some profane experience hadn't rubbed off a little more.* It was hard to have to accept him as of our own hard-headed stock, but after all there could be no better sign of his American start than the completeness of his reaction in favour of vague profits. The very heat of his worship was a mark of conversion, those born within sight of the temple take their opportunities more for granted. . . . I made a point of never seeming to cross a certain line with him, but each time we met, I ventured to make some respectful allusion to the *magnum opus,* to inquire, if I might, as to its health and progress. "We're getting on, with the Lord's help," he would say with a bravery that never languished; "I think we can't be said not to be doing well. You see I've the grand advantage that I lose no time. These hours I spend with you are pure profit. They bring me in a harvest of incentives. *Just as the truly religious soul is always at worship, the genuine artist is always in labour. . . .*"[7] (Italics mine)

In *Roderick Hudson,* James dramatizes at great length the eternal paradox of art. While life is all passion and heat and indulgence, art is all coolness and abstraction and detachment. How should the artist, then, conduct himself so that, remaining in the element, he transcends its limitations? James has no answer to it, and all that he can offer at this stage is the cold consolation of art as opposed to the misery and combat of life. In Roderick's fate James sees the defeat of art by destructive passion, and is therefore wary of its importunate claims. Leon Edel rightly interprets the novel as a Jamesian exercise in autotherapy. Obviously, James is seeking to exorcize the Roderick in him, that fever raging in his blood, and threatening to blow up all his artistic ambitions and dreams. "Roderick," writes Professor Edel, "is the artist side of James all flame and passion, yet rendered ineffectual by the very fear of his own intensities. Roderick seems to represent all that Henry James was *within* but could not allow himself to be or do. . . . "[8] A somewhat similar conflict between "blood and judgement" has been noticed in Shakespeare, and its tragic dramatization in *Antony and Cleopatra* is at once a salute to the majesty of passion and a warning in regard to its explosive destructiveness. In fact, it is an archetypal conflict, and may well be traced in Keats, in Yeats and in all such artists as are inclined to resist the blandishments of passion, and yet know the irresistible truths of man's "resinous heart."

Another side issue of the artist question in *Roderick Hudson* is the issue of the cruelty and inhumanity of genius. Here we find a potentially great sculptor on the verge of a moral collapse as a result of his hopeless infatuation, and he considers everyone expendable—his beloved, Mary Garland, his mother, his friend and benefactor, Mallet. All must somehow administer to the needs of his inconsolable heart. Genius has its petulant prerogatives. "Genius was priceless, beneficent, divine, but it was also at its hours capricious, sinister, cruel."[9] In the end, Rowland, hurt by the pride of the artist, is constrained to tell him: "It's a perpetual sacrifice then to live with a remorseless egotist."[10] The idea of the artist's inhumanity as a condition of his art is present in some of James's later novels and tales also. In *The Tragic Muse,* Peter Sherringham notices with dismay the drift of Miriam's heart after "the cold passion of art had perched on her banner."[11]

Something in the nature of art, James appears to believe, requires a certain "selfishness" if you like. Art, he declares elsewhere, should be "as hard as nails—as hard as the heart of the artist."[12]

Does the cultivation of art mean necessarily the sacrifice of all creature and civilized pleasures—money, social position, wife and children? This is one of the problems James poses in "The Lesson of the Master." Though the ironic ending of the tale may well suggest that the "lesson" of the Master lay in seizing life's opportunities as they came rather than in renouncing all the pleasures of life, the drift of James's thought, on the whole, is in favour of the view that the artist "that hath wife and children hath given hostages to fortune," a view that presumably rationalizes his own position in the matter. To Paul Overt's anguished observation, "What a false position, what a condemnation of the artist that he's a mere disfranchised monk and can produce his effect only by giving up personal happiness,"[13] the Master, St. George, replies by marrying the young man's beloved, Marian Fancourt—an act calculated to remove temptation from the pupil's path, and to save him for his promised and high destiny of a great artist! Once again in *The Tragic Muse* James comes close to saying that the artist who seeks the very highest perch needs must discard sexual love. As Lyall H. Powers sums up: "This, then, is the prevailing pattern in James—the celibate artist, the chaste muse, and their incorporeal, spiritual intercourse."[14]

Early in "The Lesson of the Master," another important question that occurs frequently in James's writing is also briefly touched upon—the question of the choice between life and art. In the preface to *The Tragic Muse* James refers to the conflict between art and the world "as constituting one of the half dozen great primary motives."[15] F. W. Dupee quotes Yeats's well-known lines from "The Choice":

> The intellect of man is forced to choose
> Perfection of the life or of the work,
> And if take the second must refuse
> A heavenly mansion, raging in the dark:

Can art, indeed, ever be a real substitute for life? Paul Overt, taken up a great deal with the handsome young woman, Miss Fancourt, is unable to see the logic of the Master's argument.

> "Well, after all, why try to be an artist?" the young man pursued, "it's so poor, so poor?"
> "I mean as compared with a person of action—as living your work."
> "But what's art but an intense life—if it be real?" She asked.
> "I think it's the only one—everything else is so clumsy."[16]

Miss Fancourt is obviously echoing St. George's views which, in a manner, hark back to Theobald's passionate statement in "The Madonna of the Future."

"No one so loves and respects the rich realities of nature as the artist whose imagination intensifies them."[17] For James, art always meant a way of meeting the muddle and chaos and waste of life, a way indeed of preserving all that was worth one's salt. That is why he speaks of "the conserving imagination" which is, at the same time, the imagination of discrimination. For whatever the artist's imagination seizes upon as truth out of life's mishmash is turned into beauty as a result of the purifying processes of art. James, however, is unable to see that though art does preserve the best that has been known and felt in the world, that indeed it creates and sums up the ideal possibilities of life, it cannot tweak life's nose to assert its independence or superiority. Keats, confronted with a similar problem, clearly asserted that in his system of values, poetry was the finest thing next to action. Even James's own friend, R. L. Stevenson, in his essay on "The Apology for Idlers" declares that though books are good enough in their own way, they are "a mighty bloodless substitute for life." Thus, James's whole apologia for art had a distinct leak. James, on the contrary, tends to believe that the artist, being removed from the press and heat of things, and having a more prescient mind, is nearer to the heart of reality than a person committed to and involved in action. Or, as Lionel Trilling puts it, the artist "may be close to the secret center of things when the man of action is quite apart from it."[18]

James at times is almost guilty of saying that it is not life, but its representation in art which is really important. All the "complexities" and "the fury and the mire of human veins" are finally resolved for him in the Yeatsian paradise of art. Though Yeats himself in his later phase bounces back to life with an athletic vigour, James, it appears to me, keeps showing a certain distrust and fear of life till the end. Undoubtedly, some of his own statements in this regard tend to create misconceptions. In one of his letters to H. G. Wells, he makes a statement which, on the face of it, is astounding, to say the least. "It's art that makes life, makes interest, makes importance, for our consideration and application of those things, I know of no substitute whatever for the force and beauty of its process."[19] Obviously, he cannot mean anything so silly and crude as this that art precedes life, or that it undercuts life. What he seems to have in mind is that the ideal possibilities and reaches offered by art to fine consciousnesses constitute the only type of life worth caring for. And art makes life in the sense also that it returns its debt to it in the form of increased perceptions. All this, if that is what he means, is correct, and yet one cannot escape from the feeling in James that the novelist is somehow offering art as an alternative to life. Some of the artist-based tales and novels do seem to promote such a view. If critics and readers tend to disregard the subtler meanings of his various and clashing pronouncements on art, it is because the Jamesian practice often gives a lie to his declared views.

His attitude, for instance, toward the aesthetic movement of Pater, Wilde and Symonds is hardly free from ambiguity. He does mildly satirize its excesses and extravagances in *The Tragic Muse* and in "The Author of Beltraffio," and yet there is a distinct craving for its avowed objectives. He is wholly in sympathy with the movement's concern for form, elegance and style, though he objects to its lack of high seriousness and moral purpose. It does occur to him that whenever form or style becomes an object in itself, it leads in the direction of frivolity, and yet he himself cannot quite master the impulse to run to excess. Mark Ambient's creed in "The Author of Beltraffio" is somewhat questioned, though his "passion for form" receives James's unqualified praise.

> This was the taken stand of the artist to whom every manifestation of human energy was a thrilling spectacle and who felt for ever the desire to resolve his experience of life into a literary form. On that high head of the passion for form—the attempt at perfection, *the quest for which was to his mind the real search for the holy grail*—he said the most interesting, the most inspiring things.[20] (italics mine)

Clearly, the idiom and imagery of this nature would tend to invest James's pursuit of art with a mystic ambience. And yet in all this kind of rhetoric, he is nowhere near an apprehension of the reality beyond the grave. His concerns remain desperately and resolutely mundane.

James's quest for form, however, is at once a question of architectonics, ethics and epistemology. It is a quest for formal beauty and grace, for the ideal geometry of relationships, and for the modes of apprehending human reality. Since his concept of the form stipulates that the whole shall contain the parts, just as the parts shall make up the whole, the form, then, is not merely an outer shell, but an integral part of one's vision. Or, to put it differently, the form eventually becomes the vision. That is why indeed the Jamesian pursuit of form assumes a compulsive character, and seems to acquire mystic overtones.

At the epistemological level, the question of form is related to the theme of appearance and reality in James. The baffling and teasing nature of the manner in which man apprehends reality lends it a special significance. If the senses preclude any other form of apprehension, and the appearance of things alone is our certification, then obviously the appearance itself is reality. If the form in art or literature is not a mere costume to cover the view, or a scaffolding to hoist it, it is perhaps the view per se. Such appears to me to be the rationale of James's accent on form. Inevitably, it leads in the direction of what F. O. Matthiessen has called, "aesthetic idealism."[21] Dorothea Krook sums up the problem in these words:

> That art concerns itself to render the world of appearances, that these appearances exist only in the consciousness, indeed are the content of the consciousness, of human observers; that the world of art therefore is a beautiful representation of the appearances present to a particular consciousness under particular conditions, and the artist's overriding task is accordingly to exhibit in the concrete, with the greatest possible completeness and consistency, as well as vividness and intensity, the particular world of appearances accessible to a particular consciousness under the specific conditions created for it by the artist: these are the elements of James's theory of art.[22]

Meanwhile, it will be interesting to see how James seeks to reach the heart and ideal of reality, that is to say, the essence of experience and the finished form of things. This he does in a variety of ways. First of all, he makes his chief protagonists super-fine, if not super-subtle, in the quality of their being. To meet a Christopher Newman, a Lambert Strether, an Isabel Archer, a Milly Theale or a Fleda Vetch is to explore the limits of inner refinement, as also incidentally, "the limits of metaphor."[23]

However, it should not be difficult to see that what we have here is a closed-in quest rather than a flight beyond reality, a reaching-in rather than a reaching-out or a reaching-beyond. James apparently is both intrigued and charmed by the ramifications of human consciousness. The expansion, the rotation of aspects, the correspondences, the luminosities, the sophistries and the subterfuges—all these make man's consciousness an endless theme for variations on life. It will be readily seen that consciousness in James is not a free, flowing, spontaneous stream as in Joyce or in Virginia Woolf, but an energized, animated, awakened state of mind which permits the protagonists to live to the fullest pitch of private life, and to cultivate the garden of sensibility, redolent of the fragrance of memories and associations, of dreams and desires. It is such crowded and enlarged consciousnesses which at their highest reach are lit up with a million candles, as it were. However, this again, as I have said earlier, has little to do with spiritual epiphanies. James's intense concentration tends to give his artistic quest a feeling of the numinous. It is as if he has a premonitory apprehension of reality as engineered in art. In fact, the *affective* glow of his later rounded compositions is a distinct evidence of the presence of high emotion even though it comes to us distilled as through a fine sieve. James himself speaks of the same thing when in "The Lesson of Balzac," he refers to "the mystic process of the crucible, the transformation of the material *under aesthetic heat*"[24] (italics mine).

Again, it may be argued that the effort to interpret reality in a tangential and oblique manner, as in James's later work, is emblematic of the mystic strain in the novelist. One has to read between the lines and break the code as in Sufi poetry or in Zen philosophy. The obstacle, the riddle, the feint, the parry, the detour, the mask—all these, we know, are part of the hoary paraphernalia of mysticism. It is through these alone that the imponderables are reached, if they are, indeed, reached at all! Perhaps the door and key imagery, or the imagery of voyage and light to be found increasingly in the later works would indicate an imagery of mystic quest. But I suggest the mystic James in the wings is also a mirage. His efforts at penetration do not extend beyond the waking consciousness. All "the wayside traps set in the interest of muddlement"[25] are really the means to intensify the theme. For we know James often created complexity for the sheer challenge it offered to his inventive and "grasping" imagination. In short, "the indirect vision" is a question more of indirect style than of revelation or transcendence.

Alternatively, in order to achieve density, he keeps adding layer upon layer of meaning so that the skyscraper of consciousness causes in the end a kind of spiritual vertigo. There is, undoubtedly, in the later James the danger of the language or the form carrying on by itself, leaving the reality cold in the street. This happens when the mind begins to convert all solid things into a state of pure consciousness, when indeed a scruple is stretched to the point of evaporation or extinction, and the pursuit becomes bizarre, quizzical and quirkish.

However, often we are saved by the skin of our teeth as we stand teetering over the abyss of the void. For usually James holds on tenaciously to the thread; he does not forget the concept of the frame or the principle of "internal relationship." After the detours and the traps, things fall inevitably into their proper place and proportion. The perspective, so to speak, is restored. In this single-minded persistence and rigorous discipline of form, the balance of subtlety and sanity is, on the whole, scrupulously maintained.

Similarly, if Stransom in "The Altar of the Dead" is James's voice, one may not draw any mystical conclusions from his worship of the dead, or his reverence for the abiding mystery of death. These private, personal pieties and holinesses are simply part of the Jamesian ethics. Commenting on "The Altar of the Dead," S. G. Putt writes: "If James had other worldly experiences, they emerge in his fiction as the raptures or ecstasies of a rooted earthbound consciousness."[26] Again in "The Great Good Place," which has sometimes been regarded as a study of some heavenly mansion, a bower of paradisal bliss uncomplicated by money, fame or woman, there are, both in style and language, hints enough to suggest James's concern with the reality beyond the grave.

> Everyman must arrive by himself and on his own feet—isn't that so? We're Brothers here for the time, as in a great monastery, and we immediately think of each other and recognise each other as such, but we must have first got here as we can, and we meet after long journeys by complicated ways. Moreover, we meet—don't we—with closed eyes.[27]

> Those things were in the world—in what he had left; there was no vulgarity here of credit or claim or fame. The real exquisite was to be without the complication of an identity. . . .

> This key, pure gold, was simply the cancelled list slowly and blissfully he read into the general wealth of his comfort all the particular absences of which it was composed. One by one he touched, as it were, all the things it was such rapture to be without. He had not had detachment, but there was detachment here—the sense of a great silver bowl from which he could ladle up the melted hours. . . .

> It was a part of the whole impression that, by some extraordinary law, one's vision seemed less from the facts than the facts from one's vision. . . . [28]

Without sharing Clifton Fadiman's great enthusiasm for the story, which he compares with *Pilgrim's Progress* and *The Divine Comedy,* I endorse his view that "the place is no ethereal heaven—James is almost devoid of any religious sense—but a theoretically achievable utopia. . . ."[29]

The visionary quest, then, boils down to finding that unique equation in life which will protect a sensitive psyche against the brutal blasts of reality. As for the reversal of the natural order of things—the "vision" creating "facts" rather than the "facts" creating "vision"—it is nothing more than James's belief expressed in his memorable definition of "the real" and "the romantic" in the preface to *The American,* which I have had the occasion to quote in an earlier essay. The definition, for all its felicity of phrase, has a misleading air about it. It seems to suggest an acute awareness of the reality beyond, whereas, for all practical purposes, James is referring to those vague, unrequited yearnings of the heart and fantasies of the mind which are not necessarily our "intimations of immortality." Indeed "the real" and "the romantic" so interpenetrate in the end as to suggest a marriage of antinomies. Or, as Georges Markow-Totevy puts it:

> Reality with James lies always elsewhere than where one first saw it. Although he is himself unable to explore all the possibilities of the new approach, he already shows future writers the simultaneous contours of the apparent and the hidden, the reassuring and the threatening aspects of significance. In other words, James opens the way to an integral realism with an essentially psychological basis of questioning and wondering: a dimension for which the word "realism" is no longer an adequate description.[30]

In this essay, so far, I have tried to maintain that for James the only reality worth the artist's powder is the reality of the facts as presented to a unique consciousness. The "madness" of facts may well lead the artist a merry dance—the facts become opaque beyond a point—but it is only in art again that he can structure and envision that "madness." In "The Middle Years," Dencombe, another Jamesian alter-ego, talks of "the madness of art." "We work in the dark—we do what we can—we give what we have. Our doubt is our passion and our passion is our task. The rest is the madness of art."[31] However, this "madness" is not the madness of a Blakean visionary, or of some inspired "fool" of God. It is all centred round the intractability of facts, and the perpetual chipping away at the rock-reality of life to make it yield its meaning. In a manner, it is even a "scientific" pursuit, in that James too, like Wordsworth, sees the essential poetic truth that is "in the countenance of all Science." The artist, above all, is concerned with that truth.

There is, however, a critical view that James himself is never quite certain about the *bona fides* of art. In fact, he even questions not only its strategy, but also its rationale. Its healthful aspect is viewed suspiciously, and it is almost equated with disease. Art, in short, is considered a pathological exercise, if not a mere will-o'-the-wisp. Too long a view of it cannot but distort one's vision, and undermine one's judgement of life. And since art is essentially an exercise of the imagination, it is fair to ask if the imagination itself does become a dangerous decoy, and man's enemy, beyond a point. If such a view of art is indeed to be found in Henry James, then it is not too far removed from the view of William James who, as Lionel Trilling observes, "came to suspect that the preoccupation with art was very close to immorality."[32] That James does show at times a certain anxiety in his relationship with art is true; that he tends to undermine the very structure he is raising by casting a sly, ironic glance at the entire proceedings could be easily illustrated. However, these wayside doubts—the result of an ingrained scepticism—do not, to my mind, destroy or nullify his faith in the health and energy of art. Those are, at best, to be treated as occasional voices clamouring to be heard. They do not in the end command his ear. L. B. Holland, for instance, maintains strenuously that James in *Partial Portraits* shows a plain distrust of art. "Time and again in the essays," he remarks, "there are clear suggestions that art is morally dangerous, irresponsible or immoral either because of its content or because of the very nature of its manipulation."[33] And Professor Holland, supporting the Follett theory about *The Sacred Fount*, adds that James in caricaturing his own art questions "the validity of all creation" and "the authority of art." This, as I have shown elsewhere in this volume, though a legitimate critical premise, is, nevertheless, too far-fetched to be true. If James had seriously believed in anything of this kind, he should have as a conscientious person cried halt after *The Sacred Fount*. Instead, he goes on to create some of his greatest experiments in fiction with a view to encompassing visions of human reality. Obviously, art, though a dangerous siren, is not repudiated. On the contrary, it is increasingly called upon to buttress up the embankments of life. It is perhaps possible to argue that in *The Sacred Fount*, which, among other things, deals with the theme of the creative act in art, the power of sexuality in relation to the creation of art is indirectly affirmed. Or, as Harold T. McCarthy puts it, James insisted that art "should multiply our relations with life."[34] The idea that since art is all "manipulation," and since "manipulation" is a cardinal sin in Jamesian ethics, art must, therefore, be suspect or corrupt, is to confuse the issues of art with the issues of life. Art is also artifice, and necessarily involves manipulation, but it has no design upon us except that of affording aesthetic pleasure. Or, as A. N. Whitehead affirms, art is the imposing of a pattern on experience, and our aesthetic enjoyment is nothing but a recognition of that pattern.

Art then, far from being a kind of self-abuse (though in practice, it does become so in some of James's later tales), is regarded by the novelist as the only refuge of fine and sensitive spirits. "It muffles," says James, "the ache of the actual."[35] The idea of salvation through art is not unique to him, for the entire Bloomsbury group came also to view art in a similar manner, though the intensity of the quest and the presence of religious imagery in James's later works tend to give a mystic gloss to the whole thing. In his story, "Collaboration" he writes: "Art protects her children in the long run—she only asks them to trust her. She is like the Catholic Church—she guarantees paradise to the faithful."[36] In his book,

Nietzsche, Henry James, and the Artistic Will (1978) Stephen Donadio, arguing for the Nietzschean influence, says that art alone ensures moral and aesthetic transcendence.

To conclude, James's tenacious and intensive pursuit of art has nearly all the marks of a religious passion, but it would be a mistake to regard it as a mystic breakthrough or something of that kind. At best, it could be described as "a kind of aesthetic mysticism,"[37] the way Flaubert describes it in a letter to Louise Colet. Or, the Jamesian passion may be equated with the kind of vision a painter like Velasquez had—a painter adored by James, incidentally. Referring to Velasquez in her seminal little book on Henry James, Rebecca West uses an imagery that would have wholly pleased the Master. "The Artist," she observes, "at the moment of creation must be like a saint awaiting the embrace of God, scourging appetite out of him, shrinking from sensation as though it were a sin, deleting self, lifting his consciousness like an empty cup to receive the heavenly draught."[38]

11

The Ethics of Relationship

In *The Great Tradition,* F. R. Leavis argues with considerable force why he elects to place Henry James along with Jane Austen, George Eliot, Joseph Conrad and D. H. Lawrence amongst the greatest novelists in the English language in preference to Dickens, Trollope, Thackeray, Hardy, Meredith and several other equally engaging writers. His chief criterion, which, as we know, was employed strenuously throughout his stewardship of *Scrutiny,* is the quality of the moral sensibility an artist brings to bear upon his material, and the manner in which he is able to make it significant and typical at a given moment of history in the life of a class, a people, a race or a civilization. All other achievements and perfections—aesthetic form, style, pictorial beauty, entertainment, humour, irony, plot, character-portrayal, etc.—could not make up for the lack of that central concern with the moral health of the individual and the community which in Dr. Leavis's view constitutes the distinctive mark of great art and literature. In short, the concreteness and richness of the rendered continuities within which moral natures operate and seek hospitality alone would make a novel worthy of the highest consideration. Viewed thus, James's fiction undoubtedly belongs in "the great tradition" of the English novel which, unlike the French, for instance, has all along been more concerned with moral beauties and perceptions, paradoxes and ambiguities than with passion or sex as such. Only the Russian novel of the nineteenth century equals it in the quality of its ethical engagement, and surpasses it in the quality of its metaphysical concerns. Obviously, James's eventual distrust of the French novelists whom he admired otherwise for their splendid technical achievements, as also for their realism, fullness, vivacity and vigour, stems from the feeling that in the final analysis, Flaubert, Sand, Maupassant and Zola fail to bring out the moral poetry of life that survives all appetites, and transcends them. In Balzac alone, as late as 1905, he finds that richness of relationships and community of moral interests which make for the felt felicities of fiction. No wonder, both the sun-lit and serene moral realism of Turgenev and the stern, troubled and roused moral universe of George Eliot's novels appeal to his sensibility more and more as he begins to realize the true nature and genius of the novel as art form. This idea undoubtedly is strengthened when he goes, as Dr. Leavis puts it, "to school to George Eliot,"[1] though "the admired Turgenev" is not as negligible an influence in this respect as he thinks. The later James is Dr. Leavis's anathema because of the "cobwebiness" of his style, yet his moral antennae are even more sensitive than ever before, as he comes to deal with the cognitive processes of involved and vibrant consciousnesses.

The genius of the novel, as distinct from the romance, lies in its ability to comprehend and present a variety of interests and attitudes, or to render the choreography of human relationships. In his excellent study, *The English Novel from Dickens to Lawrence,* Raymond Williams, for instance, shows how the novel's growth in England is umbilically linked to the new genre's capacity to mirror and interpret the complicated and tortured web of human relationships in a society convulsed by the industrial upheaval. Commenting on this process, he writes: "Thomas Carlyle, who did more than anyone else in his generation to communicate this sense of history—of historical process as moral substance and challenge—came to think that the novel was outdated, that it could be replaced by history. He was of course to be proved wrong, but only by the transformation of the novel in very much the direction of his central argument. It was by becoming history, contemporary history—but a history of substance, of process, of the interaction of public and private life—that one important kind of novel went to the heart of its times."[2] Clearly then, the novel's fortunes rested upon its tensile framework which could bear the burden of involved relationships without going under. Henry James's own brother, William James, enunciated his philosophy of pragmatism in terms of such relationships. For him, the very "knowledge *about* a thing is the knowledge of its relations."[3] And without such a knowledge, no ethical perceptions are earned. Thus, Henry James's increased admiration for George Eliot could be accounted for accordingly. He realized how any imaginative study in relationships became, ipso facto, a study in ethics or values. Indeed, his own theory of the novel, which he perfected around the time he was taken up a great deal with George Eliot, stipulates an ethical base in that all ethics are finally a question of multiplying and meaningful relationships. What is more, the novel's structure or form itself profited from the interplay of relationships and values. Edith Wharton remembers James telling her once in Paris apropos of a French play: "The trouble with eliminating the moral values is that almost all the dramatic opportunities go with them. . . . "[4] In short, the dramatic imagination at its finest, as in Shakespeare, had to be a moral imagination also. James's view of the novel being dramatic, one can see the importance of ethical thought in his fiction.

Again, James's New England background, whichever way we interpret it, was bound to affect his moral imagination. The two opposed views present the novelist as a puritan to the backbone, and as one who completely overcame and repudiated his ancestral heritage. For instance, Rebecca West sees "the grim New England faith like a cold drop in his blood."[5] F. W. Dupee too regards James as a full-blooded puritan. F. O. Matthiessen, however, thinks otherwise. "James himself," he writes, "did not have the heritage of American Puritanism. He spoke of not being a New Englander as a danger after all escaped."[6] I think a more balanced view of the problem would be to regard him as a reformed and refined puritan who, whilst frowning upon the harsher and sterner aspects of the Calvinistic faith, imbibed its spirit of moral rectitude and courage. Perhaps the phrase that best describes this state is the one used by an anonymous critic. James, he wrote, gave off "the faint aroma of the Puritan tradition."[7] A certain central discipline of moral values, even perhaps a streak of moral rigour, persists in James till the end, but this is seldom allowed to assume a grim or menacing posture. On the contrary, the later fiction, on the whole, erects an ethics of moral continuities, accommodation, hospitality and understanding, without sacrificing the essential verities and values of life. In such novels as *The Ambassadors* and *The Golden Bowl,* he seems to have realized the limits of human nature. The darkening vision, which now regards the pit and the abyss as ineluctable dangers, is, nevertheless, "light enough" to admit of moral beauties, born as a result of sympathy, pity and forgiveness—qualities engendered in the process of living. Man's moral health, James seems to say, can best be preserved in a condition of perpetual engagement with life. Who loses and who wins is a question that becomes irrelevant in the face of the dark depths that confront man at every stage of his life. In the community of evil, we may not insist on moral victories won at the expense of the spirit, or even of the flesh.

In fact, both moral rigidity and moral chaos are regarded with utter disfavour from the start. As we have seen in some of the preceding essays, whenever an American heroine insists upon a morality of flagellation, of fire and brimstone, as does Euphemia in "Madame de Mauves," James leaves us in no doubt as to his attitude towards such heroics. A morality that has hardened into a fixed stance, and become part of one's *persona,* is about as lovable a thing as a blunt and rusty nail. There is indeed something inhuman about a stoicism that is death-oriented. The abrasive processes of life demand a catholicity of spirit, if one has to have a measure of the sun in this world. Something of Euphemia's chilly and stony ethics is undoubtedly to be found even in such an endearing heroine as Isabel Archer, though her redeeming qualities—spontaneity and generosity of impulse, a rich and poetic imagination, a vibrant sensibility and an aristocracy of spirit—prevent her from becoming a monster of morality. In any case, stoicism as a doctrine or philosophy is unsuited to the novel of relationship. A linear or one-dimensional ethics naturally is inimical to a fiction built around the complex of varied responses and attitudes. The ability to see the rich *chiaroscuro* of life and to project the same through an act of empathy constitutes the very health of all dramatic fiction.

If moral rigidity is frowned upon, moral hysteria is held up to scorn in James's work. Olive Chancellor of *The Bostonians* is a clear example of what happens when one is possessed by a proselytizing or crusading passion. Such a loud and rampant morality is basically hostile to happiness, and makes its own poverty an excuse for emotional or psychological imperialism. With a rare insight James equates Olive's thwarted sexuality with her evangelical politics, and shows the psychic links between the two. To a somewhat lesser extent, he shows a similar relationship between the repressed sexuality of Mrs. Wix and her over-aggrieved and self-righteous morality in *What Maisie Knew*. Undoubtedly, whenever a character becomes a morality figure, James's irony steps in; for such a person is unable to see straight and whole. Even Laura Wing of "A London Life," though shown as genuinely appalled by the moral horrors of the situation in which she finds herself placed, is possibly deluded to some extent, and James seems at least to hint about her moral astigmatism. Similarly, Fleda Vetch's moral queasiness in *The Spoils of Poynton* has led several critics to believe that her character is conceived and developed in a spirit of irony. It is not a position that I fully accept, for Fleda also represents, like other Jamesian heroines, a rare degree of fineness; yet James perhaps could not resist the temptation to show that a moral nature which tries to overreach itself is also by no means the best spectacle in the world. Some sacrifices do not even bear a close, psychological scrutiny. In short, it would not be too much to say that James, on the whole, is against any legislating or sermonizing or strangulating morality. He has little sympathy for Olympian or absolutist ethics.

This should not, however, be taken to mean that James stands for an ethics of convenience, or that he discounts regulative and normative ethics. On the contrary, he comes down upon the transgressors or violators of evolved morality even more heavily than he does upon its scowling pundits and pontiffs. If his New England background means anything, it signifies the presence of an unmistakable ethical sense which will not be subverted or compromised under severe tests. If anything, the moment of crisis is also the moment of moral beauty and moral integrity. In fact, it is often the moment of the birth of a moral conscience. This happens so frequently in his fiction that Conrad rightly styles him as "the historian of fine consciences."[8] We shall see later how rich and responsive consciences under pressure and assault develop into fine consciences. Here, it should suffice to say that moral laxity and apathy, moral obtuseness and opaqueness, moral chaos and horror in varying degrees constitute the sum of sin in James. On the whole, these failings are associated with the Europeans in his novels and tales, just as the failings resulting from moral aggression are associated with the Americans.

As in the case of Conrad, James's primary concerns in his fiction are ethical rather than psychological. The extended psychological probings and dissections are, at bottom, an effort to understand and express the values and truths of daily life achieved in the teeth of evil, absurdity and irrationality. The interest in the involved geometry of human motives, fears, dreams and desires clearly stems from an ethical concern. This is much more evident in his later fiction than in his earlier compositions which, despite some splendid moments of moral affirmations and epiphanies, remain principally the work of a romantic and aesthetic imagination on the prowl. To be sure, James realizes the need for ethical conflicts in the interests of drama right from the time of *Roderick Hudson*, but the nuclear impulse is aesthetic rather than moral. In such later novels as *The Ambassadors*, *The Wings of the Dove*, *The Golden Bowl* and *The Ivory Tower*, for instance, the aesthetic and the moral aspects of the creative impulse are closer to each other, though perhaps even here the identification is not as instantaneous and complete as, say, in the case of Arthur Miller's plays. I recall here what I said a few years ago about the nature of this process vis-à-vis Miller and James in a paper on the American playwright. I quote the relevant excerpt:

> I am not concerned here with the dialectics of creativity, nor even with the architectonics of art; they are only relevant here in so far as Arthur Miller is a writer in whom the bridge between what Kierkegaard calls, "the first sphere" (aesthetic) and "the second" (ethical) is traversed almost instantaneously, if not simultaneously, with the act of creation. The immediacy and the externality here are subsumed in a moral vision springing to life through instant choice and decision. The time-lag, if any, is so brief as to seem to suggest the reversal of the "spheres." That is to say, in Miller the nuclear explosion appears ethical rather than aesthetic, such being the moral energy of his plays. I think the point will become clearer if we compare him with writers like Henry James or Conrad who too are intimately concerned with the questions of choice and commitment, action and consequence. Whereas they warm up to the ethical centre in their stories through levels of awareness painfully arrived at and crossed, Arthur Miller brings things to the boil instantly, not only because a playwright, unlike a novelist, has no space for extended dramatics, but because the primary cause in him will brook no delay. Or, to put it differently, whereas for a James the creative exercise may begin in "delight" and end in cognition, if not "wisdom," for Miller, it inevitably begins in disturbance and debate. There is no room here for the play of the imagination *qua* imagination, and the work is never an aesthetic artefact, sovereign and sufficient. In fact, Miller may well have voiced the well-known Shavian sentiment that as for pure art, he would not have bothered to put pen to paper.[9]

However, this comparison should not be taken to mean that the aesthetic always overtops the moral in James, or that it somehow undermines it. J. H. Raleigh in a brilliant analysis of James's Lockean empiricism observes: "Each person is his own arbiter and must arrive at moral decisions by an appeal to his own experience, which, in this case, usually means sense impressions, and, finally, morality becomes purely esthetic. The consciousness most sensitive to impressions is liable to be the most moral. So in James there is an equation between the esthetic and the moral sense, and the individual who most appreciates the beauty of a Renaissance painting is also the most moral."[10] This is well put, even though the Jamesian view taken this way shows the circumscribed or narrow range of his moral vision which opens the route to solipsism. I do not think Dorothea Krook to be quite correct when she affirms the victory of the moral over the aesthetic in James's work:

> The sense of beauty is one thing, aestheticism, the 'touchstone of taste' (as James is to call it in a later work), is quite another thing. . . . The conflict of the aesthetic and the moral in a highly

civilized society is to emerge in James's later novels as one of his great themes, perhaps his very greatest. In *The Portrait of a Lady* it receives only its first and more or less tentative statement. . . . But for its definitive rendering we have to wait until *The Golden Bowl* where we will find the whole fable directed to the single end of exhibiting the triumphant supersession of the aesthetic by the moral.[11]

The fact is that while the intensity of James's pursuit does give the reader an idea of the moral becoming more imperative and imperious than the aesthetic in his later novels, there is no complete liberation from aestheticism. For James, the two become eventually aspects of the same reality. Joseph Warren Beach is nearer the mark when he says that "in its essence, James's morality is indistinguishable from his esthetics—that his ethical system of values is essentially an esthetic system. What he is concerned with, from the beginning to the end of his writing, is *the fine art of living.*"[12] The meaning of Strether's shy love for the beautiful Madame de Vionnet, and his rejection of the Spartan and cold ethics of Woollett would be lost if we were to believe in "the triumphant supersession of the aesthetic by the moral." Strether's victory—if it is a victory at all—is certainly moral, but one securely allied to aesthetic values. Even Beach to my mind errs when after equating the moral and the aesthetic in James, he goes on, in a later chapter devoted to James's ethics, to remark that in his work there is no "moral indifference," only "neutrality." "The author," he writes, "in this method shows himself no *parti pris*. He passes no judgements upon his characters. He does not even ask you to pass judgement; he simply invites you to the enjoyment of his picture."[13] The fact that James is, like all great writers of dramatic fiction or literature, able to employ "negative capability" with perfect ease does not eliminate the idea of his own preferences, judgements and strictures. As I have shown elsewhere in this volume, there can never be any complete or total objectivity or neutrality in art as in life. And James, most certainly, is not "neutral" where the moral choices and commitments are involved. Could there be any doubt as to what he thinks of persons like Dr. Sloper, Olive Chancellor, Gilbert Osmond or Rose Armiger? Even in the case of such beautiful sinners as Kate Croy and Densher, Charlotte Stant and Amerigo, James's sympathies, despite some ironic streaks in his treatment of Milly Theale and Maggie Verver, are clearly manoeuvred in behalf of the innocent victims of sexual intrigue and passion.

As a rule, the dramatic imagination of James is never fully engaged till the moral situation in the story has reached an almost unanswerable crisis. In story after story, the chief protagonist is placed in such a tight corner that he or she must struggle to the last ounce of spiritual energy to be able to wrest a sum of viable values from the darkness and chaos around. At the elemental or existential level, it is a struggle for identity; at the moral, a struggle for definition and equations and insight. Such a moment of truth arrives for Isabel Archer in "the night of the vigil," for Fleda Vetch after Owen's passionate outburst in London, for Milly Theale after the interview with Lord Mark in Venice, for Maggie Verver in the scene where the golden bowl is dashed to pieces by the cornered Mrs. Assingham. After a sensitive psyche has been sorely tempted and tried, it cannot but battle its way through darkness and gloom into the noon-day of decision. The question of options and choices is important, for no nature is fully challenged without the presence of moral tensions. In fact, Henry James's view of the matter comes very close to William James's opinion that no moral beauty is born till the choices are narrowed down for the struggling psyche. "An act," he says, "has no ethical quality whatever unless it be chosen out of several all equally possible. . . . The ethical energy *par excellence* has to go farther and choose which interest out of several, equally coercive, shall become supreme."[14]

Take, for instance, the case of Catherine Sloper in *Washington Square*. Here we watch with sympathetic interest the drama of a simple, affectionate and docile girl acquiring, under spiritual stress, a moral energy that very nearly unsettles the massed forces of sophisticated cruelty and hypocrisy. Caught in a cruel, archetypal dilemma, she has to choose between a stern, unbending father whose judgement she implicitly trusts, and a scheming lover who has so worked upon her generous and shy nature as to have secured a firm lodgement in her affections. Her position is doubly difficult and doubly pitiable in that she has till now no reason to question either of the two opposed trusts and loves. She would wrong neither of the two persons, and yet, should she choose, she needs must sacrifice one or the other. And this rightly strikes her as a cruel, gratuitous fate mocking her dreams. Simple natures such as hers are not made for heroic conflicts, and if they are not challenged to the bone, they do not erupt or explode.

> "But we can wait a long time" said poor Catherine, in a tone which was meant to express the humblest conciliation, but which had upon her father's nerves the effect of an iteration not characterized by tact.
>
> The Doctor answered however, quietly enough: "Of course; you can wait till I die, if you like."
>
> Catherine gave a cry of natural horror.
>
> "Your engagement will have one delightful effect upon you; it will make you extremely impatient for that event."
>
> Catherine stood staring, and the Doctor enjoyed the point he had made. It came to Catherine with the force—or rather with the vague impressiveness—of a logical axiom which it was not in her province to controvert; and yet, though it was a scientific truth, she felt wholly unable to accept it.
>
> "I would rather not marry, if that were true," she said.
>
> "Give me a proof of it, then; for it is beyond a question that by engaging yourself to Morris Townsend you simply wait for my death."
>
> She turned away, feeling sick and faint; and the Doctor went on: "And if you wait for it with impatience, judge, if you please, what *his* eagerness will be."
>
> Catherine turned it over—her father's words had such an authority for her that her very thoughts were capable of obeying him. There was a dreadful ugliness in it, which seemed to glare at her through the interposing medium of her own feebler reason. Suddenly, however, she had an inspiration—she almost knew it to be an inspiration.
>
> "If I don't marry before your death, I will not after," she said.[15]

Catherine, a New England daughter, can never bear for a moment any kind of duplicity or deceit. Everything with her has to be open, free, before the world, in the clear light of the sun. And we watch the quality of her beautiful "deep-welling sorrow" as it envelops her—a "sorrow of the purest and most generous kind without a touch of resentment or rancor."[16] No doubt, at times a cold anger grips her, but always her heavenly patience holds her in check. James shows brilliantly how, when possessed by love, even a frigid, unattractive girl begins to glow with charm. There are as usual no scenes of passionate love here, though there can be no doubt about the transforming quality of sexual love. And finally, when her tragic betrayal is complete, and she would not, like other Jamesian heroines, let the world indulge in sentiments of pity, her father rightly remarks that she needed no "moral poultice." She is perfectly capable of standing up to her misfortunes; her spiritual strength will not be subverted. However, in her "admirable old maid" fate, we may perceive some hints of a lurking Jamesian irony. Here has a heart grown cold in doing duty to a rigid ideal, making a warped virtue its anchor-sheet in life! Happiness, James appears to be saying, is not born of ingrown stoicism, but of resilience and understanding.

However, in that well-written but neglected novel *Confidence* (1879), which undoubtedly is botched up by James in the end in the interest of a fanciful resolution, we have an example of moral evasion on the part of the novelist himself. The hero, Bernard Longueville, finds himself in a moral cleft when he discovers that he is desperately in love with Angela, a woman he has earlier presented with the best of motives as light and wanton to her suitor, Gordon, who had commissioned him, as a trustful friend, to report on her. And now the horror of his position, which would naturally strike Gordon as one of infernal deceit and doublecross, sickens him.

> It filled him with a kind of awe, and the feeling was by no means agreeable. It was not a feeling to which even a man of Bernard Longueville's easy power of extracting the savour from a sensation could rapidly habituate himself, and for the rest of that night it was far from making of our hero the happy man that a lover just (coming) to self-consciousness is supposed to be. It was wrong—it was dishonorable—it was impossible—and yet it *was;* it was, as nothing in his own personal experience had ever been. He seemed hitherto to have been living (by proxy) in a vision, (in reflection)—to have been an echo, a shadow, a futile attempt; but this at last was life itself, this was a fact, this was reality. For these things one lived; these were the things that people had died for. Love had been a fable before this—doubtless a very pretty one; and passion had been a literary phrase—employed obviously with considerable effect. But now he stood in a personal relation to these familiar ideas, which gave them a very much keener import; they had laid their hand upon him in the darkness, he felt it upon his shoulder, and he knew by its (pressure) that it was the hand of destiny. What made this sensation a shock was the element that was mixed with it; the fact that it came not simply and singly, but with an attendant shadow in which it immediately merged and lost itself. It was forbidden fruit—he knew it the instant he had touched it. He felt that he had pledged himself *not* to do just this thing which was gleaming before him so divinely—not to widen the crevice, not to open the door that would flood him with light. Friendship and honor were at stake; they stood at his left hand, as his new-born passion stood

already at his right; they claimed him as well, and their grasp had a pressure which might become acutely painful. The soul is a still more tender organism than the body, and it shrinks from the prospect of being subjected to violence. Violence—spiritual violence—was what our luxurious hero feared; and it is not too much to say that as he lingered there by the sea, late into the night, while the gurgitation of the waves grew deeper to his ear, the prospect came to have an element of positive terror. The two faces of his situation stood confronting each other; it was a rigid, brutal opposition, and Bernard held his breath for a while with the wonder of what would come of it. [17]

Here are the elements of a first-rate moral drama, full of the type of complexity James loves to depict in his later fiction, but the tragic drift of the story is unnecessarily violated, and a beautiful situation is allowed to lapse into a popular magazine denouement.

Later, a Strether, however, will face the full consequences of a moral position which, though full of ambiguity, vindicates him not only in his own but also in our eyes. James, in the final phase, will not stretch his ethics to suit a desired end. Indeed, in a great deal of his later fiction, the ends are chosen as much by the author as by the protagonists who *must* work out their moral natures to vindicate their psyches. These "morally inflammable" heroines, in particular, will not rest till they have met, full in the face, the brutal assault of life. It appears to be James's contention that no moral heights are attained till sensitive consciousnesses are exposed to possibilities of engagements and commitment.

I have hinted earlier in this essay that in James such sensitive and lively consciousnesses, when affronted, baited or bruised, are apt to acquire fine consciences. This process is dialectical in that no conscience comes into play till a certain quantum of consciousness has been attained. It is at that level or degree that all the accumulated impressions of life begin to exert their silent but undeniable weight, and the imperious voice from within will brook no delay or compromise. Consciences, too, are not, generally speaking, received as gifts in James; they are earned in the process of suffering, struggle and confrontation. Their authenticity may be measured by the quality of their music. Delicately strung, they come alive at the softest touch.

However, as James feels, there are dangers in nursing overstrung consciences. Ralph Touchett speaking to Isabel Archer tells his beautiful and suffering cousin that an overworked conscience can often be an embarrassment in the end. "Don't question your conscience so much—it will get out of tune like a strummed piano. Keep it for great occasions. Don't try so much to form your character—it's like trying to pull open a tight, tender young rose." [18] In the case of Euphemia we are shown the ruin and misery caused by a strangulating conscience, while in Fleda Vetch, the very fineness or nicety of her conscience appears to have assumed menacing proportions. She very nearly is smothered by her own fanciful scruples.

Despite the pervasive nature of the Jamesian irony, it is possible, I think, to visualize the complex of virtues and values endorsed by James's moral imagination. It is not a codified system, but a gathered sum of moral perceptions and insights evolved through a continual and strenuous process of adjustment. There is nothing bold or new or revolutionary about this ethics. On the whole, the graces of civilization, intelligence and sophistication which James prizes above all, and the daily pieties of life such as good faith, fidelity, pity etc., which we find enshrined in his work are all conceived and worked out within the traditional framework of Christian bourgeois ethics. No wonder form, catholicity and cosmopolitanism on the one hand, and freedom, sacrifice and integrity on the other, emerge as ultimate values in his scheme of things. While the first set of values has European moorings, the second is clearly related to his New England roots. It is in their mutual interplay and accommodation that James seeks a vision of viable ethics.

The accent on form and style in life is obviously of aesthetic concern, and is another aspect of his well-known dread of vulgarity and coarseness in all its forms. This dread itself takes at times a vulgar aspect so that we feel the misery of an attitude that cannot look at the raw, irresistible and heaving swell of life without disgust or dismay. For too much of fineness is as coercive, and, therefore, unethical, as too much of brashness. James is certainly aware of the tyranny of mere form, both in life and in art, and the French ethics of form comes in for a fairly rough treatment in such novels as *The American* and *The Reverberator,* yet his own attitude is not completely free from formalism. The taint of aestheticism is unmistakably there.

James's love of freedom, again, is typically ancestral in its force and flavour. There is, undoubtedly, the quality of beauty and heroism about the Jamesian heroine's sustained pursuit of the life of the spirit, and her desire to preserve her liberty in this behalf. However, as I have shown earlier in the volume, the notion of freedom as an abstract and fixed quality ignores the fact that in the final analysis freedom is but, as the Marxists assert, recognition of necessity. James is too deeply immersed in liberal bourgeois illusions to realize the force of this argument. Where freedom means the right of a person to attain the farthest reaches of his or her being without being subjected to personal manipulation, overt or covert, there can be no quarrel. What is often forgotten is the fact that this right has meaning only within the social and historical context, that some societal pressures and necessities alone help preserve and expand it. "To will oneself free," as Simone de Beauvoir observes, "is also to will others free."[19]

Another ultimate value in James is one of sacrifice. Its place in his ethics may be measured from the fact that it becomes a part of not only his vision of life, but also of his "poetics." From Rowland Mallet and Christopher Newman down to Isabel Archer, Fleda Vetch, Lambert Strether and Milly Theale, we watch a procession of persons involved in sacrificial retreats. Though a shade of irony seems to undercut some of these sacrifices—unconscious heroics may never be eliminated even from the purest of human motives—it would be wrong to infer that these acts of renunciation are without a positive victory. The whole drift of Jamesian thought suggests that the capacity to suffer for an earned vision of life is about the highest virtue one may aim at in our creature existence. In a manner, perhaps, it could be suggested that, as in Shakespeare, if Christianity enters the Jamesian world in any significant sense, it posits the paradox of sacrifice. The finest spirits, James seems to imply, crave crucifixion from deep and obscure urges, but there is always in some form a subterranean longing to add to the sum of human happiness through such symbolic acts of sacrifice. Even where the death-wish is a strong component of that act, as in the case of Milly Theale, the desire to leave a slightly happier world behind through a gesture of the soul's magnanimity may not be ruled out. It may even be possible to view the emergence of conscience in Jamesian protagonists as a fulfilment of a deep-seated desire for sacrifice and death. Paraphrasing Freud's notion of conscience in *Eros and Civilization* Herbert Marcuse writes: "This inner-directed destructiveness, moreover, constitutes the moral code of the mature personality. Conscience, the most cherished moral agency of the civilized individual, emerges as permeated with the death instinct. . . ."[20]

The theme of moral integrity in a world of ready convenience and easy compromise is one of the greatest recurring themes in James's fiction. How is a "dove," for instance, to spread her "wings" in a menacing sky? How is a "princess" to mend the cracks in "the golden bowl"? How is an "ambassador" to conduct himself when his "embassy" is imperilled through a change in his allegiance? The answer for James lies in the voyage within. By constructing a complete inner world, sacrosanct and inviolable, impervious to obtrusive and gross reality, the protagonist manages in the end to salvage a great deal of the wreckage. Christopher Newman converts this defeat into a moral triumph, and, as James puts it, "one's last view of him would be that of a strong man indifferent to his strength and too wrapped in fine, too wrapped above all in *other* and intenser reflexions for the assertion of his rights."[21] Similarly, Milly Theale achieves her spiritual identity when she turns within for an answer to her predicament. Perhaps most consumptives or stricken persons, James seems to suggest, achieve a peaked awareness of things before death, a heightened and spiritualized view of reality such as we find in Ralph Touchett or in the Keats of the final sonnets and odes. There is, of course, some force in the view that in turning her face to the wall, Milly opts out of the "absurd" world of man, but most of these retreats are, in fact, efforts to live life at higher altitudes of consciousness, to draw breath in a rarefied air. While the immediacy of life is missed, the intensity of introspection is gained. It is the life of the spirit, and the intelligence is seen at its most luminous. One hears the music of the mind in a world within a world.

There is, to be sure, the danger of an isolationist, and even egotistical, attitude in such retreats to the fragrant arbours of sensibility, and in James the danger is real in view of his pronounced aestheticism, but, it will be readily seen, the novel of relationships which he writes cannot sustain itself on an ethics of isolation. The moral health of an individual in James depends upon his ability to keep the conduits of emotions flowing, even when the pressures of life have driven him to private sanctuaries of the mind. In a perceptive study of the problem, Naomi Lebowitz in *The Imagination of Loving,* pointing out the essential similarity between James's ethics and Lawrence's, remarks that "the formation of dynamic relationships" is vital in any novel of "interrelatedness." "The unpardonable sin for both," she adds, "is deadening a circuit."[22] This is correct up to a point only, for one cannot imagine the basis of the "circuit" being identical. Lawrence's open and healthy sexuality is in marked contrast to James's frigidity and voyeurism. Nor is James's imagination entirely of "loving," as we have noticed in the essays on James's irony and sense of evil; yet there is no doubt that the compositional fulcrum in James stipulates a developing ethics of relationships. There is this positive core which prevents his "imagination" from becoming one of complete "disaster."

My criticism here of James's ethics has, however, a different genesis. For all the fine qualities of civilized life and values of relationship, one misses in James the concept of agape or human brotherhood. There is no extension of understanding beyond the set of privileged human beings he deals with. The vision does not include the poor and the deprived, the slighted and the disregarded of the world. His humanitarianism is severely circumscribed, and does not become an all-embracing affair. We see virtually no servants in a fiction that deals with the country houses and city saloons, simply because James is aware of them not as human beings but as means and ministrants. Even "Brooksmith" is more a sentimental fantasy based on inverted and warped values than a sympathetic study in master-servant relationships. A vision such as Shakespeare attains in Lear's speeches on the heath is something utterly beyond Henry James. The "poor naked wretches" to whom his worshipful prayer is addressed have no place in the novelist's world-view. His ethics, then, are essentially a complex of personal pieties and loyalties, something akin to E. M. Forster's set of values based upon the sanctity of mutual trust and obligations. That the ambit of these ties and relationships is narrow does not, however, make them the less authentic. After all, it's not given to everyone to reach out his hand across the globe. It is enough that James stresses the beauty of relationships in a section of society that by nature and force of circumstances least effects or honours such relationships. Where its own members prey upon each other as of necessity, it is something to underscore the value of these personal graces and ties. Manfred Mackenzie has argued that James finally moves on from "cabal" to a "community of love," realising that the pursuit of identity and "honor" was ultimately dehumanising. He even invests Milly Theale with a halo, calling her a "virginal knight" or "white soul,"[23] And the Ververs, father and daughter, reaffirm for him "a pastoral of prodigious spirit."[24] I cannot somehow share the view of this order of transcendence in James. After seeing the pit and the pitch, he may turn to private prayers and altars, but there is no evidence of *agape* in the final vision. Only the ethics of personal pieties holds and sustains his protagonists.

It should be clear from the above that though the Jamesian ethics are rooted in traditional Christian thought, they are by no means strictly related to any theological belief or doctrine. Nor is faith in God a necessary component of such an ethics, though He is not excluded from the overall scheme of things. James would not have endorsed the well-known view of Dostoievsky that "if God does not exist, everything is permitted." He would have rather said with his brother, William James, that "whether a God exist, or whether no God exist, in yon blue heaven above us bent, we form at any rate an ethical republic here below."[25] In a manner, this connects with the existentialist view that in the absence of God, the only absolutes we may depend upon are the moral energies released by man in the process of "becoming." Such a proximity of views does not make Henry James an existential humanist in the sense that we understand this type of humanism; nor could perhaps his ethics be described as "the ethics of ambiguity" in the sense Simone de Beauvoir uses the expression, yet I have no doubt he would have agreed with her when she writes:

> Far from God's absence authorizing all license, the contrary is the case, because man is abandoned on the earth, because his acts are definitive, absolute engagements. He bears the responsibility for a world which is not the work of a strange power, but of himself, where his defeats are inscribed, and his victories as well. A God can pardon, efface and compensate. But if God does not exist, man's faults are inexpiable.[26]

The ethics of relationships which James erects and apotheosizes in his work, considered thus, constitute an ethics of autonomy and relativity. The God of his scowling forbears is absent, though a more tolerant and relaxed Deity, indulgent, if not somnolent, may well be instructing mankind in his pages to look to itself for all its comforts and consolations!

12

The Question of Style

The question of style in Henry James is so central to our understanding of his fiction that one is surprised to see James criticism peculiarly evasive and shy in this respect, despite broad and, at times, even acute swipes at it. To be sure, since the advent of the New Criticism, Stylistics, Semantics and Structuralism, many a passage from James has been subjected to penetrating and extended treatment,[1] and all these efforts have opened up new territories or vistas, yielding us fresh and provocative insights into the work of one of the most rhetorical and poetic imaginations in the English language. It is not, however, sufficiently realized that the idiomatic energy in James has complex, organic and obscure aspects which overlap each other in such a manner as to render any sample or splinter analysis, however acute, at best a little chink through which a tentative vision may be obtained. The sheer volume, variety and opulence of his prose make it almost impossible for anyone to catch more than a glimpse, unless, perhaps, a novel-by-novel and a tale-by-tale analysis is undertaken strictly with a view to deciphering the *leitmotifs* in the involved rhetorical universe of his fiction. Even then, no complete picture is likely to emerge because of the ambivalence and the clashing ironies in his work. Thus, the assertion of René Wellek and Austin Warren that "it is not difficult to analyze the style of such pronouncedly 'mannered' authors as Carlyle, Meredith, Pater or Henry James"[2] is, at least in respect of the last-named, questionable. Again, while his imagery and symbolism as constituents of his prose style have received attention,[3] and have served as favorite quarry for the excavation of archetypal themes and myths, the style as a complex of semantic and verbal structures, yielding a polyphony integrally related to the music of minds, and the style as a stance of the Jamesian psyche, and as a correlative aspect of the Jamesian world-view, have not, I think, been fully explored. This essay is, then but a small, tentative effort in that direction. It seeks to trace briefly the fecund subtlety and progression of James's style over the years, and to account for its peculiar graces and idiosyncrasies which have more often been wondered at and grudgingly admired than really understood.

In talking of James's style, particularly the style of his later novels and tales, critics have as often the peculiar mechanics and mannerisms of his story-telling in mind as the verbal or idiomatic patterns of his prose. Quite often, therefore, the discussion involuntarily shifts from one aspect to the other. In a way, perhaps, this is unavoidable in view of the organic and poetic relationship between the two. After all, in a word of literature, the question of architectonics cannot be separated from the question of words—the medium through which the edifice is raised. Nevertheless, in this essay, my principal concern will be with the rhetoric of James's fiction, and I use the word in its limited, linguistic sense. Naturally, therefore, the prose excerpts used as illustrations will help show the idiomatic energies informing James's vision rather than the structural devices. Only novels and tales considered as complete artifacts can show the "other" style.

It should be clear enough at the outset that when a novelist happens to be so intensely conscious of language *qua* language as James is, the question of style assumes philosophic and epistemological dimensions. One is at once driven into such problems as those of cognition, nescience, communication, tautology, limits of metaphor and the like. In an essay of this size, I can, at best, take notice of these things in an oblique manner, though, as I have tried to show in the essays dealing with the Jamesian themes, all these concerns are really the heart of the matter in James. Thus, theme and style, in the final analysis, become indivisible, for what the mind seeks as reality or truth is, in essence, an order of images, and if, as Swift says, "proper words in the proper places make the true definition of a *style*,"[4] then the arrangement of words into images is an exercise whose meaning connects us with the ultimate quest. Style is, thus, at once a mode of comprehending reality and an aspect of reality. Its *organizational* character gives it this unique distinction. Or, as Meyer Schapiro says: "Investigation of style is often a search for hidden correspondences explained by an organizing principle which determines both the character of the parts and the patterning of the whole."[5] In other words, in James the style is not merely a tool or a medium, a dress or a mask, an excrescence or an extravagance. It is truly organic and poetical, having a cognitive function much in the same way that Shakespearean style has.[6] It is in this sense that a Jamesian novel or *nouvelle* could be regarded as an expanded metaphor. The style *becomes* insight.

Again, before we start examining the dialectical development of James's style, a couple of points relating to the question of style as such have to be clarified. One of these is the validity of using an author's style for the purposes of interpreting his psyche and his world-view. Undoubtedly, since Buffon's well-known adage, "the style is the man," the aura or aroma of the writer's personality as a felt presence in his language has been universally acknowledged in one way or another. Although the words he uses are drawn from the common pool of language, there is always a certain freshness about the way or manner they emerge in clusters of images and in associational patterns from a particular consciousness. This is not typical of poetry only, for no two persons thinking exactly alike have ever expressed themselves at any length in exactly the same sum or order of words. Such a thing may even lead us to regard thought itself as having style. However, it is safer to assume that since there can be no thought without words, the peculiar placement or disposition of the words gives a chromatic quality to our thought. In short, in any language other than the one used in scientific literature, the writer's personality gets refracted through the prism of words. The connection between style and psyche as also between style and *Weltanschauung* has received a further impetus since the extensive use of Stylistics as a demagogic discipline. Leo Spitzer, in particular, stipulates an organic relationship between stylistic idiosyncrasies and states of mind, though Wellek and Warren warn us against this omnibus assumption. Even if, sometimes, the peculiarities of style may turn out, on analysis, to be a part of "a disguised genetic psychology,"[7] I think it does not radically alter the force of the argument that somehow a style gets evolved as a heart or a soul gets written down. In the case of James, the conclusion is inescapable. In talking of the soliloquies in Shakespeare's tragedies, Arthur Sewell views soliloquies as a "characteristic address" of the hero. One could perhaps use the phrase to describe the place of style in James's prose. For here, the style is but a disposition and a stance of the artist's being. It is his "characteristic address" whereby he notifies his inner being. There is, in other words, no such thing as a "neutral or transparent style," and Susan Sontag in her essay, "On Style," goes on to show after Sartre how even the celebrated "white style" of Camus's prose is not free from the silent impress of personality. Similarly, the bare, clinical, adjectiveless style of Robbe-Grillet or of Michel Butor is shown up, for what it's worth, as a style of a disengaged personality. Paradoxically enough, not to have a style is also to affirm a kind of style! "Style," writes Sontag, "is the principle of decision in a work of art, the signature of the artist's will."[8] And though it will have a certain amount of arbitrariness in it, it will also have a certain kind of inevitability about it.

James criticism has recognized three phases in the novelist's journey from complexity to complexity. For, as it is, even the James of the earliest compositions has a degree of subtlety and sophistication that is singularly attractive. The style, of course, does not as yet present any serious problem of explication. It has, apart from vividness and freshness, an assured urbanity and aplomb, a kind of elegant, well-bred air about it. It is, if I may say so, even at the outset, an ambassadorial prose having patrician moorings. It requires of the reader no more than a certain knowledge of the high idiom employed. Its complexity beats only the untutored mind. The obscurity here is not germinal or nuclear. It is obvious that the youthful James reared in American affluence and European culture has come to regard wit, charm, effect, poise and polish as ends in themselves. The style correspondingly reflects the values of ease and elegance, of culture and continuity, of irony and detachment. Its limpidity is clearly a sign of an untroubled psyche on the whole, while its poetry is the poetry of dream and initiation. A classical sense of proportion is obligingly stretched to accommodate a romantic imagination. To be sure, there are some shallows and rapids which the style cannot negotiate, and there are a few distressing clichés and gallicisms which are purely meretricious, yet the packed energy of his muse breaks through, and the general effect is one of beauty and power.

The style of *Watch and Ward*, his first novel, is unfortunately without much distinction or charm. It has a certain deadness and fatigue about it. It is stilted and cumbersome, priggish and pompous, and shows James at his weakest. For instance, describing Mrs. Keith, Roger's first love, he writes: "This lady had completely rounded the cape of matrimony, and was now buoyantly at anchor in the placid cover of well-dowered widowhood."[9] This kind of style has a verbal extravagance which stems not from an involved or indirect vision as in his later fiction, but from a sense of inner emptiness and vacancy. The imagination has not bitten deep into reality, and remains furtive and unengaged. However, its furtiveness shows up in the style in the form of distinctly erotic imagery, a fact noticed by nearly every critic. The persistent use of the "lock and key" and the "bow and arrow" imagery, apart from that of "sowing," shows not only James's libidinous fantasy-world, but also what, for want of a proper Freudian expression, I should like to call "the Lolita complex"—a thing that erupts with considerable force later in the James of *What Maisie Knew, The Awkward Age* and so on. In this sentence, the hero, Roger Lawrence, is thinking of the effects of exposing his 12-year old "ward," Nora, to her cousin's overtures: "The ground might be generally tickled to receive his own sowing; the petals of the young girl's nature, playfully forced apart, would have the golden heart of the flower but the more accessible to his own vertical rays."[10] The vaginal-phallic imagery here is too pronounced to escape notice.

The style of *Roderick Hudson,* however, shows a distinct leap forward. Since his *donnée* is intrinsically engaging and viable, James's language at once becomes luminous and athletic, supple and sumptuous. In later life, James was none too proud of the style of this book, and when he revised it for the New York Edition, he made several changes, which, as Clara F. McIntyre shows in "The Later Manner of Henry James," were almost uniformly unhappy, if not disastrous. They tended to obfuscate the meaning, the prose losing a great deal of its warmth and vigour. Of course, all the revisions that he carried out in other novels were not equally damaging; most of those in *The American* and *The Portrait of a Lady* were, in fact, positively purposeful, and obeyed a figurative logic which was entirely in keeping with the altered needs of his psyche. However, the earlier style, clear, limpid, flowing, without many twists, turns and dodges, but sophisticated nonetheless, is the style that evokes for the reader the poetry of Rome and the aroma of Christina Light's luminous and breath-taking beauty. Here is a fine example of the early style which while being highly figurative retains an essential clarity. It is already a psychological style. Rowland Mallet is musing over his last, private interview with Mary Garland for whom he retains a shy secret desire.

If the interview had but stirred the waters of bitterness he wished to ignore it for Mary's sake; and if it had sown the seeds of reconciliation he wished to close his eyes to it for his own—for the sake of that contingency, for ever diminished and yet for ever present, which hovered in the background of his consciousness with a hanging head, and yet an unashamed glance, and which had only, like a sentry in a narrower niche, to shift from one foot than the other, in order to become a fresh bribe to patience. . . .[11]

By and large, this style continues up to the time of *The Portrait,* and *The Princess Casamassima,* though with each passing year the metaphors multiply and become more and more involved. And it is a well-known fact of rhetoric that the use of metaphors suggests "an indirect vision" and that James turns to this trope whenever there is a significant shift in thought or in perspective. What Marius Bewley says about the prose of *English Hours* could well be said of the style of *The Europeans* and other earlier novels and tales. It has "the light," he remarks, "of Constable and Turner."[12] There is the same poetic feeling for line and colour, the same glow and wash of emotion, serene and chaste, largely untroubled by Gothic eruptions, though vaguely suggestive of packed darkness here and there. Does this mean, on the whole, that during these formative years of his craft James is at peace with himself? I think it does. The mere presence of incipient evil in some of these books does not indicate as yet the darkening of the vision. The expansive, felicitous, opulent and luxuriant prose suggests a world of country houses and London drawing-rooms, a world, in short, of achieved graces and sheltered values. The formal, rounded structure of the sentences, as of the books, betokens not the rotundity of vision, but the diplomacy of sentiment. Even the ironies of this period are light and airy, as a rule, so that the irony in style is more a question of wit than of vision.

By the time of *The Bostonians,* the style has also acquired a certain "epigrammatic swiftness and hardness,"[13] in the words of Irving Howe. There is even a certain kind of dryness that is intended to offset the lushness of prose. This is the middle period of James's development extending from *The Portrait* to *The Tragic Muse,* a period favoured by F. R. Leavis and several other critics. Essentially, it is a continuation and refinement of the earlier style, rather than a new phase. The style now has an inner strength, and no longer depends upon extraneous effects. There is an increased control or discipline over the rhetoric employed. The poetry is not diminished, though it no longer tends to run away with the situation. The style has a rich glow and warmth, resilience and elegance, as for instance, in *The Princess Casamassima.* The "moral realism" of these books is reflected in their muscular and supple but knotted language, as Lionel Trilling has shown. James has reached the end of the initial journey. All the gathered essences and beauties of the evolved style are felt in their fullness.

Though the effect of his style in this phase is visible in many a facet and form, it is particularly felicitous in evoking the poetry of place and character. The celebrated description of Gardencourt in *The Portrait,* done in the "impressionistic" style, apart from being a "framed" picture yielding aesthetic pleasure, is a pictorial correlative of Isabel Archer's romantic hungers and aristocratic dreams. It answers the deeply felt desires of the young woman from Albany reared in a house with drawn blinds, and in a country of democratic vistas. A similar feeling for the place is to be seen in the later phase also, and we recall memorable and evocative pictures of Mr. Longdon's house in *The Awkward Age,* of the Venetian palace in *The Wings of the Dove* and of the Fawns in *The Golden Bowl.* Undoubtedly, James's love of spacious lawns and gardens, of richly appointed rooms and houses is an aspect of a psyche at home in an atmosphere of culture and well-tended existence. Negatively, it shows a dread of the wilder and fiercer aspects of life. No wonder we have few pictures of nature as such in his fiction. The style's graciousness too has a smooth, cultivated quality about it. It is trimmed to perfection, and enveloped in aromatic airs.

As for the minor characters, those that are conceived in irony and delight, as for instance, Mrs. Penniman in *Washington Square,* Henrietta Stackpole in *The Portrait,* Miss Birdseye in *The Bostonians,* the tendency in James is to fix the portrait in a few bold, memorable and epigrammatic phrases. These characters, being "types," lend themselves to such a capsuled treatment.

Take the witty but apt introduction to Henrietta Stackpole. The peculiar American flutter and restiveness of Isabel Archer's pert and uninhibited friend, combined with her freshness and naivete, are set down in these words:

> She rustled, she shimmered in fresh, dove-coloured draperies, and Ralph saw at a glance that she was as crisp and new and comprehensive as a first issue before the folding. From top to bottom she had probably no misprint.[14]

Miss Birdseye is cryptically summed up thus:

> She looked as if she had spent her life on platforms, in audiences, in conventions, in phalansteries, in *séances;* in her faded face there was a kind of reflection of ugly lecture lamps. . . . [15]

And again:

> She was heroic, she was sublime, the whole moral history of Boston was reflected in her displaced spectacles; but it was a part of her originality, as it were, that she was deliciously provincial. . . . [16]

However, a character like Isabel Archer is developed through a rich and varied and multiplying imagery which, reflecting her changing fortunes and growing perceptions, is drawn from gardens and flowers, swift carriages and voyages, cages and caves, water and pools, light and rays, etc.

Her nature had, in her conceit, a certain garden-like quality, a suggestion of perfume and murmuring boughs, of shady bowers and lengthening vistas, which made her feel that introspection was, after all, an exercise in the open air, and that a visit to the recesses of one's spirit was harmless when one returned from it with a lapful of roses.[17]

"A swift carriage, of a dark night, rattling with four horses over roads that one can't see—that's my idea of happiness."[18]

Ralph Touchett to his mother about Isabel:

"She has started on an exploring expedition, and I don't think she'll change her course, at the outset, at a signal from Gilbert Osmond. She may have slackened speed for an hour, but before we know it she'll be steaming away again. Excuse another metaphor. . . ."[19]

And now in Osmond's house:

She could live it over again, the incredulous terror with which she had taken the pleasure of her dwelling. Between those four walls she had lived ever since, they were to surround her for the rest of her life. It was the house of darkness, the house of dumbness, the house of suffocation. . . .[20]

Then with the dying Ralph at Gardencourt:

She had gone forth in her strength; she would come back in her weakness, and if the place had been a rest to her before, it would be a sanctuary now. She envied Ralph his dying, for if one were thinking of rest that was the most perfect of all. To cease utterly, to give it all up and not know anything more—this idea was as sweet as the vision of a cool bath in a marble tank, in a darkened chamber, in a hot land.[21]

A similar pattern of developing imagery can be traced in respect of other heroines and heroes also. In short, the style becomes the character.

The passages quoted above do not really make difficult reading at all. There is, in fact, a light, nimble touch where the minor characters—part of the Jamesian "furniture"—are concerned. There is even a hint of what James elsewhere called "blessed economy." In the middle phase, therefore, the complexity of the style is still viable, and is largely related to the complexity of the theme and the technique. His passionate interest in the whimsies and vagaries of the human heart, and his unfailing aesthetic and moral delight in unfolding the involved dramas of conscience, make the style at times acute, packed and dense, though it is seldom burdened with thought to the point of exasperation as in the novels and tales of the final phase. Sentences, taken apart, present few problems of explication, but a long row of sentences in the same key gather an accumulated mass of meanings, requiring of the reader a sustained and close attention.

The earlier style is also rich in aphorisms and epigrams. Tossed off with visible delight and dexterity, they are examples more of meretricious wit than of a mode of comprehending and communicating reality, as, for instance, in Bacon's *Essays*. Quite often, they have a Wildean air about them. Nevertheless, they do reveal James's love of symmetry, order, poise and polish in life. It is easy to see that in those epigrams and aphorisms, as in his sustained and drawn-out dialogues, James exploits antithesis, parallelism and counterpoint to great advantage. The contrapuntal mode may well give a clue not only to the musical base of his novels and stories, but also, especially in his later work, to his search for values. Words and their manipulation, as the study of Semantics and Stylistics reveals, are, in the final analysis, questions of epistemology. It may be added that the Jamesian use of italics and play upon prepositions, though certainly overdone, are not merely verbal pyrotechnics. They signify the author's way of meeting the essentially tentative and ambiguous nature of human reality.

The style of James's later fiction, often referred to as "the indirect style," "the third style," "the mandarin style" etc., has naturally been the subject of consider- able controversy since James's own time. Any analysis of the reviews and notices that appeared at the time of publication of those teasing and enigmatic books would show that the critics, by and large, were not slow to sense the element of newness and even modernity in the James of the final phase, though baffled and dismayed by the turn his genius had taken. Even such a perceptive and sensitive "Jamesian" as Edith Wharton felt that the Master's hold on reality had slackened, if not slipped, and that he was spiritually depleted, as it were. F. M. Colby's well-known attack (1902) on James's style as a "fig-leaf" or a "verbal hedge" to cover his thinness and lack of passion, a style "puffed up with its secrets,"[22] set the tone for this type of criticism. And in various forms this criticism has been with us from the beginning, and nothing that later critics like Van Wyck Brooks, Pelham Edgar, F. R. Leavis, Maxwell Geismar, S. Gorley Putt and others have said against the style has materially added to the indictment, through we are the richer for their insightful views in some other ways. The case against the later James—when we talk of the later James, we inevitably, and above all, mean the later style—was neatly and perceptively summed up by W. C. Brownell in a long critique that appeared in *Atlantic* (April 1905), though he understood and admired the artistic integrity of James's supreme effort at a breakthrough. "The reader's pleasure becomes a task, and his task the torture of Tantalus,"[23] he concluded. Now, I do not know of any "Jamesian" who has not, at one time or another, felt embarrassed by the tortuous and gratuitous meshes of the later style, and wished that the novelist had escaped the vulgarity of extravagance and over-refinement. But also, I know of none who, notwithstanding all such lapses, has not felt drawn to it out of some deep compulsion. The misery and the miracle of the later James abide! To show him up as a long-winded Polonius of fiction is, therefore, to misunderstand both the raison d'être and the complex code of this type of style.

One thing that needs to be emphasized is that the change in his style is not so striking as is commonly believed. In all this spinning and weaving from phase to phase, there is always an authentic, residual and invariable style which remains constantly in attendance. Its features include poise and rotundity, amplitude and opulence, eloquence and poetry, irony and innuendo, aphorisms and epigrams, quips and quibbles, shades and nuances. To these are added integral imagery and emblematic embroidery during the middle phase, hieroglyphic complexity and poetic density during the final phase. The essential style endures.

However, even if the change is not really qualitative, it is real enough to warrant a proper scrutiny. Several reasons have been advanced, the most important being James's new method of dictation, colloquialism, shift in vision and psychological pressures. Even his "impediment of speech"[24] referred to by Joseph Warren Beach could be a possible source of the styles's compensatory volubility and tortuosities. Now, a change from longhand to the method of dictation invariably affects one's style. His secretary, Theodora Bosanquet, tells us that the practice, begun in the nineties, became increasingly "a confirmed habit, its effects being easily recognizable in his style, which became more and more like free, involved, unanswered talk."[25] Linguistically, there is a marked increase in the incidence of qualifying clauses and parenthesis, punctuation, pronouns and adverbial phrases as analysts like Vernon Lee, Ian Watt, R. W. Short, David Lodge and Wayne C. Booth have shown, but, I think, it is safer to regard these idiomatic symptoms as the result rather than the cause of the obscurity we find in the later style. In which case, the conclusion is inescapable that the dictation method is a contributory factor, not a fundamental aspect of the change in question. Though begun as a matter of convenience, it admirably met the requirements of an imagination that was increasingly straining at the leash. Also, it is possible to view the increased use of parenthesis, for instance, as James's hypersensitive awareness of and regard for the swarm of doubts and shy contingencies that clamoured for utterance at every turn of one's thought. In short, the new idiomatic habits may well be related to his world-view. Similarly, the peculiar evasion of the language in the later fiction may be taken as an example of his concern for personal privacies, as also of his notorious sense of caution and habit of prevarication in day-to-day life. The verbal vagueness may again be an armour of a sensitive mind that makes a play of things and calamities. Take the following passage from "Crapy Cornelia" which, though not a very happy example of the poetry and felicity of the "third style," is, nevertheless, representative enough to show, as no other style could do, the muted agony, uncertainty and deviousness of its Prufrockian hero, White-Mason, who undoubtedly has something of his creator's nature.

> He had ever felt that an indispensable presence—with a need of it moreover that interfered at no point with his gentle habit, not to say his subtle art, of drawing out what was left him of his youth, of thinly and thriftily spreading the rest of that choicest jam-pot of the cupboard of

consciousness over the remainder of a slice of life still possibly thick enough to bear it; or in other words of moving the melancholy limits, the significant signs, constantly a little further on, very much as property marks or staked boundaries are sometimes stealthily shifted at night. He positively cherished, in fact, as against the too inveterate gesture of distressfully guarding his eyeballs—so many New York aspects seemed to keep him at it—an ideal of adjusted appreciation, of courageous curiosity, of fairly letting the world about him, a world of constant breathless renewals and merciless substitutes, make its flaring assault on its own inordinate terms. Newness *was* value in the piece—for the acquisitor, or at least sometimes might be, even though the act of "blowing" hard, the act marking a heated freshness of arrival, or other form of irruption, could never minister to the place of those already and long on the field; and this if only because maturer tone was after all most appreciable and most consoling when one staggered back to it, wounded, bleeding, blinded, from the riot of the raw—or, to put the whole experience more prettily, no doubt, from excesses of light.[26]

If James does not exactly have the Flaubertian quest for the *mot juste* (notice, for instance, the somewhat awkward and intrusive phrase, "that choicest jam-pot of the cupboard of consciousness"), he certainly brings his whole inventive imagination to bear upon the paradigms of words as they reverberate in his ears, and express for him the wide spectrum of human consciousness spanned over luminosities and intensities, darknesses and twilight zones. In fact, the *chiaroscuro* effects and the chromatic tonalities that make up the tangled web are, on the whole, James's salute to the ambiguities and imponderables of life, though they do tend to cause a spiritual dislocation when the rhetoric overtops theme or character.

Again, though dialogues of the earlier novels also have a characteristic subtlety and charm, it is those of the later fiction that have a truly organic character, reflecting the shifting vision of James. Mere grace and wit and word-play are now not enough; acuteness, ambiguity and necessity come in to lend density to thought. He is still not above a certain kind of meretriciousness in these dialogues at times, but where his imagination is fully and dramatically engaged, there is a Shakespearean quality about them. Normally, dialogue is used by a novelist to express the style of a character, to authenticate the experience of communication. But James uses it in a variety of ways to reinforce his themes, as also to suggest the fundamental inability and failure of communication, and the limits of rhetoric. The style of the dialogues is, at times, apposite to the long passages of indirection that precede or follow them; at times, it is in sharp contrast to them. The dialogues then become exercises in parenthesis. They reveal as much as they conceal. Concealment is thus both a device and a necessity. The portentous and loaded dialogues of these novels and tales are as much weighted down with words as with breaks, blanks and absences.[27] In fact, the tentative, half-shy, bitten-off statements, the unasked questions and smothered, fractured replies create a hum of hints and echoes. Again, the dialogues have a peculiar effect of coiling and uncoiling, something like a "tedious argument of insidious intent." By a sudden shift of emphasis, James creates tension, foreboding and atmosphere. Sometimes, when the Jamesian irony is at work, the style has the sting of a sly, sharp, backhandish slap.

How virtually the same words—and James is in the habit of repeating favourite phrases and turns of idiom in different novels and tales—can have the effect of Shakespearean finality at one place, and of trickery and pyrotechnics at another, may be seen in the snippets of dialogues set down below. The first forms the concluding lines of *The Wings of the Dove*. Densher and Kate are struggling to unstitch the tragic web woven by themselves:

> Prompt was his own clearness, but she had no smile, this time, to spare. "Precisely—so that I must choose."
> "You must choose."
> Strange it was for him then that she stood in his own rooooms doing it, while, with an intensity now beyond any that had ever made his breath come slow to him, he waited for her act. "There's but one thing that can save you from my choice."
> "From your choice of my surrender to you?"
> "Yes"—and she gave a nod at the long envelope on the table—"your surrender of that."
> "What is it then?"
> "Your word of honour that you're not in love with her memory."
> "Oh—her memory!"
> "Ah"—she made a high gesture—"don't speak of it as if you couldn't be. I could, in your place; and you're one for whom it will do. Her memory's your love. You want no other."
> He heard her out in stillness, watching her face, but not moving. Then he only said: "I'll marry you, mind you, in an hour."
> "As we were?"
> "As we were."
> But she turned to the door, and her headshake was now the end. "We shall never be again as we were!²⁸

There is a terrible and desperate beauty about this exchange. Kate's last words are spoken from over the edge of an abyss, as it were, and leave her gaping into the void. Its very bareness and repetitive pattern make the dialogue so taut and tense. "The characteristic dialogue of the later novels," as Austin Warren says, "avoids the long speech—turns, indeed, to stichomythia."[29]

The second piece is the concluding bit of dialogue between Mr. and Mrs. Gedge in the story, "The Birthplace."

> His wife still watched him; her irony hung behind.
> "Then we're just as we were?"
> "No, not as we were."
> She jumped at it. "Better?"
> "Better. They give us a rise."[30]

Since the whole idea of the story about Shakespeare idolatry is an academic exercise rather than a felt experience, the words quoted above have a mechanical ring. They do not warm up to an inevitable conclusion as in *The Wings*.

The question of James's colloquialism has again not been properly understood. It is true, an oral style follows speech patterns, and the method of dictation lends it a certain tang and raciness. But, if by colloquialism we mean something "belonging to familiar speech, not used in formal or elevated language" as the *C.O.D.* defines it, then this colloquialism is a very different order of thing. If the plea is that he uses only the idiom of the upper classes with which both he and his characters are "familiar," this restricts the meaning. Also, it is not true that the language of the London drawing-rooms and salons always approximates the Jamesian high style. More often, it is the exuberance and excess of the author's own verbal wit which spills over and envelops all. Lord David Cecil, therefore, is right when he observes: "Henry James, for instance, makes all his people talk in exactly the same way—it may be incidentally observed—in which no one in heaven or earth ever talked except Henry James himself. But his characters are not lacking in vitality, for they live less through their own talk than through their creator's insight into the workings of their mind and conscience."[31] Nor is there any slang in his style in the manner we find it, for instance, in Mark Twain or in Whitman. That spitting, waspish energy that we find in their street-idiom is simply not there. Of course, we have in abundance, what may be styled as "U-Slang," the pet and code words of the upper classes, particularly in relation to their "collective mating-calls,"[32] to use S. Gorley Putt's expression. But this type of slang becomes mere tittle-tattle after some time, for it is the ersatz language of a spiritually depleted and morally defunct class. To be sure, here and there in the later style, as F. W. Dupee affirms, we have a dash of cheeky and "raffish jargon,"[33] even a cockney phrase which helps deflate the pompous pyramid of formal speech, but this is again a trick of style, not an aspect of it. Perhaps, Lionel Trilling comes nearest to the mark when he writes in a letter: "What I am chiefly conscious of is his desire to shape a prose that has the beat and intonation of the way people talk—or at least the way he himself talked!—rather than of the way people commonly write."[34] To me, his colloquialism is really a question of the thought processes as informed by speech rhythms and periods. It still remains a severely formalized style entirely in keeping with James's patrician values. At any rate, it is a "James dialect" one way or another.

Another feature of the later style is the manner in which James effects a wonderful cohesion of language, theme and form in his fiction. This is particularly true of *nouvelles* and tales, though, of course, a novel like *The Ambassadors* which, as E. M. Forster observes, reveals "like *Thais,* the shape of an hourglass,"[35] also has this kind of integral relationship. The style, for instance, of "The Aspern Papers" has the effect of winding stairs, that of "The Altar of the Dead" the effect of solemnity and funereal sombreness, that of "The Turn of the Screw" the curious effect of wheels within wheels, that of "In the Cage" the effect of constraint and inhibition, etc.

I return, then, to the question of the reasons that appear to have impelled James in the direction of "the indirect style." Apart from the dictation method and colloquialism, there are, as I have said earlier, other more organic factors involved in the process. Assuredly, a shift in vision is perceptible in the work composed in the nineties and afterwards. For one thing, more than ever before the fecundity of dream-life is recognized as a source of vision and vitality. This necessarily involves a plunge into the poetic world of rhetoric involving analogy, trope and symbol. Also, as we know, James becomes at this stage more than ever involved in the exploration of the mystery of evil which is at once of sexual, sociological and metaphysical nature. Since the rock-face of evil will not admit of a direct, frontal assault, the resort to "indirection" becomes imperative. Again, the later James is uncertain about the nature of reality, having moved away considerably from the earlier certitudes. The extensive use of irony, not merely verbal and thematic as in the earlier novels, but visionary, also testifies to the nature and the manner of this quest. If the style becomes tangential and elliptical, tenuous and tensile, the reasons lie in his sustained ambivalence. The marriage of thought and language, though not always happy, is certainly not a marriage of convenience. The style does not, as a rule, sabotage the theme from within or undermine its spiritual potential. It no longer is the dress of thought; it is, in a manner of speaking, the thought become word. It will not be easy to illustrate this peculiar aspect of his style, because a sentence or two, perhaps even a whole paragraph, cannot show the mechanics and the dialectics of this phenomenon. Taken apart, the sentences will, at best, illumine themselves; they will not invade the reader's mind in an insidious or insinuating manner. It is the slow, gathering force of the passage and the pages which will work upon the imagination and enlist it as a secret ally. The style, then, becomes not merely a means of thematic expression, but also a mode of revelation. Epiphanies may still be rare—James's method discourages sudden illuminations and explosions—but the accumulated mass of what I should call *laminated metaphors* does reach in the end the point of "criticality," to use a word from nuclear physics. In which case, the obscurity of style has, as in the poetry of T. S. Eliot and of W. B. Yeats, a visionary aspect.

It may thus be asserted that the progression of the Jamesian style has been from the horizontal to the vertical, from the overt to the covert, from the elegant to the elliptical, from the functional to the mythopoeic. Once again, it may not be fanciful to compare this development to a somewhat similar, though differently motivated, development in the style of Shakespeare. The poetry of *The Wings of the Dove* and of *The Golden Bowl* has an obvious correspondence to the gnomic, sibylline quality of the poetry of *The Tempest*. Walter Allen sums up the later style thus: "James makes his sentences dense with as much meaning as he can get into them, but the meaning exists on several planes at once; it is a fusion of meanings, so that to attempt to unravel a James sentence is akin to analyzing a complex stanza in poetry."[36] One recalls in this connection T. S. Eliot's well-known words in his essay, "The Metaphysical Poets": "The poet must become more and more comprehensive, more allusive, more indirect, in order to force, to dislocate if necessary, language into his meaning."[37]

James's later style has been compared to the expressionistic style of such painters as Van Gogh and Edward Munch on the one hand, to the Mannerist style of the early sixteenth-century Italian painters like Rosso, Pontormo and Parmigianino on the other. Expressionism emphasizes the subjective side of reality, and seeks to capture the tangled and confused world of fantasy, dream and thought which the outer objects and stimuli set into motion. The style is, thus, bound to become involved, distorted and fanciful in its effort to paint the gropings and meanderings of the mind and the wrenchings of the soul. The smooth classical style would fail to do justice to such distortions and plunges and flights. Similarly, the Mannerist style, which was, in fact, a reaction against the High Renaissance style, was essentially a subjective and "spiritual" style, and aimed at a grasp of the transcendental reality through indirection and stylization. This may best be illustrated in the figure paintings of El Greco, one of James's favourite painters, where, as Walter Friedlaender puts it, "the space always has something irrational and illogically organized about it." Continuing, he observes: "The whole bent of anticlassic art is basically subjective, since it would construct and individually reconstruct from the inside out, from the subjective outward, freely, according to the rhythmic feeling present in the artist, while classic art, socially oriented, seeks to crystallize the object for eternity by working out from the regular, from what is valid for everyone."[38]

In terms of the development in James's style, this would mean a shift in his world-view. While the patrician way of life prized formalism, surface, conformity, proportion and consonance, the altered vision of reality could not be rendered in the elegant prose of the earlier days. Would not, thus, the burgeoning of the Baroque and the Gothic in the Mannerist style indicate James's half-conscious revolt against the decadent values of the upper classes? This "revolutionary" style does seem to undermine their smooth and smug universe, which he never rejected at the conscious level. Perhaps the peculiar restiveness, tension and pressure we feel in the later fiction is a direct consequence of his unconscious ambivalence. In an able and perceptive analysis the Mannerist element in James's later style, L. B. Holland rightly relates it to the style of Matisse, Picasso and Rouault, despite James's "disturbed hesitations"[39] before it, in Roger Fry's phrase. Obviously, James's sensibility around the turn of the century was, in some ways, in consonance with the advanced aesthetic sensibility of the period. In fact, even in *The Tragic Muse* there are passages in the Mannerist style, showing a Hogarthian sweep and a Bruegel-like imagination.

Here is Nash predicting a grand, stunning, but vulgar future for Miriam on the stage:

> Its vulgarity would rise to the grand style, like that of a London railway station, and Miriam's publicity would be as big as the globe itself. All the machinery was ready, the platform laid, the facilities, the wires and bells and trumpets, the colossal, deafening newspaperism of the period—its most distinctive sign—were waiting for her, their predestined mistress, to press her foot on the spring and set them all in motion. Gabriel brushed in a large bright picture of her progress through the time and round the world, round it and round it again, from continent to

continent and clime to clime; with populations and deputations, reporters and photographers, placards and interviews and banquets, steamers, railways, dollars, diamonds, speeches and artistic ruin all jumbled into her train. . . . [40]

That the later style has its own peculiar weaknesses and insufficiencies can be illustrated in a dozen ways. Perhaps the best way to do so would be to see it parodied.[41] Even otherwise, some of James's own passages tend to create a feeling of self-parody unconsciously, for, as I have shown elsewhere, he could not have mocked his own craft. These weaknesses include verbiage, attenuation, preciosity, stylization, circumlocution, meretriciousness, trickery, staleness, etc. They crop up in the style chiefly when the germinal ideal of the tale is not rooted in reality, but in his closed cranium; when indeed he allows his maverick and promiscuous imagination, instead of common experience, to invent the material. In thus reversing the order of reality, he deifies individual consciousness as a sovereign entity unanswerable to any outer framework of facts. When this happens, the style will naturally assume an exotic or inebriated form to hide the lack of felt experience. Sometimes the foliage of words is simply a device to extract a drop of sap from some dry twig of knowledge. A vertiginous skyscraper, indeed, is sought to be erected on a pinhead. Or, to put it differently, one has at times the feeling of a magic flower bursting out at the end of a coloured stick. The show is brilliant, but the sleight-of-hand can deceive none.

I think one of the major troubles with the later James is that he appears to have had almost a horror of writing a plain sentence. It would have amounted to a literary faux pas or an idiomatic vulgarity for him. Where fastidiousness becomes inhuman, the style too assumes monstrous forms. The weakness for the ornate and the extravagant is responsible for yet another well-known Jamesian sin. Nearly all his characters talk in the same high and subtle idiom, thus blurring frequently the contours of individual personality. This, in fact, would mean that James is incapable of rendering different streams of thought in their own native style, or of individualizing the idiom of different characters. There is, of course, some point in the argument that since he deals only with one set of people whose idiom is highly standardized, there cannot be much room for individual shades and nuances. This, to my mind, does not fully explain the nature of this oddity which stems from the desire to hit a "sixer" off every ball that is to be bowled on the Jamesian pitch.

Again, the later style has the tendency to run to unwarranted stylization and preciosity, thus creating needless "muddlement" and obfuscation. The art then turns to artifice, and the style becomes musty and mildewed. The stuffiness suggests cobwebs covering old bric-a-brac.

However, all these faults are not as pervasive and as stultifying as is generally assumed. Take, for instance, the charge of verbiage or overstatement. The relentless volley of words in most cases is wholly in keeping with the psychological pressures and confusions inherent in the situations James is attempting to explore or analyze. The multiplicity of aspects and the ever-receding nature of human reality would, indeed, require a language rich enough to cope with these phenomena. What is more, a kind of understatement is dexterously played off against overstatement. Often there is a controlling principle of economy within this lush and luxuriant prose. Or, to it put it differently, the later style is a unique blend of overtures and avoidances, of overtones and undertones, of sounds and silences. It is an orchestrated style which, when fully engaged, has the resonance of a great symphony.

That the later style, being highly figurative, more aptly captures the poetry or essence of things may be seen from the revisions made for the New York Edition. That here and there one change or another strikes us as clumsy and meretricious should not obscure the fact that in a large number of cases, the changed text is more expressive of the character or the situation in question than the earlier. I cannot, therefore, agree with Leon Edel when in an afterword to the 1879 text of *The American* he observes: "The late revisions may be interesting to study for the light they throw on the novelist's creative process; but they are extremely artificial."[42] Perhaps, the two printed texts do not give us a full idea of the nature of these revisions. As Professor Edel knows, the typed manuscript at the Houghton Library, Harvard University, which James corrected in his own hand, is literally strewn over from cover to cover with scores of deletions, revisions and additions. Almost each page is a jumbled graph of insertions and superscriptions. Even grammatical changes abound. Obviously, James undertook this massive labour with a view to bringing the text closer to his poetic intentions. Let me give a couple of examples.

Revised 1879 Text

Her clear gray eyes were strikingly expressive; they were both gentle and intelligent, and Newman liked them immensely; but they had not those depths of splendour—those many coloured rays—,which illumine the brow of famous beauties. Madame de Cintré was rather thin, and she looked younger than probably she was. In her whole person there was something both youthful and subdued, slender and yet ample, tranquil yet shy; a mixture of immaturity and repose, of innocence and dignity. . . . [43]

New York Edition (1905)

Her wide gray eyes were like a brace of deputated and garlanded maidens waiting with a compliment at the gate of a city, but that they failed of that lamplike quality and those many-coloured fires that light up, as in a constant celebration of anniversaries, the fair front of the conquering type. Madame de Cintré was of attenuated substance and might pass for younger than she probably was. In her whole person was something still young and still passive, still uncertain and that seemed still to expect to depend and which yet made, in its dignity, a presence withal and almost represented, in its serenity, an assurance. . . . [44]

Now, clearly, there is at least one false and unhappy phrase in the altered text—"attenuated substance"—the archaic "withal" somehow sounding perfectly in its place. The changes, to my mind, bring out more fully the rich and elusive beauty of Madame de Cintré than the earlier text whose concluding sentence is a string of clichés to be found in any picture magazine. The romantic ambience of her personality being one of the novel's principal concerns, the revisions here are wholly justified.

Revised 1879 Text

> The Marquis was with his wife when Newman entered their box; he was bland, remote, and correct as usual, or, as it seemed to Newman, even more than usual. "What do you think of the opera?" asked our hero. "What do you think of the Don?"[45]

New York Edition (1905)

> The Marquis was with his wife when Newman entered their box; he was as remotely bland as usual, but the great demonstration in which he had lately played his part appeared to have been a drawbridge lowered and lifted again. Newman was once more outside the castle and its master perched on the battlement. "What do you think of the opera?" our hero none the less artlessly demanded. "What do you think of the cool old Don?"[46]

Even here, there is one gratuitous phrase in the altered text—"none the less artlessly"—but the entire metaphor of the drawbridge, the castle and the battlement, etc., is an immense improvement upon the businesslike functional language of the earlier text. We realize how perfectly the new image agrees with the intent of the situation as it obtains now, and as it would in the future. Apart from its romantic associations, which are entirely in tune with the fairy-tale atmosphere of the novel, it is a figure of war—the impending one between American openness and French duplicity.

Nor is all his extended analysis in the later novels always a matter of pedantic industry. In the entire range of Anglo-American fiction, there is little to compare with the virtuosity of his tracker mind which, equipped with highly sensitive antennae, follows the faintest trail of an emotion or idea to its dark psychological lair. In fact, each point is rotated in the great globe of the mind, and the angles of departure, intersection, collision and coalescence are drawn with the precision of a mathematician. Each nodule of experience, so to speak, is drained of its psychic potential to the last drop. A style which is attuned to such purposes, as, for instance, the style of *The Ambassadors,* cannot be simple, bare and direct. It has to be pleated and textured and scented, above all. What James said of Gautier in 1873 is true of himself: "He loved words for themselves—for their look, their aroma, their colour, their fantastic intimation."[47] The trouble comes when he cannot be satisfied with this density of effect, and begins to produce a filigree work, wire-drawn to the point of exasperating ambiguity. Ironically enough, then his very virtue—the feeling for words and their inherent beauty, music and power—turns into a vice and a weakness! The prismatic and visionary quality of rhetoric is lost in a froth of words. This weakness crops up again and again in those later stories where one feels that it is not the ideas that are *driving* James, but James who is *driving* the ideas.

Finally, could these idiosyncrasies of the later style be interpreted psychologically as a kind of ersatz satisfaction of a sexually starved life? Could it be that the author's own lean and lukewarm response to passional immediacy was responsible for the prodigality and embroidery of the style? As it is, most readers and critics have felt an emotional vacuum, and even some frigidity, at the centre of the Jamesian universe. Or, could we relate the fantastic fecundity of the later style to the eruption of a delayed sexuality? One is reminded of the later poetry of W.B. Yeats which derives its tremendous force from erotic energy and libidinous ribaldry. In James, the sexual imagination is voyeuristic and devious and cold, seeking gratification through a style prone to rhetorical self-abuse, depletion and idiomatic aphrodisiacs, whereas in Yeats, the style becomes, as a result of sexuality, realistic, earthy and warm. The whole question of the style seen thus needs an extended "Jamesian" treatment, and may well be taken up as a cognate study.

Whatever, therefore, our view of the matter, one thing seems to be pretty obvious. James could not have written the later novels and tales in any other style. There is a ring of inevitability about it. Its built-in complexity then assumes a compulsive quality. It *alone* could have translated for him the huge and vague continents of dreams and desires, the pulls and pressures of an agonized psyche, the stinging doubts about the nature of reality, and the dark mystery of evil in the world. Any paraphrase, simplification or effort at reduction would not only destroy its beauty and poetry, but also its dialectics. David Lodge in his *Language of Fiction*[48] carries the point perhaps too far when he claims for the language of fiction the same kind of inevitability and untranslatability that is normally claimed for poetry, but if there was ever a fiction that came very near to achieving a word order that simply could not be disturbed without a grievous injury to its content and meaning, it is the later fiction of James. Or, to put it differently, just as the clinical, skeletal and gaunt, though supple and sinewy, style of Hemingway is essential to the truth of his experience, the rich, ornate, textured, formalized, ironic and teasing style of James is essential to the truth of his vision. One is reminded of his retort to William James, who in a letter concerning the perversity of the style of *The Golden Bowl*, asked him to switch over to a "fourth manner," "just to please Brother."[49] In his reply, James talks of the style's inevitability and bemoans the "constitutional" inability of his brother to "enjoy" the kind of fiction he was then writing, and adds: "I see nowhere about me done or dreamed of the things that alone for me constitute the *interest* of the doing of the novel—and yet it is in a sacrifice of them on their very own ground that the thing you suggest to me evidently consists. It shows how far apart and to what different ends we have had to work out (very naturally and properly) our respective intellectual lives."[50]

For James, then, the style was one's way of understanding and conducting one's being. He would have entirely endorsed the view of Wittgenstein that a language is a way of life.

13

Aspects of Love and Sex

James criticism in general has endorsed the popular view that the novelist's *vital* energies went into the making of his fiction at the expense of his life. This, in brief, is a reversal of Oscar Wilde's well-known aphorism that he had put his genius into his life, and his talent into his works. Also, such a view of James seems to echo the oft-quoted pronouncement in a letter to H. G. Wells that for him, it is "art that makes life," though, as I have argued earlier,[1] he was not offering art as a substitute for life, but as an instrument of refinement and richer perceptions. However, notwithstanding such a gloss, James's life and James's literary productions do present possibilities of a deep division, even of a continual combat, if one may say so. That is to say, while his life went in one direction, his art appeared to go in another. These issues can best be seen (not resolved, for nothing in so complex a writer as James can be resolved) in the light of the *sexual imagination,*[2] which, as I hope to show later in this essay, constitutes the exercise and health of his art, whatever its miseries and insufficiencies in actual life. Indeed, the paradox of James's power compels one in the end to look for the clues to his energies in an area where manifestly the search ends up in a cul-de-sac as soon as it begins. It is not as though what I have to offer will be a key to the complex code of life, ethics and art engineered by James with a cunning that nearly imperils the virtue of his exercise. Surely, he "covered his tracks" so well in his work that even when we appear to be close to the buried essence of things, the element of nuclear ambiguity unsettles our conviction, if not our response. In turning, therefore, to the question of love and sex in a writer whose image is that of a Victorian prude, notoriously nervous in relation to passion and marriage, I propose to authenticate the presence of the sexual imagination in him as a driving force almost from the start, though it is in the final phase that it seems "to burst, with a latent extravagance, its mould,"[3] despite all dodges, screens and blinds. The jokes regarding his squeamishness and virginity[4] will not cease for all the raking of the pit by Leon Edel in his massive five-volume psychological biography, but, I think, it is possible to intuit and perceive the nature and force of the libido in his art. Considering finally that his novels and tales were the only offspring he was destined to have, it may not be too fanciful to establish an organic link between his starved and wasted sexual life and his potent and fecund sexual imagination. The Prufrockian aspect of James, in fact, suggests a whole Freudian paradise of erotic dreams and desires, apart from a deep-rooted fear of "the surrenders that sexual relation seemed to entail."[5] His art, so to speak, battens on his lean and hungry life, and as it ripens, it becomes ever more coercive, devious and willful. We may even stipulate a Jamesian poetics of proxy and voyeurism. But of this later.

In trying to relate James's unique powers to his sexual imagination, I do not mean to suggest that such an imagination is wholly sovereign, intolerant of a compeer or rival. In fact, in any creative artist, we usually witness a syndrome of imaginations, and it is not easy to isolate one from another. The collateral imaginations—religious, moral, political, sociological, romantic, aesthetic etc.—then so group themselves though an organic process of mutual sacrifices and accommodations as to present a unitary character. Clearly, though the imagination may turn predatory at some stage, as James's sexual imagination seems to do in the end, the remaining components do not disappear from the scene. They remain in business because of the benign piracy of the coercive imagination. It may even be argued that since the sexual imagination is, in any case, common to all artists and creative writers in the Freudian sense, its nature in a work of art is constitutive. As such, there is no need to prove its presence in James or in any other artist. "All the ladders start," as Yeats affirms brutally, "in the foul rag-and-bone shop of the heart." Nevertheless, where an imagination begins to operate indirectly, casting ironic shadows over the proceedings, it becomes necessary to examine its disguises and masquerades, particularly where it seems to constitute the kinetics of a work of art.

In order to understand the operative energies of any great writer, it is essential that we posit a poetic relationship between his dream work and his life, as psychoanalytic criticism, in general, does. But, more importantly, there is a need to establish a reverse relationship whereby the mock world of art can be shown, in its turn, to shape his responses and overtures to life. In a writer like James, this is of particular importance in that he stipulates a perpetual tension between the artist as man and the man as artist. Thus, in considering the nature of his art, we are obliged to come to terms with his subterranean or submerged self. In a dramatic artist, such a self surfaces not only in imagery and rhetoric, but also in the nature and disposition of plot. In fact, when personality is extinguished as a conscious exercise in a work, it erupts more meaningfully in the mechanics and medium of its art. In the end, the precarious balance abides. In the preface to his *Golden Codgers,* Richard Ellmann writes: "A secret or a tacit life underlies the one we are thought to live—one of the pleasures of writing novels and poems is that the subsurface life can be drawn upon without incurring the responsibilities of autobiography or history, yet with happier obligations imposed by an art form." And he goes on to talk of "the 'mysterious armature' as Mallarmé called it, which binds the creative work," and of the aesthetic heat that shapes "the fiery clay" into "the wrought jar."[6] I suggest that this "armature" in James comprises sexual strains. Or, to put it differently, the sinews of his art are the sinews of sex as, indeed, they are in Shakespeare and in other major writers.

Now, whatever the nature of James's "obscure hurt," sustained in the years of his adolescence, it appears to have caused a psychic wound whose pervasive power may be seen symbolically as late as "The Jolly Corner." Clearly, Edmund Wilson's theory of "the wound and the bow," though reductive as a study of art and neurosis per se, has a visible and demonstrative relevance to James's work in particular. Even if the young James was not physically maimed, the castration complex at the unconscious level was to remain an abiding presence, distorting the structure of his sexuality, pushing the libido into exotic eroticism on the one hand, into narrow, devious and destructive variants on the other. As we shall see, the entire brood of Freudian monsters was in full cry, as the novelist, retreating more and more into the sanctuaries of the imagination, fashioned "palaces of thought" and "pagodas" of art in gothic extravagance. The trauma of the "obscure hurt" resulted at the very start in the apotheosis of art. Or, as R. P. Blackmur observes, James made "a sacred rage of his art" much in the manner of Abelard after his injury.[7] Apparently, the prodigality of the Jamesian imagination owes not a little to the missed intensities of sexual experience. In proportion as his life became vapid, decorative and ritualistic, his art became rich, fantastic and subtle. That is to say, as James grew older, his sexual imagination became more coercive and fabulous. And if writing, "which consists in allowing a fluid to flow out from a tube upon a piece of white paper," acquires "the symbolic meaning of coitus,"[8] as Freud avers, then the Jamesian industry assumes a particularly sexual character.

All the evidence Leon Edel has so painstakingly, and often insightfully, gathered in relation to the link between James's stories and James's "women" and "boys" goes to prove that the figure in the Jamesian carpet is woven from tangled sexual skeins. Clearly, his cousin Minny Temple, who ravished his romantic imagination and inspired two of his greatest heroines, Isabel Archer and Milly Theale, became, soon after her youthful death, an abiding sexual metaphor in his work. She is "the Bright Absentee" of Emily Dickinson's imagination, inveigling the artist into a vision of virginity and worship. In his later tales, she surfaces as a nubile "nymphet" (Maisie, Nanda, Aggie, Jeanne de Vionnet) whose virginity is both a bait and a beatitude. Thus, Minny Temple, in the end, is rarefied into an abstraction, though she remains a compelling presence, if only because ideas moved James more deeply than men or women. As for Woolson and other literary ladies including, possibly, Edith Wharton, Violet Hunt and Rhoda Broughton, James's mildly flirtatious and flippant attitude seldom rose above the academic and epistolary level. However, while its "playful" nature had a truly Freudian aspect, and the ravages beneath the surface seen by Leon Edel in such tales as "The

Aspern Papers" and "The Altar of the Dead" are real enough, no woman appears to have brought James to the boil.[9] His diversionary imagination at once set up decoys, and ingested all the passion. An inner mechanism converted the situation into sensuous thought. This, incidentally, accounts for the Donne-like quality of the rhetoric in his later fiction. But where James's "boys" are concerned, the position is far more complex, intense and disturbing. The erotic idiom and tactile imagery of the letters to Anderson, Fullerton, Hugh Walpole and Persse did suggest a strong streak of homoeroticism in the Master, but neither "The Pupil" nor "The Great Good Place"—often cited as examples of homoerotic over-tones—can be taken as evidence of homosexuality as such. While the former is a tender tale of human relationships between pupil and teacher, forged as a result of parental venality and vagabondage, the latter, which envisions a world uncom-plicated by females and safe from emotional erosion, is essentially a utopia of the spirit where James seeks to annul the ache of identity. Despite the fact that handsome young men continued to snare his imagination in actual life,[10] we do not find a Tonio Kröger in his work. The susceptibility to youthful male beauty in old age reveals an ache and a void, but the novelist, unlike Thomas Mann or Shakespeare, creates no compulsive figure of passionate intensity in his fiction. While the letters to his young friends are certainly couched in a lover's language, the novels and tales of the period continue to centre round women, in aspects varying from spiritual charm to dark sexuality. Considering that James's later fiction, in particular, is highly coded and stylized, and also more significantly related to the unconscious, the absence of golden, godlike boys is somewhat mystifying. The irresistible conclusion is that at the deeper level, it is not male beauty which disturbs his creative vision. There is, on the contrary, enough evidence of "the female principle"[11] at work in his fiction till the end.

Of the three archetypal aspects of sexual love—hierogamous (sacred-cosmic-elemental), romantic and married—James was forever swinging between the last two, never achieving an integrated vision. This is not necessarily a criticism of his position, for in a fundamental sense, the metaphysics of ironies informing the Jamesian universe only authenticates such a partial and changing vision. To that extent, the continual tension between the categories of romantic love and married love is, in fact, a source of poetic powers in his fiction. And it is within the extremities and aberrations of these bourgeois aspects of love that we must seek answers to James's sexual problems.

To begin with, it must be understood that, though James evolved highly innovative and daring techniques of fiction, he was, so far as his social vision was concerned, working within the narrow confines of bourgeois marital ethics. Thus, the entire concept of hierogamy or sacred marriage, for instance, lay outside the range of his experience and vision. In a perceptive article, "Hierogamy versus Wedlock: Types of Marriage Plots and Their Relationships to Genres of Prose

Fiction," Evelyn J. Hinz writes: "The paradigmatic marriage for archaic man is the hierogamy, the sacred marriage, and the prototype of his sacred marriage is the union of earth and sky. . . ."[12] Such a sexual union, whose cosmic reverberations reach down and out and beyond as in the Catherine-Heathcliff union in *Wuthering Heights*, or in the Connie-Mellors congress in *Lady Chatterley's Lover,* is clearly a rude and violent threat to the church-ordained and consummated married love. In such hierogamous unions, celebrated amidst root and flower to the music of rain, wind and storm, a wilderness weds a wilderness in utter disregard of all forms and conventions of civilization. In James, on the other hand, the entire effort of the awakened and civilized consciousness is in the direction of complete refinement. Here the form of things has almost become a sacred convention in itself. No wonder there are no earth-shaking love-scenes, no stormy assaults and consummations in the fields of night. Even the celebrated Goodwood-Isabel "lightning" kiss in *The Portrait of a Lady* is not really a case of a baulked or thwarted hierogamy where the novelist pulls back the "drowning" lady from a sudden encounter with her unconscious, as Hinz seems to argue. The weighted burden of civilization, it appears, bears down upon our young heroine, and prevents her from facing the truth of her deep and dark desires. And amidst a tumult of confused cries, she bolts for Rome.[13] The fury of sexual passion will erupt in devious forms in James's later fiction, though, even then, the outward aspects or forms of civilization will be rigorously maintained.

As for romantic love, by the time of James, it had almost lost its wilder and, even, idealistic connotations. In any case, it had been, in a manner, domesticated within the structure of bourgeois marriage. That is to say, the premarital poetry of passion, with all its urgent and exotic appeal, had been assimilated in the form sanctioned and blessed by society. The American heroines of James largely operated within such a world-view. Thus, his Daisy Millers, Isabel Archers, Francie Dossons, Milly Theales and Maggie Ververs tended to view romance as innocent play, a stroll in the arbours of Eden leading to the bower of conjugal bliss. It was an exercise of the dreaming heart in natural ease and innocence. Its end was always consecrated matrimony in clear and full commitment before the world in the house of God. That is why when the crash came their spiritual travail was inevitably accompanied by moral beauty. For, as we shall see presently, these young American women were required to invest all their soulful energies in an institution which to James appeared tragically flawed, whatever its social graces and charms.

However, from the beginning the Jamesian imagination also responded richly and darkly to another kind of woman—the woman of romance, nurtured like a golden peach by exotic airs and soft breezes, drawing one into dark and desperate territories. Thus, the ineffable appeal of a Christina Light, of a Madame de Cintré and of a Madame de Vionnet is essentially romantic in the medieval Provençal tradition, though James varies the form from the femme fatale and the mystic

Diana to the eternal Cleopatra. And if this woman whom the male Mediterranean mind has nursed over the ages in song and story does not get "typed" in James, it is because the ardour of the imagination is matched by the fineness of perception and inventiveness of description and detail. It may be noticed that from *Roderick Hudson* (1875) to *The Ambassadors* (1903), she becomes more and more tractable and vulnerable, and therefore, more and more human. She becomes domiciled in the salons and châteaux of Europe. Clearly, the Jamesian chemistry of love and sex has been undergoing silent changes.

There is, of course, the "other" woman in James—Madame Merle, Rose Armiger, Kate Croy and Charlotte Stant—who is sexually more attractive, and whose adventurous nature invests sin with romance. The dark lady archetype, then, is another dimension of the lady of romance, though in her case the mystic element has been dissipated en route. She keeps troubling the Jamesian vision till the end. Even these beautiful sinners finally receive a measure of James's pity and compassion. Their passion, though destructive, is not devoid of beauty and poetry. In the imperium of sex, passion, it seems, constitutes its own health and aesthetic.

The question of married love in James is fraught with laminated ironies and ambiguities. For, though his world-view underscores symmetry, finish, and orderliness in life and society, the eruption of the gothic element in his later fiction notwithstanding, his vision of marriage seems to cast some doubt over the capacity of this institution to secure harmony and happiness. Leon Edel's view that the pitiful dependence of James's father upon his wife made the novelist look upon marriage as something enervating and debilitating, leading in most cases to spiritual spoliation, is partly borne out by the fact that his fiction is full of fractured unions and wasted wedlocks, and that there is scarcely a happy marriage in his pages. But, I think, it would be wrong to regard him as a misogamist for that reason. The mere fact that in one of the most penetrating and moving studies of married life in the English language James uses the symbol of the golden bowl to denote the rounded beauty and felicity of marriage should prove the place of this institution in the Jamesian scheme of things. The "cracks" in that cup would then be as natural as fissures in windswept rounded rocks. And ironically enough, such "cracks," in the end, ensured the stability and health of the gilded form. Its flawed nature left room for spiritual and moral exertions, and, therefore, for a limited kind of martyrdom and heroism. From the sterile and cold marriage of Euphemia in "Madame de Mauves," and of Isabel Archer in *The Portrait,* James has, in the end, moved on to the passionate marriage of Maggie Verver which, teetering on the edge of disaster, is saved by compassion, sacrifice and accommodation—some of the highest virtues in Jamesian ethics. Marriage, then, is viewed not as a dreaded hell, not even as an imperfect heaven, but as a purgatory of the human heart, offering endless vistas of personal culture and refinement within its limited orbit. Such a view is simply a subtler and more psychological extension of the

nineteenth-century American vision of marriage which finds its happiest expression in the novels of Howells, who even speaks of marriage in celestial terms, and
observes that heaven, which is nothing but the joy of self-giving, is mirrored in
each true marriage. James would have agreed with such a view except to state that
a "true marriage" is so rare a thing in life as to become a receding ideal. Again,
Howells's accent on the social and communal aspects of marriage chimes well
with James's ethics of personal relationships and social responsibilities. Marriage
as a means of reducing or conquering the chaos of passions, and of stabilizing the
self in its quest of identity is the principal theme of Howells. Indeed, as Allen F.
Stein remarks, in "Howells's work the extent to which a character is worthy of
respect is usually in direct proportion to the success his marriage enjoys."[14] Such a
facile view, however, is not part of James's aesthetic of marriage. Even a broken,
unhappy marriage such as Isabel Archer's in no way diminishes our respect for
her. On the contrary, as she ripens in agony and suffering, we are vouchsafed a
vision of her character which essentially is as tragic as it is heroic. In the Jamesian
concept of marriage, then, there are no palliatives, no easy affirmations, no
transcendences.

It appears as though the corruptions of marriage became an obsessive issue or
theme with James in his London-based novels and tales such as *What Maisie
Knew, The Awkward Age, The Sacred Fount* and "A London Life," etc. The stink
of furtive sex, the venality and vulgarity of "high" life, the playful adulteries and
fashionable fornications of the upper set, the hidden brutalities and treacheries of
the spouses, the love-cannibalism of the vampire mates etc.—all these shady and
ugly manifestations of married life do present a dark and disconcerting picture.
This would seem to present marriage as a licensed club, not as a cultivated garden.
Its squalor and moral horror would naturally show up married love as a
convenience, a decoy and a sham. But the point to grasp in these stories is that
James is presenting a very special set of people from the upper classes for whom
marriage has become an abstract "game of chess," and who have abused an
institution which, though imperfect in itself, is, nevertheless, capable under
different circumstances of engendering great moral perceptions and truths. James,
the moral and social critic, is at work in secure knowledge of the value of marriage.
Indeed, the nuptial imagery, in general, has a positive charge, and the marriage
metaphor, in particular, has mystic overtones, though no overt theological
connotations.

However, where unbridled passion and concupiscent marriage in relation to
art and to the artist's health and exercise are concerned, James does show a certain
diffidence, if not dread. His first notable novel, *Roderick Hudson,* presents sexual
passion as something inimical to the life of the imagination, and of cultivated
detachment, so essential for a practicing artist. And since the artist is, in one sense,
"a remorseless egoist,"[15] as Rowland Mallet observes, he was likely to be more
demanding, even more cruel, than others in marriage. This view persists in some

of James's later productions such as *The Tragic Muse* and the stories of writers and artists like "The Author of Beltraffio" and "The Lesson of the Master," etc., though the gathering ironies do add new shades to it. Thus, the artist as a celibate monk serving the veiled goddess of art in worship and prayer becomes an operative image in James.

Why sexual motifs and fantasies erupt with such a shattering force in the final phase of James is not difficult to guess. A whole lifetime of slaughtered dreams and desires, of ignoble retreats before passion, cannot but explode in the end. The Jamesian unconscious throws up in rich profusion all manner of erotic images. The ageing Master becomes, thus, a classic example of repression and of the revenge the unconscious takes in its turn. No wonder, arrested and baulked sexuality is now unable to flow in a free and open manner. It seeks hospitality in nooks and corners, in dark lofts and cellars. And because it carries a tremendous charge, where and when it surfaces, it assumes an obsessive and compulsive quality. As Herbert Marcuse, discussing sexual perversions in general, observes, "The perversions seem to give *promesse de bonheur* greater than that of 'normal' sexuality. . . . The perversions seem to reject the entire enslavement of the pleasure ego by the reality ego."[16] Hence the taste for *fleurs du mal*.

Though Freudian depths and distempers may be seen in nearly all his novels before the final phase, particularly in *Watch and Ward* (displaced eroticism), in *Roderick Hudson* (the narcissistic libido and *thanatos*), in *Washington Square* (oedipal fixation), in *The Bostonians* (sexual repression and lesbianism) and in *The Portrait* (sexual frigidity and phallic fear), it is in his later novels and tales that the more grisly and shaggy creatures of the Freudian menagerie may be seen in full fury. James, the snooper and the voyeur, is abroad in such novels as *What Maisie Knew* and *The Sacred Fount*. There is a distinct relish of things veiled and forbidden, of peeping through the key-hole. Sex by proxy or ersatz eroticism and cerebral sex now become the lean satisfactions of a prodigal imagination. The way young Maisie's burgeoning sexuality is baited, roused and teasingly dramatized, or the way James's sexual imagination "turns the screws" to seemingly involve two innocent children, Giles and Flora, in a vision of "hell," and the manner in which the Jamesian narrator lets his salacious imagination run riot over the supposed sexual intrigues in *The Fount* show the strains that make up the tapestry of James's sexual imagination. Of course, James's interest in dark sexuality was partly triggered by his fascination with Ibsen around that time.

Two other aspects of aberrant or devious sexuality in these two novels—the "nymphet" fixation or the "Lolita" complex and the vampire motif or love-cannibalism—again testify to the ravages within. Of these, the Jamesian "crush" on little girls—his *jeunes filles en fleurs*—is particularly intriguing and interesting. There is, indeed, quite a small procession of these vestal virgins[17] in his fiction. Nora of *Watch and Ward,* Pansy of *The Portrait,* Maisie, Aggie and

Nanda of *The Awkward Age* and Jeanne de Vionnet of *The Ambassadors* constitute a row of nubile virgins presented to our eager imaginations in a highly provocative imagery and idiom. Maisie, for instance, is described as "a deep little porcelain cup in which biting acids could be mixed."[18] Aggie offered as a bait to town wolves, is "the fruit—grown to the perfection of a peach on a sheltered wall."[19] Again, both Aggie and Nanda figure in the highly erotic passage quoted below. Nanda, in particular, is primed for passion, and is all set to dig her teeth into London life and draw blood.

> Both the girls struck him as *lambs,* with the great shambles of life in their future, but while one, with its neck in a *pink ribbon,* had no consciousness but that of being fed with the *sweet biscuit* of unobjectionable knowledge, the other struggled with instincts and forebodings, with the suspicion of its doom and the far-borne scent, in the flowery fields, of *blood.*[20] (italics mine)

Again, Jeanne de Vionnet appears to Little Bilham in *The Ambassadors* as a bouquet of pale pink petals to be opened to some great golden sun.

The increased incidence of erotic imagery after his "sexual breakthrough,"[21] and "the menopausal mood" as Geismar wittily terms James's roused voyeuristic interest in virgins, spinsters, homosexuals and snoopers, has been noticed by different critics. However, it is revealing to see that even his first novel, *Watch and Ward,* is heavily erotic in meaning and tone.

There are, indeed, any number of Freudian images, and their incidence increases alarmingly as the "winter" of James's "discontent" arrives, and the grey years begin to cast their long and dismal shadows. These may roughly be divided into images of (*i*) *nature* (sowing and tilling, vertical rays and flames), (*ii*) *water* (pool and tide and wave; boat and oar, rowing and diving), (*iii*) *garden* (fruits and flowers: apple, peach and plum; petal and pollen), (*iv*) *animal* (lamb and dove; tiger and hawk), (*v*) *architecture* (house and window, door and handle, bolt and key, lock and key, fork and screw, cave and tunnel, pit, pagoda and tower), (*vi*) *sports* and war (bow and arrow), (*vii*) *money* (casket and jewel, mint and coin), (*viii*) *utensil* (cup and bowl, spoon and ladle), (*ix*) *religion* (the garden of Eden and the Serpent, the lance and the holy grail). The genital and copulation imagery and the imagery of deflowering persist in various forms and figures in James's productions till the end. The marine imagery, in particular, is pervasive in James,[22] and as Freud and Jung argue, water and sexuality are interlinked at the unconscious level. In addition to these archetypal sexual images, there are chromatic images of a similar nature. Lyle Glazier, for instance, notices the sexual connotation of the red, pink and yellow colours in *The Ambassadors.* The red colour "defines Strether's psychic depth against which his puritanism marshalls the force of his inhibitions . . . redness is associated with sexuality which is primitive, pagan, bluntly physical, but *not* in the least depraved or decadent. . . . For a merely prurient sexuality, James uses yellow. . . . "[23] Again, in relation to Jeanne de Vionnet, the colour pink is used, and it is suggestive of "innocent passion and adolescence."[24] Sometimes, James even uses popular slang to describe a phallic image. Philip M. Weinstein thus quotes Lord Warburton's "big bribe" and Goodwood's "way of rising before her"[25] as examples of hard and raw sexuality which Isabel dreads. And significantly enough, James begins to use erotic imagery not only in the context of love and sex, but also in that of other areas of experience. To quote a couple of examples, in *English Hours,* when speaking of a shopping interlude in London, he talks of the "sense of the importance of *deflowering,* of *despoiling the shop*" (italics mine).[26] Again, on the eve of the staging of *Guy Domville* in London, fears of its possible fate are expressed in a letter to Minnie Bourget in an imagery that is purely sexual. The play becomes in James's excited reverie "a white Christian virgin thrown to the lions and the tigers."[27]

Also rampant in James's later fiction is the imagery of food. In Freudian terms, the "transference" symbolically assumes the form of "infantile oral and infantile anal" in such a novel as *The Fount* which, as most critics believe, has an agonizing autobiographical aspect.

It is strange, however, that even as James plunges more and more into the pits of "evil sexuality"—adultery, fornication, incestuous, oedipal and homoerotic impulses etc.—and "the imagination of disaster" takes over the proceedings, as it were, he also becomes more and more conscious of the beauty and power of passion. If the one strain finally leads to the tragic syndrome of sex, power and money in his unfinished novel, *The Ivory Tower,* the other is apostrophized in Strether's well-known address to Little Bilham in Gloriani's garden in *The Ambassadors.*

And this brings me to the two complementary images of sexual starvation and sacrificial sex in James. In such wasted and trapped figures as Olive Chancellor of *The Bostonians,* Mrs. Wix of *What Maisie Knew,* the governess of "The Turn of the Screw," the telegraphist girl of the story called "In the Cage," Herbert Dodd of "The Bench of Desolation," John Marcher of "The Beast in the Jungle," and Traffles of "Mona Montravers," the novelist has indirectly dramatized his own sexual miseries. Here is a life of feckless fantasies, of cerebral orgies, of masochistic and sadistic erosion, of an empty, long and confused journey into twilight regions. Figure after figure of deprivation and depletion crowds the canvas in the end.

The idea of sacrificial sex begins with Rowland Mallet of *Roderick Hudson.* His later incarnations include Christopher Newman of *The American,* Isabel Archer, Fleda Vetch of *The Spoils of Poynton* and Lambert Strether. In these protagonists James has embodied his philosophy of sacrifice when values and vision triumph over appetite. They are nearest to the Jamesian conscious, just as the starved figures are closest to his unconscious.

And finally, it may be rewarding, I think, to study the Gothic structure, indirect technique and involved style of the later James in terms of his Freudian fixations. Why the novelist was driven into fantastic forms, and why he evolved a Byzantine rhetoric may well be a question of sexual "compensation," apart from its metaphysical and epistemological aspects. A verbal voluptuary here plays with words, fondles phrases, savages the syntax, costumes his nouns and verbs, drapes and deflowers his elegant, feminine sentences. Indeed, a whole linguistic paradise is set up by an imagination which has all along sought to gather the ambience and essence of things at the expense of felt experience and reality. Norman O. Brown, like Huizinga, whom he quotes in support, sees language primarily as "play" of love and sex. As he puts it, language "is an operational super-structure on an erotic base."[28] Its metaphorical character makes it a "playful" activity. James's excessive "play" with words, structures and tropes etc., thus, lends itself to a Freudian treatment.

How James himself reacts to the theme and treatment of sex in French and Italian novelists will also help show his attitude in the matter. It is true, he is shy of naming things and of "the verbal terms of intercourse,"[29] and he often resorts to euphemistic expressions. However, in his essay on Guy de Maupassant (1888) he observes: "A healthy, living and glowing art, full of curiosity and fond of exercise, has an indefeasible mistrust of rigid prohibitions."[30] Again, in the essay on D'Annunzio (1904), he makes it clear that though he admires the poetry of passion in that novelist, a sexual scene which is there for its own sake cannot but lead to "vulgarity." "From that moment it depends on itself alone for its beauty," says James, "it endangers extremely its distinction so precarious at the best."[31]

In an essay on Henry James, André Gide complained of the lack of sexual passion in the American novelist's protagonists. "They are," he wrote, "winged busts; all the weight of the flesh is absent, and all the shaggy, tangled undergrowth, all the wild darkness."[32] Apparently, there is a lot of truth in this statement, and, indeed, that is how James strikes one on the *surface*. But, as I have tried to show, there are dark "jungles" and prowling animals in almost all his major novels and stories of the final phase. Indeed, there is such a great deal of "the shaggy, tangled undergrowth" that one is tempted to say: "Yet who would have thought the old man to have had so much sex in him?" That he remained in actual life a distant sniffer, a remote connoisseur of sex, a lover *manqué* perhaps, even a horrible virgin, does not prove the absence of sexual passion in his work. On the contrary, it authenticates it for that very reason. Leon Edel neatly sums up the situation thus: "The Master plays with fire but he does not burn his fingers."[33] I may add that this remark simply echoes what James himself observed in another context in an early *nouvelle, Eugene Pickering* (1874), which has a strong autobiographical aura. He was "charmed by the smell of brine and yet afraid of the water."[34] And as we have noticed, the water imagery has always its own tale to tell.

14

The Politics of the Master

Each great writer acquires an image that owes its energies to certain felt airs and essences associated with his creative imagination. The cut and quality of that imagination, its character and code, its reach and ambit, finally determine its dynamics. The image is uniquely answerable to such a dialectic; it sustains itself through a certain "chemistry" of effects, and, at times, through a certain aesthetic "mysticism." In short, it attains en route an unmistakable ambience. Considered thus, Henry James figures to the responding imagination as a writer of such rare refinements, subtleties and felicities as to become in the end a kind of ultimate artist. To be sure, his fastidiousness has in some later tales a distressing aspect, and his "transcendence" a false ring, but where the Jamesian imagination is true to its inner energies and does not let the human situation turn cold or abstract or static, the compact between reader and writer has the quality of a shared dream. Its ceremoniousness has a purposive aspect; it becomes a kind of aesthetic tender. The "great good place" holds and compels.

With such an image before us, it is difficult to imagine Henry James in relation to any kind of politics, feudal, parliamentary, radical, charismatic or messianic. Indeed, we are tempted to rule out any Jamesian truck with it. Somehow the thing seems wholly out of character. And yet the novelist, as we know, did produce some novels and tales that have a distinctly political atmosphere and tone, even when they tend to pull in other directions, as though politics were an interloper in that "house of fiction" or "a pistol-shot in the middle of a concert," to use Stendahl's famous phrase. In any case, a work of art need not be overtly political to show the presence of a political imagination of sorts. In the larger sense of the word, politics are *constitutively* there in the body of a book that has anything to do with the fate of persons and societies and civilizations. And James, above all, was continually engaged in vast enterprises of the human spirit, relating man to family, society, culture and country. What, then, is the character of James's politics, if that is what we must call them, what are their compulsions, what are their aspects?

To begin with, it will be noticed that nearly all critical comments on James's politics are in the nature of stray remarks or parenthetical observations or wayside variations, and even where, as in Lionel Trilling, in Stephen Spender and in Irving Howe, to mention three outstanding James critics, the novelist's political vision—or the lack of it—receives a fuller and pondered treatment, the critical effort is confined to one or two novels. There are several penetrating critiques on the so-called political novels, but all these splinter studies do not add up to a consistent and coherent picture of James's politics. There is a need, therefore, to consider the problem in its essence and in its totality. Any consideration of his politics will, then, have to be a complex of comments authenticating in some manner the politics of the fabulator and the politics of the man. Eventually, we may even reach the conclusion that James had no great interest in politics, or that his politics varied from book to book, yielding no discernible pattern, but to do so we have to close with all those presences and "ghosts" that seem to mist the mirror, as it were. If "the figure in the carpet" remains vague and unrealized, that too may have a political moral of its own.

Broadly speaking, there are three kinds of critical comments on the subject of James's politics: (*a*) that he was temperamentally a deeply reactionary and conservative writer who subscribed openly and continually to the ideals of a patrician, elitist, aristocratic society; (*b*) that he had a strong, hidden, but inherited, familial streak of radicalism that erupted time and again in his deeply pondered works; (*c*) that he was essentially innocent of politics *qua* politics, that he did not understand the "psychology" of political thought, and that his few forays into the world of politics were simply aesthetic exercises of a ravaging but disengaged imagination. Admittedly, all these views are not mutually exclusive, and most critics do add codicils and clauses to voice their reservations when they encounter strange contradictions in James's attitudes. In any case, in a writer whose ambiguities and ironies are constitutive both at the level of vision and of technique, it may not be profitable to posit reductive positions. We may recall James's own well-known words: "Nothing is my last word about anything. I am interminably super-subtle and analytic."[1] Still, the general impression remains that James had no politics other than a sum of conservative values and attitudes. This is a fairly acceptable, though not quite accurate thesis. The trouble arises when we begin to ponder the question of politics in its larger, expansive, "spiritual" sense. James was not a visionary of empires and dynasties, or of political democracies and utopias as such. He was, on the other hand, a visionary of the republic of the imagination and the spirit. In that vision, the politics of the street, of the hustings, and of the gun were subsumed, though never fully absorbed in the manner of a Tolstoy. James, as we shall see, remained an American Balzac whose conservative sympathies and radical understanding were in a state of continual combat. Since he lacked a dynamic and dialectical sense of history, the Shakespearean "moment" did not arrive.

Before we come to the specific books and the specific issues that may be said to fall under the rubric of politics, one fundamental question has to be considered.

That is the question of the archetypal allergy of the aesthetic temperament to politics per se. Apart from the fact that it becomes a major theme in *The Tragic Muse* in particular, it raises certain collateral issues of great importance. Rebecca West refers in passing to "a nagging hostility to political effort" in James, and we will do well to examine the problem in its larger aspect.

It is often averred that the business of politics is too ugly and abrasive to attract the general run of intellectuals, writers and artists. There is something in its nature that is inimical to their moral and spiritual health. To cultivate a life of the imagination, to traffic in ideas, or to withdraw into the sanctuaries of thought is to see, as in a glass, darkly, the essential hopelessness and helplessness of one's passage in a world of heat, din and dirt. Again and again, the brutal business will require a falsification of the self, a sacrifice of values and a desecration of the pieties and protocols of civilized life. No sensitive psyche may survive in that kind of moral squalor without paying a fearful price. The erosion in the end will make the whoring mind an eternal impostor in retreat before the assaults of reality. Such a prospect, no wonder, turns off at least those artists who see their salvation in what G. E. Moore styles as "the states of mind." To put it differently, their allergy to politics may imply three things at once: a temperamental retreat, an ethical distrust and an aesthetic diffidence. Politics, then, become something inferior and wretched and wasteful, not worth their time, energy or powder.

Now this picture, though true in essentials, is somewhat naive, if not simplistic. For the fact remains, no one is so fatally and ineluctably attracted to politics as a certain type of intellectual or artist. Ironically, the mind that shies away at the level of immediacy and engagement is also the mind that is uniquely susceptible to its murderous charms at the level of ideas and ideologies. There is, indeed, something vicious in the manner in which the possessed mind subverts the structure of feeling and sentiment. The tyranny of thought is, in certain ways, tragic and eternal. The larger the imagination, the deeper will be the pull of politics. The desire to penetrate the mystery and mystique of power is, then, an ontological necessity. And when the quest spreads to become the great dream of politics in its widest sense, it comprehends the entire complex of human relationships—which is another way of saying that in this sense politics at once subserve and transcend the immediate business of governance. And what intellectual, whether writer, artist or scholar, is then not involved in that high dream? Indeed, in a certain inner and organic manner, not even the loudest politician is so truly in it as the artist whose involvement is spiritual and therefore all the more coercive. While the politician's tenancy is temporal, the artist's ministry is essentially religious. Indeed, the ideological and psychosomatic nature of politics draws in compulsively each such imagination as has the power to register the multiplying imponderables of existence. I trust that it was this kind of *angst* that made the Swiss writer Gottfried Keller say that everything is politics, or that prompted Thomas Mann to make the memorable statement, "In our time the destiny of man presents its meaning in political terms." Still, there is always a fatal tendency in the artist to draw even public affairs into the theatre of the mind and to play out the "drama" there. But all such retreats into the arbours of the imagination in the end cannot sustain him. The wild call of reality erupts grotesquely to make nonsense of his *nirvana.* There is the intolerable burden of unspent thought that cries out for dissipation. Thus may the imperium of ideas be broken to ensure sanity and moral health.

Essentially, this is a somewhat hurried sketch of the archetypal aesthetic sensibility in its widest, most universal sense. It remains to be seen how far James fits into this frame. Perhaps one way to do so is to understand briefly the dynamics of the novel as such, for, apart from other things, such a consideration leads us to the Lukacsian concept of "totality," a concept that helps us to understand the changing sociology of the novel. The search for "totality," "coherence" and "meaning" in an atomized class-society that characterizes the fictional hero since the advent of "critical realism" is, ipso facto, the writer's own quest for the key to the energies that bind the factual world despite the continual assaults on its integrity and viability. The novel that appropriated the myth and the epic was, in reality, a historical phenomenon. In all its earlier disguises—fable, romance, fantasy, utopia, etc.—it strenuously hankered after a "lost" paradise. No wonder, then, the search for wholeness and authenticity became the secret springs of the novel even in its most fantastic forms and aspects. As Michel Zeraffa says in *Fictions,* "With the novel society enters history and history enters into society," and the novel becomes, as in Balzac or in James, "a virtual fusion of the ideas of History, Society and the State."[2] The novel as art form itself becomes an *integer* in a disintegrating world and seeks to assume the role of a harmonizer. For Zeraffa, novelists like James, Joyce and Mann employ "a kind of imaginative sociology"[3] and their empathetic imaginations are able to penetrate the laminated layers of social reality and to disentangle the web of social relationships. In another recent study, Monroe Berger, a distinguished social scientist, shows how the integral link between the novel and bourgeois values and dreams is, at bottom, a political act. This is what the Marxist critics like Ralph Fox, Raymond Williams, Arnold Kettle and Fredric Jameson have been saying in their own way. To quote Berger, "Politics in its broadest sense refers to the relations among power, moral ideas and social institutions"[4] as in a novel like Ignazio Silone's classic *Bread and Wine.* Similarly, it has been argued lately that James's "blanks" and "silences" reveal more than they hide in terms of both *class* and *gender,* and "a political subtext of class relations" and "the structure of class relations that form a major aspect of the political content of any period" would indicate James's covert biases and values."[5] Taken thus, James's Dickensian and Balzacian novels of the eighties and even the "muslin dramas" of the nineties take us deep into that world where the dark trinity of money, sex and power presides in various guises. In his unfinished swan song, *The Ivory Tower,* James seems to be on the threshold of a visionary breakthrough, but the moral tragedy of ill-gotten millions remains merely a requiem for the passing away of classical continuities and felicities. That is about as far as he could go; the vision falters, remaining amorphous and unrealized.

Though James was a writer who wrote prodigiously and strenuously for nearly half a century, and whose enterprise covered a variety of genres, and though stray political comments will necessarily find their way into that vast imperium of letters, it is not easy to reduce them into patterns and wholes. Nor is it, I believe, safe to do so. The exercise will spring a leak somewhere and falsify the picture. For such a congeries of comments made in response to certain situations in the novels and tales, or to certain situations in real life, may not always fit into our notion of a writer's *Weltanschauung*. And since James seems to encourage the reader and the critic into fanciful and extravagant exercises, we have to be doubly on guard. The lure of Jamesian sirens is too well known to need additional comment. However, there are some novels and tales and travelogues that lend themselves to a more overt political scrutiny in terms of their vision and aesthetic, and our business ought to be with these books. That is where the politics of the fabulator stem from a certain unified and organic imagination, at least within the structure and confines of each separate volume. Even the discordant or subversive notes will eventually fall into the achieved harmony of such books.

The Bostonians, The Princess Casamassima and *The Tragic Muse* do not really constitute a political triptych as such. That is to say, they are not animated as a group by any single governing thought in the manner of, say, Disraeli's "Young England" trilogy of *Coningsby, Sybil* and *Tancred*. If they belong to the same aesthetic impulse—naturalistic fiction—they do not embody a cohesive political vision. Even in terms of their aesthetic, it is difficult to consider them in the naturalistic vein in equal quantum or measure. *The Princess Casamassima,* for instance, will not so readily wear the tag, for the romantic and "mystic" strains are loud enough to be heard all through. In *The Bostonians,* on the other hand, the satiric impulse is so cold and calculated and ratiocinative in character, and the method so spruce and dry and comic as to drown most such reverberations. In short, even the ironies of the two books operate along separate lines and owe their energies to disparate visions. Still, since all these novels were written within a space of three years and display a certain kind of ideological consanguinity, it seems natural to take them up as a group. Of the three novels, surely *The Princess Casamassima* is the most political, and *The Bostonians* the least, in intent and execution, but in the larger sense all these novels have been somewhat loosely included in the category of political fiction. And there is that obscure *nouvelle, Covering End,* which has unaccountably drawn few insightful comments, though in any consideration of James's politics the volume should have figured prominently, if not centrally.

To begin with, the so-called political novels of James are not in the mainstream of the political novel in England and America. These are, if one may say so, the "by-blows" of a novelist who happened to be inveigled into an enterprise somewhat in the manner of a sailor in a foreign port. And yet the ravishment of the enlarged imagination for the nonce was so complete as to have called forth the full force of his moral and spiritual energies. These political "strays," then, have the verve and vigor of illicit offspring, and they help show certain sleeping depths in James.

It may also be helpful if we pause for a moment and consider one or two definitions of the political novel in order to clarify the issue. In a pioneering effort, M. E. Speare gave too diffuse and eclectic a definition to be of much use. For him, basically, it is "a work of prose fiction which leans rather to 'ideas' than to 'emotions,' which deals rather with the machinery of law-making or with a theory of public conduct than with the merits of any given legislation; and where the main purpose of the writer is party propaganda. . . ."[6] Again, Joseph Blotner gives a somewhat similar, though more controlled, definition: "Here a political novel is taken to mean a book which directly describes, interprets or analyzes political phenomena. Our prime material is the politician at work: legislating, campaigning, mending political fences, building his career."[7] Clearly, both these definitions fall short when we consider politics in their larger sociological, sexual and metaphysical aspects. However, Irving Howe, a noted James critic, is nearer the mark when he writes, "By a political novel I mean a novel in which political ideas play a dominant role, or in which the political milieu is the dominant setting."[8] This definition is appropriately elaborated thus: "At its best, the political novel generates such intense heat that the ideas it appropriates are melted into its movement and fused with the emotions of its characters."[9] What Howe seems to be saying is that ideas *qua* ideas, even when aired in the context of the story, do not make a novel political till they are interiorized and converted into the stuff of felt, warm, human reality. In other words, as an aesthetic artifact, the political novel deals not with ideas but with the energy and poetry behind them, with their spiritual potential. To me, a political novel means an aesthetic product of the political imagination, and the political imagination is an imagination that seeks to confront, assault, subdue and order the existing socio-political reality in behalf of a political vision or a complex of political values. It remains to be seen how far the Jamesian specimens succeed in turning ideas into affects and ideologies into poetries of the spirit and the imagination, on the one hand, or into subversive sirens, on the other.

It appears to me an important fact that with the exception of *Covering End*, all James's putatively political novels were written almost at one "go," so to speak. This brief burst of political "sentiment," at least at the time of their composition, has something to do with his aroused interest in two things: the naturalistic form and the deeper, larger sociology of the novel. However, this aesthetic symbiosis of these two French influences—Zola and Balzac—as usual is subsumed in the enveloping Jamesian poetics in such a manner as to make it subservient to the novelist's imagination of fusion. Both the form and the sociology are stretched to accommodate clashing visions and ambiguities.

It is, again, a matter of further interest that all these three novels owed their impulse to specific books that James happened to read at that time. While *The Bostonians* is inspired at once by Hawthorne's *The Blithedale Romance* and Daudet's *L'Evangéliste*, *The Princess Casamassima* and *The Tragic Muse* lean considerably on Turgenev's *Virgin Soil* and Mrs. Humphry Ward's *Miss Bretherton*, respectively. That the Jamesian imagination, like the Shakespearean or the Keatsian, is in fullest play often when it is ignited by a collateral source or a cognate imagination is a matter for separate discussion, but the coincidence here may well serve to reveal James's intentions and attitudes. The literary climate seemed to have spurred him into the writing of these novels. In the case of *The Princess Casamassima,* there are other weighty reasons also, not the least significant being the presence of all manner of political exiles and anarchists in London and the wide coverage of their activities in the daily press.

Notwithstanding all these facts and inferences, the impression remains that James was drawn to the political theme not out of any deep compulsion or conviction but out of the imperatives of a voracious, promiscuous and grasping imagination. It was characteristic of such an imagination to appropriate ideas and subdue them to its own purposes and requirements. In short, instead of allowing the ideas to consort with the imagination, he let his imagination prey upon ideas. In this context, one is inevitably reminded of T. S. Eliot's well-known statement about the fineness of James's mind, which no "idea could violate." Clearly, this tribute is so misleading in certain ways as to suggest the very opposite of what it portends. If the ability to resist not merely the *imperialism* but also the *imperium* of ideas is considered a great virtue, then surely Eliot did not do justice to the novelist. Indeed, one may even go on to question the health and culture of a mind that surrenders its sovereignty not even to an idea that it manifestly accepts and adores. Such a clinical and cold detachment, if possible at all, is a sign of the arteriosclerosis of the mind. It only affirms moral frigidity and unearned intellectual hauteur. But happily, as we know, such is not the case where James is concerned. He had, in fact, an enormous appetite for ideas despite his own pronouncements to the contrary, but he had also, as I have said earlier, a unique talent for domesticating them—which is something quite different from the interpretation usually put on Eliot's pronouncement.

It is time, then, we turned to the novels and some other books that apparently reveal political content and culture and convictions in a somewhat less disguised manner, though the well-known Jamesian ironies and "indirections" are bound to undercut whatever formulations we are finally able to adduce or establish. Obviously, there is little of special concern to us in James before the publication of *The Bostonians.* In one sense, nothing that a writer may produce, from a fairy tale to a crime thriller or an electronic utopia, is free of *"politics,"* or, to be more

accurate, of certain political attitudes and predilections. But since we are considering the question in a specific sense, *The Bostonians* will clearly be our first port of
call. Finally, as I hope to show, even this novel is basically not a product of the
political imagination as such, though its "sociology" arouses political questions
and debates.

Although *The Bostonians* was, as we know, kept out of the New York
Edition—a decision which James regretted in later life—it has been restored its
place in the Jamesian canon largely due to the belated attention it received at the
hands of such eminent critics as Trilling, Leavis and Howe, among others. If we
keep in mind the social vision and aesthetic of these critics, it becomes clear why
this novel and, of course, *The Princess Casamassima* and *The Tragic Muse*, which
had wrought such havoc on James's fortunes, suddenly assumed a central importance in the development of his *oeuvre*. Plainly, it was the discovery in James of a
deeper concern with the larger issues of life and society—something involving not
merely the fate of "the lords of life," but also the fate of evolving societies and
cultures and civilizations—than had been imagined. *The Bostonians,* then, brings
us closer to certain socio-political insights in James, even though the involved
imagination is not profoundly radical in the sense of being qualitatively fresh or
innovative or prognosticative. Of course, in one sense, it is a modern novel, for it
deals with what feminist critics like Kate Millet and Mary Ellmann call "sexual
politics," but the real point to grasp is the subversive nature of ideas when they
harden into an ideology.[10] And here James might well have used any other
messianic idea—religious, as in Daudet's novel, or tribal or racial—to dramatize
the fundamental cruelty of public ideas when they distort the very structure of
private sensibilities. *The Bostonians* may, then, be described as a political novel
manqué.

There is also another side of the public issue that in modern times has
assumed grim and pervasive proportions. And that aspect is the interlock of sex
and power. There is in this bind an integral, inner, almost intuitive relationship
between two of man's most powerful and destructive drives. The Freudian and the
Adlerian positions are not really mutually exclusive. Sex as power and power as an
extension of sex appear to be deeply intertwined. In *The Bostonians,* the problem
has yet another dimension, for the lesbianism of Olive Chancellor is not simply a
question of baulked or blocked sexuality; it is as much a question of the will to
power, the will to order the universe in response to a driving idea. She is indeed
possessed by the twin demons that ravage her own sensibility and nearly destroy
the happiness of those involved with her. The sin of manipulation—a cardinal sin
in Jamesian ethics which, incidentally, L.C. Knights emphasizes above all in his
consideration of James's politics—is, as we know, a recurring theme for the
novelist, but in the case of Olive the moral offense is complicated by deep sexual
politics that are at once private and public. There is even a certain kind of "wild
justice" in her approach to counter "the assault of reality," to recall a Jamesian

phrase from another context, and, undoubtedly, in the tragedy of her wasted life James sees "the expense of spirit," though I think there is also a muted feeling for this daughter of the Puritans. She has "a rich moral consciousness," in James's own words, but there is also a fatal tendency in her to turn that fine instrument into an engine of oppression against both self and society. This kind of moral imperialism, which seeks to colonize other minds through all manner of "blinds" and "feints" and rationalizations, in the end cracks up under the weight of its own contradictions. The archetypal Antigone aspect emphasized by Cargill in particular is, of course, there in a subdued manner, for Olive's urge for "martyrdom" is unmistakable. However, it may be noted that this is a quality that inheres in several of James's heroines from Euphemia de Mauves and Isabel Archer to Milly Theale and beyond. The purity of passion we witness in Sophocles' heroine, or even in Jean Anouilh's existential interpretation of Antigone's character, is, however, of a different order and pitch. The complex of idealism, thwarted sexuality and death-wish has altogether a higher charge, and the tragic magnificence of the spectacle is not to be seen in James. Still, we see in Olive some evidence of the larger vision at work.

It remains now to see how far James views the question of female suffrage as a radical political movement that is potentially disruptive of the evolved social fabric in America. The Jamesian reference to "the decline of the sentiment of sex" is to be understood in that context. That the movement has been caricatured and its grotesque excesses ridiculed, however, seems to hide the equally important inference regarding the basic truth of its raison d'être. For it is unthinkable that James should go against the whole drift of his own sentiment in regard to women in general. All through his fiction there is a clear celebration of "the female principle," and the young woman, in particular, carries even a vision of salvation, if not of transcendence. For him the suffragettes become suspect only when they become "angry bellows" full of hot wind and abrasive rhetoric, thereby forfeiting their inborn felicities of grace and sweetness. So James is not finally protesting the rationale of the movement as much as the distortions that it effects when its metaphysic gets the better of human emotions. The decline of "the sentiment of sex" that Basil Ransom equates with "the passing out" of "the masculine tone" is not really a one-sided affair. The hysteria of the roused American female is also seen as the obverse of the sexual and economic aggrandizement of the American male. The matter may also be viewed in another manner. Verena Tarrant, to my mind, is treated by James as a counterpoint in the sense that she represents the strong lurking urge in man that Irving Howe calls "pastoral."[11] That is to say, she does not only provide the ground for the control of both her body and soul by two competing forces, but she is also, more importantly, a symbol of femininity in its restorative, invigorating and sweetening aspects.

A word about Basil Ransom—quite frequently this Southern "gentleman" has been taken by critics to be James's alter-ego. Of course, the qualities of classicism and order and the settled serenities of culture that as a member of the leisurely, aristocratic class he seems to represent are dear to James, but the aesthetic of ironies that the novelist structures so strenuously and consistently in this book will be a gratuitous exercise if Ransom is to remain whole and inviolate. True, it is Olive Chancellor who gets the rough edge of the Jamesian irony, but the whole complex of ironies is so judiciously worked out as to suggest a fair and proper distribution on the whole. Ransom is spared the heavier strokes, though James seems increasingly in the end to turn the hose in his direction. His conservatism is perhaps a smaller menace to happiness than the psychotic radicalism of Olive, but its potential for mischief is clearly hinted in that parting irony delivered as a coup de grâce. For the celebrated sentence that brings this novel of competing and laminated ironies to its close is a masterly summation of the case. Verena, like Isabel Archer, may yet live to see through the facade of a culture based on eroded pieties and pure aestheticism. Even the ironies of names—*Olive* Chancellor and Basil *Ransom*—may not be lost upon us if we keep our ears attuned to the music of gathering ironies in the book.

The next novel, *The Princess Casamassima,* came hot on the heels of *The Bostonians,* and it is altogether a greater enterprise of the imagination, now roused to a new pitch of understanding. Both in technique and style, it moves away from the scenic looseness and the hard, dry, polished prose of its predecessor to the saturated intensity of "the commanding centre," and a warm, pulsating prose. Even its naturalism has a different aspect, for "the environment of things," as opposed to "the environment of ideas" that Oscar Cargill notices in the later novel, now has richer specificities and, of course, more poetry.[12] Trilling's well-known observation about "the social texture" of the new novel and its "grainy" and "knotted" character is apposite, even when Trilling fails to realize fully the tragedy of "the liberal imagination."

To begin with, some Jamesians wonder how the novelist came at all to be involved in a subject of which he knew little and which he liked less. Critics are generally puzzled over the apparent absences and blanks and leaks in the gathering apparatus, and the revealed depths and spreads in the achieved book. Clearly the fabulist somehow managed to generate in the heat of composition a sort of dialectic that enabled him to balance observation with intuition, sympathy with empathy, rumour with surmise. For James's notes and letters of the period and, of course, the later preface, even as they support the idea of his general awareness of the operative radicals and revolutionaries in London, gleaned from the newspapers and similar sources, preclude any real brush with both radical thought and radical personality. The fictive exercise, then, in *The Princess Casamassima* is wholly in consonance with the typical Jamesian practice wherein minimal facts ultimately yield to their embedded energy and larger poetry, and the imagination starts hitting off its own bat, as it were. Even small scraps of experience picked up like floating pieces of paper from a pavement were potent enough to launch his avid imagination. As he affirms in the preface, albeit in his typically indirect manner, though he had no direct peep into or knowledge of the sinister and seething world of the anarchists, he trusted his "grasping imagination" to obtain full nourishment from the wandering airs and fumes enveloping the great Babylonian city of London. In short, what James's method suggested or stipulated was an *imaginative,* not an *imaginary,* absorption of reality.

Take the typology of the radicals and the revolutionaries, who seem to cut across the distinctions of birth, class and station. With an unerring instinct James has seized upon the fact that in regard to political attitudes the dream-world of the concerned psyche is as important as the idea of its class mores and moorings. Thus, it is not surprising to see Old Pinnie in the role of a psychic conservative who nourishes dreams of high patrician life for her poor, deprived ward and who will hear no word against the very powers that had ironically created such an abominable situation. It is a fine delineation of petit-bourgeois sensibility steeped in archaic sentiment, and James does full justice to its inner imperatives. Similarly, Mr. Vetch, her neighbor, for all his republican ardor and the diatribes against the British philistia, is, at bottom, an uneasy liberal when it comes to the clinch. The Poupins, on the other hand, though "in a state of chronic spiritual inflammation," are yet seen as imbued with radical idealism that is unquestionably authentic. Again, Paul Muniment (about whom there is not, oddly enough, a word in the preface), who has been taken by some critics as symbolizing the archetypal labour intellectual on the upswing to pelf and power—a potential renegade—is, to my mind, the portrait of a sincere radical whose momentary confusions and aberrations are part of the search for meaning and authenticity in a world of endless solicitations and enticements. Even in Lady Aurora, whom the Princess views as "a saint . . . as good in her way as Saint Assisi," the sentiment for the poor and the downtrodden runs deep in a spiritual manner despite the limitations of her situation. As for that wasted packet of energies, Rosy Muniment, whose working-class origin is at variance with her deep distrust of radical politics, we may see another variant of political type—the suffering spectator, excluded from the drama of life, and swinging to one extreme or another out of obscure psychological compulsions.[13] And wisely, I think, James kept his most "mystical" revolutionary—Hoffendahl—as a felt, menacing presence in the wings, not only because he knew next to nothing of such "underground" messiahs, but also because the indirect pressure of his personality is far more suggestive than any real scene the novelist could have managed to paint. Later he was to use this device in the case of Mrs. Newsome of *The Ambassadors* in a more subtle manner. And when, finally, we come to the chief protagonists of the story, Hyacinth Robinson and Christina Light, we cannot but marvel at the tireless insight of James into their confused but passionately real and poetic politics. Particularly, in the case of the "little bookbinder"—a Keatsian figure of opulent dreams and spiritual hungers subsuming a vibrant aesthetic sensibility—the novelist has dramatized the eternal misery and tragedy of the artistic temperament in collision with the forces of reality and history.[14] Indeed, James has even shown in him the dynamics of the high dream of politics in which passions share the nature of the sacred and the eternal, though these moments do not, and perhaps cannot, crystallize into a *political beatitude,* given the circumstances of his life. Thus, despite these fleeting epiphanies, he remains largely a figure of cosmic "fun"—a person blown about by the forces of jealousy and aroused dreams, a person whose politics stem not from ideas but from passions. He is a psychic revolutionary, a spiritual outlaw whose desire "to connect" with the high world beyond has something of a "mystic" force. Lionel Trilling's view that his death is truly a sacrifice, "an act of heroism,"[15] is, I think, misplaced.

Hyacinth Robinson's is, in fact, a triple tragedy—of blood, of circumstance, of temperament—and James has fused wonderfully the dramatic conflicts inherent in the situation into an aesthetic whole. The naturalism of the novel, as in Zola, partakes of the political at the thematic level, and though the "Dickensian" scenes of London life may be enjoyed for their sheer fun and vitality and heartiness—something rare in a novelist given to the moral and metaphysical ambiguities of patrician life—James has taken care to integrate these scenes into the ideational structure of the story. Their political potential lies in the dialectic of the binary class forces set up in the book. Even that gay flower of the London streets, Millicent Henning, who delights us with that energy Keats found in "a quarrel in the streets" is, nevertheless, a figure of political iconography in the larger sense of the word. She symbolizes the joyful and regenerative powers of "the lower orders" as against the self-destructive, attenuated and depleted energies and banality of the ingrown elites. Her appetite for beer and buns and bonbons, then, falls into a pattern that probably transcends the idea of cheery vulgarity so dreaded by the finical James otherwise. In herself this "shameless Philistine" administers only to the senses, but the larger meaning of her presence may not be overlooked.

But the real passional center of the story belongs in the dialectic of reversed loyalties. While Christina Light's "desertion" of her class is at one level a "play," a "game" that enables her spirit to disport itself in full freedom, a kind of "picnicking"—a "political" blow struck at the masked hypocrisies and cruelties of the patrician society she has sold her body to—at another level it seems to show, in a somewhat limited manner, the creation of a moral consciousness in a "light" vessel when it has had a brush with the metaphysic of history. No doubt she acts as a femme fatale in a narrower sense when she leads the poor bookbinder up the garden path and keeps rousing his imagination through measured draughts of "high life" to a pitch of tragic passion, but I do not think James's operative irony covers the Princess in any constitutive manner. Her recoil from the boredom of brilliance, her spiritual nausea and her "world weariness" have a psychological validity. Her "recall," as the novelist affirms in the preface, too, was to be a

psychological affair, her plunge into "th destructive element" to be the requirement of a sensibility in need of rejuvenation through a direct contact with the
forces of the breathing, heaving life of the streets. To be sure, James seemed to
have initially intended her to be a dilettante of anarchist politics, but somehow the
impression of her genuine involvement in the fate of the poor and the dispossessed
lurks, and the Jamesian ambiguity, as usual, abides. Indeed, one crucially revealing image—that of the "dove" with "folded wings"—in relation to her suggests a
Milly Theale kind of "transcendence" in the end. Such a thing, of course, does not
happen, but it does show the obscure stirrings inside the Jamesian imagination. As
for Hyacinth, the tragic bind permits him little room for redemptive exertions. He
has pledged his heart and soul, nay his very life, to the cause that his liberated
imagination now finds impossible to accept or endorse. He has pawned away his
freedom and his future only to discover that he has given hostages to an ideal in
whose virtue he has no faith. Of course, James has purposely stacked all the cards
in favor of Hyacinth's spiritual apostasy. He is seduced by the glittering world of
romance and money and mansion even as his sire's blood begins to fume in his
bones. The conflict has a Shakespearean range, though the act of suicide, inevitable in terms of the dramatized imperatives, still gives off a hollow thud. It is an
absurd death, a wanton cease, but not inauthentic for that reason. Here we find a
sensitive and lacerated psyche drawn to the uttermost reaches of existence and
poised hopelessly on the edge of a precipice, experiencing something like a feeling
of metaphysical vertigo. "After such knowledge," what life? Self-slaughter becomes a philosophical necessity even as it remains in the domain of the absurd.

How are we, then, to view James's own politics as embodied in this book? It
is clear that despite his ability to fully dramatize the opposed points of view, his
sympathies get refracted through certain images and passages of prose in the
crucial moments of the story, not to speak of the general drift of events engineered
by the fabulist in him. For instance, Hyacinth's impassioned plea in behalf of "the
monuments and treasures of art, the great palaces and properties, the conquests of
learning and taste . . . based if you will upon all the despotisms, the cruelties, the
exclusions, the monopolies and the rapacities of the past," to quote one example,
is almost in the same vein as the famous passage in James's *Hawthorne* on the
glory and beauty of the European institutions vis-à-vis the meagreness and provincialism of American life. James is essentially a poet of civilization in a restricted
sense, and in the end he cannot transcend the limits of aesthetic sensibility.[16] At
any rate, he is unable to realize that even "dark," revolutionary movements can
end up, through the logic of circumstances and the energies of society, as
"legitimate orthodoxies."[17]

But I have yet another view to offer. If Roderick Hudson is James at the outset
of his artistic career, Hyacinth Robinson may well be his alter-ego in mid-life.
James's own artistic parentage was peculiarly mixed up—the Anglo-American
regard for light, air and moral beauty vexed at times by cloudy idealism, and the

Gallic regard for form, style and elegance vexed by energy and passion—and all through his fiction we see this conflict dramatized in one form or another. More importantly, given Leon Edel's idea that Roderick Hudson is the passional, explosive, Freudian side of the novelist, we may see Hyacinth Robinson, with equal force, as the hidden, unappeased, radical side of James. If Hyacinth represents the tragedy of a rich but trapped sensibility that can find no scope for appeasement in a class society until it joins the ranks of the rich, James shows a somewhat similar restiveness of the mind and the imagination till he attains a European haven for his American spirit. Perhaps much of the poetry generated in *The Princess Casamassima* is secretly linked to James's Freudian fevers.

The Tragic Muse, as several critics have affirmed, is primarily and preeminently a long Jamesian dissertation on the value, validity and virtue of art—a subject that crops up in various disguises in his fiction from the beginning. Of course, in the extended sense of the word that Jamesian usage subsumes as of necessity, the artist *in* life and the artist *of* life are not qualitatively different from the artist per se. Either way, the concern here is with that archetypal sensibility that shrinks before vast "glares" and loudnesses, before theatricalities and histrionics, and seeks inevitably a "style" of being and belonging on its own terms. In short, in its search for a personal equation within a world of endless decoys and detours, of overtures and solicitations, such a sensibility hoards up its inner reserves and is often resentful of a needless expenditure of nervous energy. No wonder that in order to dramatize his dissertation—*The Tragic Muse* remains, for all James's brilliance and artifice, a brittle book—the novelist appropriately takes up the metaphor of politics and the metaphor of theater in a conjunctive manner. Gabriel Nash, whose sterile Paterism comes in for some acute comments, is still enough of a Jamesian surrogate to frame the issue in his aphoristic manner. When Lady Agnes, who shares with Julia Darrow a vision of politics on the grand and heroic scale, asks him, "Pray, should you think it better for a gentleman to be an actor?", he replies, "Better than being a politician? Ah, comedian for comedian, isn't the actor more honest?"[18] The point really to note is that for James the business of politics as such is compulsively fraught with falsenesses and subversions, with ersatz urges and satisfactions. It amounts simply to "the humbug of the hustings."[19] It did not occur to him, of course, that metaphysically or existentially speaking life is, as Pirandello affirms, compulsively theatrical, and that no man born can escape that fate. The artist, too, in that sense, is continually wearing and inventing masks and in the end *becomes the mask* in order to get away from the world of hustlers and "money-changers," as W. B. Yeats sought to do. So, in the awesome scenario of life that the Great Impressario has improvised, we are bound, hand and foot, to enact a theatre of emotions and actions. Politics *qua* politics would, then, appear the very essence and aim of human activity. But, as I have said above, such larger formulations do not form part of the Jamesian metaphor here. There is some glimmer of the problem in the development of Miriam's character as a pure piece of theatre, as a person becoming a complete *persona,* but it does not somehow connect with the problematics of the novel in the larger political sense.

And this brings me to the point that *The Tragic Muse,* unlike *The Princess Casamassima,* shows little of that sense of social history in relation to politics that Martha Banta rightly senses in that book. The framework here is not only much narrower in terms of its spread, its reach and range, but it is also ideationally and spiritually more restrictive. In one sense, even in *The Princess Casamassima* James could have offered, as, indeed, Daudet does in *L'Evangéliste,* the imperium of religion rather than the imperium of politics as the decoying and deceiving siren, but that he did not do so argues, I think, for a certain kind of integral interest in the maelstrom of ideas and ideologies sweeping across the floor of the book. In *The Tragic Muse,* on the other hand, except for the political metaphor as an *integer,* there is no real involvement in the fate of man, society and civilization. The politics here remain the politics of idiom and expression largely. James's "theatrical case" and his "political case" are only fused in a fictive trope, and seem not to interpenetrate fully in a balanced way. I am inclined to endorse Leon Edel's view that the very title of the novel heavily underscores the "theatrical case," that "this is sign enough that James found it more compelling than his 'political case,'"[20] and that James's knowledge of politics was "factitious," on the whole. Basically, the book remains a *Künstlerroman.*

Again, the title *Covering End* reveals in more than one way James's intentions in this neglected *nouvelle.* It is, in fact, the only major tale in the Jamesian corpus to receive the full name of a cherished countryhouse, for though the house in *The Spoils of Poynton* is important, it is the mystique of objets d'art that informs the spirit of that beautiful, tightly organized book. James's passion for these abodes of elegance and ease is well known, and these "noble" mansions with their green acres and arbours keep turning up religiously in his fiction till the end. But what is really remarkable and, I think, quite revealing is their central importance in two of his politically oriented books, *The Princess Casamassima* and *Covering End.* For Medley Hall, where the titular heroine of the novel lives, is used quite plainly as an archetypal metaphor in relation to the little bookbinder's spiritual hungers. Indeed, it emerges as an *agent provocateur* to salvage the inner structure of his being. *Covering End* is, of course, thematically more symbolic, though in the end its role as a redeemer of patriarchal pieties and graces is only another side of the same coin.

And this leads us to that emblematic character whose very name, again, gives her away, so to speak. For Mrs. Gracedew is not only an object of romantic interest in the tale; she is also the agent of Captain Yule's "illumination," "recovery" and "salvation." It is, indeed, ironical that a beautiful windbag should bring a "passionate, pledged Radical" down in a matter of minutes or that, through her *grace* and honey *dew,* a political prodigal should suddenly begin to discover virtues in a house that had contracted "hereditary gout or organic rheumatism" over the course of "centuries."[21] If James himself intended any irony in this American conquest of the very fortress of British Conservatism for Conservatism itself, it somehow remains unrealized. At any rate, it is clear enough that the young and vivacious widow is another Jamesian alter-ego. Her evangelical argument is in harmony with the drift of Jamesian thought and imagery in general. "What do politics amount to," she asks, "compared with religions? Politics and programmes come and go, but a duty like this abides. . . . This is the temple—don't profane it! . . . You have got it in trust, you see. . . . "[22] That James here betrays a lamentable lack of understanding in regard to the nature of radical politics, which share with religion the mystique of power and the kinetics of conversion, is clear enough. What is even more callow is the half-formed idea of considering unearned wealth and property as "trust" for the benefit of the generations to come. This apologia in behalf of the tainted millions, which James was to question penetratingly in *The Ivory Tower,* is more or less the Gandhian idea of the rich and the privileged acting as trustees for the poor and the deprived. One ruefully recalls Napoleon's plea before the bewildered sheep in George Orwell's *Animal Farm* that the pigs eat apples and drink milk not for *their* own sake but for the sake of those they have to defend and protect! The need to preserve things of beauty and art as man's inalienable heritage is certainly not linked integrally to the concept of ancestral houses and fortunes, though James seems to think it so, as did W. B. Yeats and other later apologists. *Covering End* seems only to "cover" the philosophy of "ends"!

James's politics, as they emerge from his nonfictional writings—letters, autobiographies, travelogues, critiques, etc.—will of course yield direct insights into the workings of the novelist's mind, though they are not, and need not be, in complete accord with the politics in the achieved novels and tales. In one sense, it may even be safer to rely on the truth of the imagination as it dredges up one's desires and impulses and in the heat of composition sees, and often finds, a balanced statement. Such mutual accommodations are a necessary aspect of the process of fabulation. Still, the given views, actions and reactions of a writer in the daily business and traffic of life will have to be considered if an integrated and meaningful perspective is to be achieved. I can at best isolate a few significant statements and attitudes purporting to be political, or tending toward politics. These, I suggest, have to be taken as part of the continuing argument.

To take up *English Hours* (1905) and *The American Scene* (1907) first, it may be helpful to view these books as extensions of James's "public" life. As the eager and experienced eye takes in the pageantry and drama of places, persons and peoples, James's imagination of reporting warms up to the pitch and beauty and essence of things. Here, too, the facts often are just winked at before the coercive imagination takes over the proceedings and begins to go behind and over and beyond. For in James no fact is of any import till its ambience has been fully realized. The pieces that comprise *English Hours* were written between 1872 and 1890, and they may fairly be taken as the novelist's responses to the country of the imagination that England was for him in a deep spiritual manner. The period, as it happens, coincides with James's earlier phases up to the publication of *The Tragic Muse,* a period significant in terms of the ambit of this chapter.

Broadly speaking, *English Hours* is an ode to Conservatism from the start, though in James Conservatism is more a feeling and a sentiment than a pondered philosophy of politics. Here is a typical passage of the period from the piece on Chester. "Conservatism," says the novelist, "has all the charm, and leaves dissent and democracy and other vulgar variations nothing but their bald logic. Conservatism has the cathedrals, the colleges, the castles, the gardens, the traditions, the associations, the fine names, the better manners, the poetry. . . . "[23] It is a sentiment that is to occur repeatedly in James along with its alliterative imagery. The youthful James, "a sympathetic stranger" from America, nurses "the historic sentiment" and voices a concern for "the imperial element" that appears to him to be on the decline.[24] We may not, however, confuse James's "historic sentiment" with the idea of historic consciousness, for he is at this moment more concerned with the pageantry and panoply of history than with the movement of classes, societal relationships and such matters. At any rate, he is not involved in the romance of ideas.

The American Scene, though removed in time and space, is in a manner an extension of the Jamesian quest for cultural refinement and continuities. Irving Howe's comment that, "for all its brave recognitions of change," it is "a conservative book"[25] with its "elegiac" tone is a fair estimate, though what he says of James's sensibility "formed in the light of Emerson and the shadow of Lincoln"[26] is strangely at variance with certain pronounced views of the novelist in this book. True, James's suppressed Americanism is on the upswing in his later writings, but the political component of that upsurge remains removed from the Jeffersonian mainsprings. Even that elegant prose style is essentially an aspect of his elitist world-view. Its rhetoric at times betrays a mode of nostalgia, retreat and alienation. However, to be more specific, James's bias against the blacks and the Jews comes out clearly when one examines the imagery of monkeys and squirrels and ants in relation to his ethnic variations, his positive parenthetical observations notwithstanding. A group of "tatterdemalion darkies" lounging about the railway station of Washington reminds him of "some beast that had sprung from the jungle."[27] It is a familiar Freudian image in James, and one is appalled at the failing of the Jamesian imagination, considering the ethical and humanistic vision of the final phase. If there is one significant exception to Clifton Fadiman's view that James's "insight was so tireless that it was bound to comprehend his own prejudices," it is here. Diatribes against the vulgar and mindless capitalist class in America, or against the hustling new "aristocracy," do not amount to anything more than a show of distaste. There is never a question of examining the underlying socio-political structure and its built-in inequities and hidden terrors. As he admits in the preface to *The Reverberator,* he did not understand the American tycoon, "no fibre" of his imagination "responding to his mystery."[28] In some of his letters spanning a period of nearly fifty years, James is candid enough to admit that he does not quite understand the issue of "national destinies" and that he has lived "wholly out of the inner circle of political life."[29] Such statements can only authenticate the belief that his politics were never central in the making up of his *Weltanschauung* and that they, in sum, amounted to an "intelligent report" of some of the things around. He never felt or experienced the full force of pure political ideas.

There is in the vast Jamesian work one strange book-review published in the *Nation* of January 14, 1875. The book in question is *The Communistic Societies of the United States from Personal Visit and Observation* by Charles Nordhoff. There is nothing much in the review as such. A couple of views, however, tossed off somewhat lightly, do show James's inability to grasp the nature of Communism. He does not seem to like the "life of such organized and theorized aridity" characteristic of the splinter communistic communities and settlements, though in the concluding sentence he observes, "Mr. Nordhoff's volume . . . seems to establish fairly that, under conditions and with strictly rational hopes, *Communism in America* may be a paying experiment"[30] (italics mine). This will show how little he really cared to understand one of the dominant political ideologies coming up in Europe and seeking a foothold in America.

James's attitudes towards some of the crucial political issues of his times also need to be mentioned in passing, though even in such cases he seldom felt emotionally involved except in the case of the First World War. On the subjects of the British Empire and the Crown, his views were roughly the views of a Victorian worthy tending toward the mystique of Imperialism. He seems to have swallowed the idea of "the metaphysical magnificence" of the empire and to have seldom had a thought for those nations and races wantonly subjected to slavery and exploitation.[31] So far as the question of monarchy is concerned, he went to the extent of withdrawing a gift from a nephew who had written against that institution. However, in his own way, he decried "the fetish worship of the Queen," as Leon Edel puts it.[32] Again, he was unhappy with his niece Peggy for her anti-British stance in the Boer War, though in his own turn he viewed with distaste the jingoistic poems of Kipling. And to quote Leon Edel again, James found Bourget's "aristocratic and monarchial ideas intolerable."[33] Another strange eruption in his thought from time to time is the Napoleonic aspect—a phenomenon that surfaced, strangely enough, even on his deathbed. Reportedly, he seemed to resemble the French monarch as he lay in repose after his death! Whether this is to be treated as a hidden worship of power in the Adlerian sense or as an obscure groping for legitimacy and place in "communities of honor," arising out of a sense of "shame" is difficult to tell.[34] But in the story called "Owen

Wingrave," where James seems to support pacifism, Napoleon is viewed as an unmitigated "monster" by the protagonist. So, what is one to make of these strange contradictions in his attitudes? And one could multiply the cases—*l'affaire* Dreyfus, the Parnell episode, the John Brown phenomenon—to realize that James's deep-seated conservatism could assume many a fantastic form and that his sense of justice could show in some cases of political victimization whereas it went quietly to sleep in others.[35]

Finally, before I try to sum up the emerging argument of the essay, it is important that we take a fleeting look at the Jamesian imagery and also at the dynamics of the prose style in relation to the question of politics. As we know, both imagery and style as such have a *constitutive* base and rationale in a work of art, and as Leo Spitzer and so many other linguistic and stylistic critics argue, they are integrally and intuitively related to the writer's *Weltanschauung*. When, therefore, an author happens to be as compulsively and continually metaphorical as James is, the clues to the energies animating his art and vision may well be located in the paradigm of images, among other things. Or, as Alexander Holder-Barrell argues, James's images, particularly metaphors, are "an essential part of his expression of eternal values."[36]

In his pioneering study *The Caught Image*, Robert Gale has listed and examined, among other reiterative and obsessive images, certain splinter images that express James's overt as well as covert political attitudes. For instance, the imagery relating to the French Revolution "clearly sympathizes with the doomed aristocrats of an earlier era."[37] An odd image involving Adam Verver—that of "an old morocco case stamped in ineffaceable gilt with the arms of a deposed dynasty"—is viewed by Gale as "an unconscious fear in James of the deposing of Capitalism."[38] However, it is to the opulent imagery of wealth—gold, pearl, diamond, mansion and marble—that we must turn for his "mystic" rapport with the material objects of the world. The Indian sage Aurobindo Ghose once referred to matter as "the spirit's willing bride." For James, however, the mystique of money, on which a latter-day Jamesian, Scott Fitzgerald, dwells so lovingly in *The Great Gatsby,* is cultivated with a view to appeasing the imagination and liberating it from the gross and the mundane. It is, in the final analysis, a false aesthetics, but its validity up to a point may not be denied. In short, the incidence of the imagery of precious metal and stone and heirloom, etc., suggests strongly the value James attached to the aristocratic ideals of patrician purity, refinement and tradition.

The question of James's style, which I have examined in some detail earlier, again supports the idea that his ambassadorial prose, which matures like a period wine over the years as an act of accretion and cultivation, is, nevertheless, "high" from the start.[39] There is in its rhetorical structure a certain kind of settled ease and urbanity and elegance that would authenticate the presence of a patrician imagination. When, for instance, we compare this style to Mark Twain's, we cannot but instantly see the opposed energies animating their muses. Twain's slang and "raffish" idiom and colloquialisms violently upset feudal values and celebrate unashamedly the gusto and swing of common life. James's "spoken" style of the later period, on the other hand, is formalized, and it suggests altogether different strategies and different aims. Its oral quality is partly functional, necessitated by the method of dictation, and partly rhetorical. Additionally, the use of "U-slang"—the sexual and intellectual idiom of the upper classes—remains chiefly a device of dialogue, though in its own way it does suggest their fecklessness, emotional aridity and spiritual erosion. Here the language, removed from the heat and din and dust of the street and the pub, tends to become autotelic and circular, turning viciously on its own limited axis. The late "mandarin" style has distressed many critics and readers because of its preciosity and fastidiousness—qualities we associate with disintegrating aristocracies. Of course, the affiliations of the late style, both in language and architectonics, with Mannerist painters like Pontormo, Parmigianino and El Greco, would also make us conscious of the strange spiritual hungers in James towards the end and could hint at the unconscious radical impulses in him. For the tortured and twisted figures in their canvases reveal stylistically a society structured on suffocating elitist attitudes. Even the burgeoning of the baroque, regarded by some critics as an aspect of James's "mysticism," is more likely to turn out as an aspect of the half-conscious revolt against the grasping money-values of the new American bourgeoisie.

And now briefly to the tentative formulations and conclusions. The drift of this essay should indicate clearly: (*a*) that James's interest in politics as a ruling philosophy of life and society was negligible; (*b*) that though he had a "sentiment" for history, he had no great sense of its metaphysics; (*c*) that his knowledge of politics and political parties as such was not that of an insider; (*d*) that notwithstanding these limitations, he had the ability, on the whole, to penetrate the adversary idea and to empathize; (*e*) that his understanding of the "psychology" of politics and of its typology was not as naive as is commonly believed; (*f*) that, on the whole, he shared the prejudices and visions of his class even when he laid bare its uglinesses and brutalities; (*g*) that though he was *weltoffen* enough to at least respond insightfully to the undercurrents and crosscurrents of contemporary politics, his foraging, eager and alert imagination, which may be described as ontological and cognitive in the Shakespearean sense, failed eventually to organize disparate political urges and aspects into a viable gestalt of politics; (*h*) that his suppressed radical and democratic impulses break through the facade of his highly wrought fiction despite his elitist world-view; and (*i*) that, finally, as in the case of W. B. Yeats's poems, in James we can at best rely on the truth of each achieved novel or tale on its own terms, and that there is no finality about his political views outside of a professed general feeling for what Howe has styled as "a comely Conservatism."

In an essay on George Santayana, Paul Conkin talks about this "perennial bachelor" settled in Europe and imbibing its essences. And Conkin sums up the case for this "model conservative" thus:

He rejoiced in custom, whatever its form. He could never tolerate the revolutionary urge to overturn entrenched institutions. He loved elegance in a monarchy, in a church, in the traditional luxuries of a leisured or priestly class. He never resented privilege. . . . Orthodoxy, any orthodoxy, had unexpected harmonies and was beautiful; heresy, any heresy, displayed a vacant iconoclasm . . . and thus was ugly and fundamentally disloyal. . . . He became a historian of the human spirit and a connoisseur of its varied poetry.[40]

For *George Santayana* read *Henry James* and you have a fairly revealing close-up, except that whereas the American philosopher voiced a wholly consistent conservative philosophy in terms of Hobbes's gloomy view of human nature and Burke's idea of "organic society," the American novelist, equally resentful of the new "barbarians" on the American scene, showed here and there a subversive, radical streak.

15

The Writer as Critic

Henry James's position as a critic and theorist of fiction is by now so well established as to need no elaborate defense of that impressive body of collateral criticism and critical marginalia which subsumes all that goes under the rubric of Jamesian aesthetic. Ever since the James revival which synchronized with the rise of the New Criticism in America around the early 1940s, there has been a steady and sustained interest in the novelist's critical muses, as much for the purposes of lighting up his own astonishing productions as for the uncoding of the mystery of fabulation in general. As a result, a fairly insightful commentary in the form of articles and essays, studies and doctoral dissertations, has accumulated over the years,[1] and James the critic is no longer a fanciful "affair" of a summer day or two, a decoy that has inveigled an indulgent imagination into his backyard, so to speak. Something in the pith and grain of James's criticism suggests certain settled serenities of statement even in the midst of so much extravagance and opulence, so much quiddity and queerness. And though the contours of his aesthetic there are well defined, certain doubts in regard to its health and exercise have continued to tease both reader and critic *into* thought. Indeed, it is remarkable how even his critical *amusettes* and wayside utterances have been milked to show some figure in the carpet, when perhaps it was only the kind of "beast" John Marcher had to contend with in the end! Often, such stray pieces exhumed from the American magazines of yesteryear tend to support one thesis or another till we run into some counterargument elsewhere in the Master's canon to restore the balance. All this happened because it was difficult for the researcher and the scholar to have the entire critical corpus of the Master ready to hand. And this is precisely what the two American Library volumes *Henry James: Literary Criticism* (1984),[2] comprising 2,892 pages of text, notes and index, have now achieved, thanks to the visionary eye and industry of Leon Edel, and to the love and labour of his collaborator, Mark Wilson. With these two definitive volumes, which carry over three hundred pieces for the first time in book form, it has become possible to close with the Master in a more meaningful and authentic manner. Such, then, is the raison d'être of this exercise, where the aim is to present an overarching view of

James's views and theories as a critic, and of his method and manner and style as part of his aesthetic. A critique of his criticism involves, thus, a hunt for the buried essences, even as it involves a hunt for the underlying pattern, if any. And in this hunt sometimes a pigeon brought down with a shotgun is as important a clue to the rules of the game as a tiger brought down with a sports rifle, to use one of James's own favourite tropes.

However, before I try to gather all these fugitives into a schema, and show how James's criticism almost parallels his fiction in its operative energies and informing vision, and how it tends to follow the same laws of progression, and the same dialectic, it is important to define categories of *the creative writer as critic*. For it is within those categories that we have to settle the question of James's estate and value in the realm of criticism. When a novelist or a poet chooses to write criticism on a scale that compels attention, we are in the presence of an order of criticism that shows some radical new aspects and departures. It is this unique phenomenon that ought to be the starting point in a critique that deals with one of the finest critical imaginations, engaged at the same time in vast enterprises of fabulation.

The phenomenon of the creative writer as critic is almost as antique and as arcane in its notional purity as the phenomenon of artist *qua* artist itself. This, of course, is not the place to intuit or posit a theory of literary creation, which in any case is by now so much freighted with knowledge as to make any fresh effort an exercise in tautology. We may, at least, float a splinter formulation or two within that great stream in an effort to earn a tenuous or tentative purchase on the weight of gathered ideas, impressions and insights. Insofar as such a thing helps create a kind of "imaginative space" for us, it brings us closer, in a personal way, to the inner sanctum of art. There the mystery abides, and there we stop to marvel at the energies that go to make it, and to ponder the dialectic which authenticates its appeal. I shall not, therefore, pause to touch on that side of the problem, except where it directly impinges on the *donnée* of this critique. Which is perhaps another way of saying that when a creative writer turns into a critic also, the locus of such a swing needs to be viewed within the orbit of the governing perspective. And that perspective, I suggest, is related to the original impulse, the impulse of creativity. Essentially, then, a creative writer's criticism is an extension of his own art; it is his attempt to validate his practice on the one hand, and to secure a niche in the pantheon of letters, on the other. In most cases, it has a psychological basis also.

It should be clear at the outset that we are talking here about the *creative writer,* and not about the writer as such. There are writers of all kinds, from philosophers, historians and theoreticians to biographers, traveloguists and journalists, in continual labour and business, and some of them are even aesthetically as pleasing as the best among the poets and the playwrights and the novelists. This is because the common grid of language energises their thought, and words tend to assume an *affective* aspect in almost all kinds of writings except the purely mathematical or scientific. Fancy, conceit, wit, irony, metaphor, myth, symbol, whimsy, lyricism—these and nearly all other components of rhetoric are pressed into service to take the thought to its highest reaches in as felicitous an idiom as possible. However, the difference lies in the fact that such writers are, as a rule, not involved in the aesthetic of words, or, more importantly, in structuring a mock world of reality, whatever the quality of their prose style. The principle of organization in art, or in creative writing, is so different from the principle in noncreative writing as to leave little doubt about their separate rationales. Thus, when a historian or a philosopher or a sociologist or a psychologist permits himself the luxury of literary criticism in passing, as is the case with a Macaulay, a Marx, a Freud, we are in the presence of a phenomenon whose virtue, value and validity constitute a distinctive order of hermeneutic. Our business here limits us to the critical enterprise, sallies and forays of the writers who are artists at the same time, and whose criticism is a cognate exercise answerable to aesthetic imperatives. On another occasion one could even go on to talk of the *creative critic as writer*.

Ideally, all hermeneutic ought to lead us to certain universal insights and observations, whether the critic in question is a putative critic such as Aristotle, a poet like Keats, or a philosopher like Nietzsche, and at a certain irreducible level, a convergence is not only possible, but also ineluctable. However, as I have tried to maintain, there are orders and forms of hermeneutic which are precipitated by divers urges, and which, therefore, have a characteristic élan and flavour. A creative writer's criticism, as we all know, has often a kind of freshness and tartness and verve which we miss in the critic or in the critic *manqué*. He brings to bear upon it something of that *secondary imagination* which constitutes the health of his exercise. What we get, therefore, is a peep into the experience and the process of creation, which other types of critics are seldom privy to. I am not trying to suggest that it is a higher or a better kind of criticism. In fact, as it happens, it can be at times confused and misleading in a certain way. What I do suggest is its uniqueness and its splendour, whatever its miseries and insufficiencies otherwise.

To begin with, it is necessary to observe that when the question of the creative writer as critic crops up, we are basically considering it, or, at least, ought to consider it, in relation to those *major* writers who are *minor* critics, or for whom criticism is not a primary passion, or even a rival discipline. This would, in effect, mean that such writer-critics as Coleridge, Matthew Arnold and T. S. Eliot, to name three great poets who are also great critics and law-givers, should ideally be left out of our discussion, precisely because they are a *sui generis* case, and do not fully authenticate the idiosyncrasy or quiddity of our premise. Each one of them would have earned an honoured place in either of the two disciplines if he had elected to write in one alone. It is revealing, for instance, to note that no creative writer except T. S. Eliot figures in *20th Century Criticism: The Major Statements,* by William J. Handy and Max Westbrook. Such a "double" does not necessarily lead to a division of energies; on the contrary, it often helps create an inner, organic and stereoscopic view of art. Nonetheless, my point is that just as a minor writer best illustrates the temper or spirit of an age—a critical view that has been advanced in all seriousness—a great creative writer but a journeyman critic best defines the type of criticism we are considering here. He alone compels us to close with the subject, compels us to seek the link between creativity and criticism. Where the balance is so perfect as in the great poet-critics, there is no need to plumb the depths. What we are after is a kind of scent that leads us into the by-ways of criticism. We may leave the highway alone for the moment.

I trust the problem can be stated in another way also. Where a creative writer's image either blots out the image of the critic, as in the case of W. B. Yeats, of Wallace Stevens, or of Theodore Roethke, or overshadows it, as in the case of such novelists as Henry James, Virginia Woolf and D. H. Lawrence, and such poets and playwrights as Robert Frost, W. H. Auden and Arthur Miller, among others, we have before us the problem of "the creative writer as critic" in its truest terms. It is not merely, I think, a question of quantum and incidence and intentionality, though these things too have their relevance; the more important aspects are the nature of the talent involved, and the dynamics of the exercise. And there, I repeat, it's not an Eliot, but a Yeats or a Frost who queers the pitch of the question for us, as it were. We know, more or less, where Eliot belongs; we know his theories and views and judgements; and we consider them against the background of the critical heritage since Plato and Aristotle. We prescribe such critics in our courses because of their seminal importance. They have helped shape the Western critical sensibility. But when we come to, say, a Yeats, Frost or Stevens, we seldom seek to relate his critical efforts to the mainstream. We know this will not do. His very stance, style and idiom put him in a category apart. We are, in short, dealing with a critic whose surplus energies as a creative writer have spilled over, as it were. For him, criticism is a sort of by-blow, an offspring of a brief affair between a poem and a poem, or a novel and a novel. And since the exercise has the flavour of *fleurs du mal,* it naturally shows a coiled energy and a certain daring. This kind of criticism, in short, is not a spouse with whom the writer has to do daily business and duty, but a mistress who inveigles him into another territory. Hence its raffishness and its gnomic character, its extravagance and its exotic appeal. As I have said earlier, such a criticism shares the nature of poetry. "The Muses," says Yeats, "resemble women who creep out at night and give themselves to unknown sailors and return to talk of Chinese porcelain." As we may notice, this kind of critical comment on poetry has a sibylline charm, and could have come only from a practicing poet, fully immersed in the mysteries and rituals of his craft.

Having briefly stated the problem of the poet or the novelist as critic, it is now possible to view the Jamesian critical *oeuvre* at once as a thing of surplus energy and overflow, and as a collateral exercise, independent not in impulse, but in condition and circumstance. It is not the purpose of this critique to go extensively into the mysteries of James's art as such, or to show how at a given point in his progress as a novelist, his criticism served as a *surrogate* activity, or even as a regulatory, normative exercise to direct his fictive imagination. Still, it is helpful to posit such a premise, and proceed to the position that just as there are three acknowledged phases in the novelist's progress as an artist, there are three somewhat similar phases in the artist's progress as a critic. Whether we choose to call them by the familiar names of the early, the middle and the final (or Matthiessen's major) phase, or style them as periods of insightful apprenticeship, achieved craftsmanship and visionary formulations—the archetypal Shakespearian-Keatsian pattern—is immaterial so long as we keep in mind the point that in James's case, it is actually a march from complexity to complexity, though the pieces and reviews written at the start of his writing career, when he was barely twenty-two, show a complexity not of idiom and style, not even of thought and theme, but of intention and purpose, of manner and stance.

Leon Edel and Mark Wilson have, however, for good and sufficient, though unstated, reasons, broken up this mass of critical material (which includes theoretical essays, long commentaries on individual writers, and book-reviews of varying pitch and purpose on all manner of writings from fiction, poetry, drama and criticism to biography, memoirs, letters, travelogues, etc.) into such sections as "Essays on Literature," "American Writers," "English Writers," "French Writers," "Other European Writers," and "Prefaces to the New York Edition." And in this arrangement they have followed the alphabetical order and, within that order, the chronological calender, to present as complete and comprehensive a picture of the writer in question as we may hope for. And I do not see how such an arrangement can be improved upon if the aim is to show James's views on the writers of his day. For in this manner, each individual writer's progress can be monitored despite the inevitable gaps relating to his productions that somehow did not receive James's critical attention. In most cases, at any rate in the case of most major writers, whether American, English or European, there are long, authoritative critical essays, some written in the form of obituary appreciations (it appears as if the death of some loved or revered writer moved James to a new pitch of the metaphysic of criticism), and we have here in James's inimitable prose profiles of artists as men and women, and critiques of writers as artists or creators.

Since the aim of this critique is to present a somewhat unified picture of James, the practicing critic, I propose first to isolate some of the major Jamesian ideas on the nature and genius of the novel as they emerge in the course of nearly fifty years of reviewing and writing, and then to set down briefly some aspects and features of my argument. It is important, then, to proceed from the tentative and breezy formulations of the earlier years to the pondered and provocative statements of the final phase, whether the review or the critique or the essay in question relates to an American writer, or English, or French. National traits are simply matters of detail; they do not, as a rule, underpin James's vision of the novel, which develops as a consequence of his brush with some of the finest fictive and critical imaginations of his time. James's own imagination was seldom unilinear or monistic despite the impression to the contrary; if anything, it responded richly and avidly to the variety of fabulations, even as it struggled to appropriate ideas from disparate sources to form a cohesive theory of fiction. Broadly speaking, the Anglo-American novel as a product of *the moral imagination,* and the French novel as a product of *the aesthetic imagination,* served as examples to show that an ethic of aesthetics was as necessary as an aesthetic of ethics. It is within such parameters that the Jamesian imagination sought the meaning of art, and its raison d'être.

On the art of the novel, then, and on several related issues that inevitably crop up in relation to this art form, James has a sufficiently large commentary in the form of formal essays, direct pronouncements, imbedded comment, stray remarks, analogical observations, etc. It is a formidable body of informed opinion and impressions gathered in a slow maturing of the critical vision over a period of nearly half a century. Hardly any aspect of the magic and mystery of fabulation escapes James's imagination of engagement. But before I turn to some of those aspects which make him almost a seer of fiction and a scientist at the same time, it may be of interest to note his view of the critic's position and business in the realm of letters, and his "philosophy" of criticism as such.

In the course of his long industry, James had the occasion to comment on some of the major critics of his time, and the long essays on such critics as Matthew Arnold and the French Taine, Sainte-Beuve and Scherer, in particular, enable him to dwell on the dynamics of criticism, and offer views that, in certain ways, forestall the modern theories of the New Critics, linguistic and stylistic critics, on the one hand, and of the Geneva critics and the phenomenologists on the other. All these ramifications are naturally not part of this limited critique, though they do help establish his *modernity* in the field of criticism in the same way his novels and tales do in the realm of fiction.

In an important essay called "The Science of Criticism" (1891), James regards "the critical sense" as something "absolutely rare," and the critic as the artist's "brother" in vision and exercise, a person made absolute through the energies and economies of his own craft. As he puts it, "In literature criticism is the critic, just as art is the artist."[3] In his essay on Maupassant (1888) James again implies that just as a tale is "a direct impression of life"[4]—a view more fully and insightfully aired in "The Art of Fiction" (1884)—a really creative work of criticism is a direct impression of a poem, play or novel as it invades the responding imagination. In each case, the intervening temperament or sensibility or psyche brings the sum of impressions to a focus. And he quotes Maupassant's statement to the effect that "every theory is a generalised expression of tempera-ment asking itself questions."[5] And finally, in the article on M. Scherer as a critic, written as early as 1865, James insists upon the same virtues in a critic that he does in a novelist. It is "the moral sense" leading to the "spiritual force" that "animates, coordinates and harmonizes"[6] the mass of opinions and impressions, whether the "vessel" is one or the other. That is why his criticism and his fiction eventually form a continuing grid of moral energies.

The emerging Jamesian "theory" of the novel, as it begins to acquire critical weight, and assume the dimensions of a "philosophy" of fiction in his critical writings, may briefly be summed up as follows:

The novel, to James's way of thinking, had become through a process of natural development the freest form of fabulation, and it could, therefore, appropriate the multiple and complex aspects of the human reality in a manner no other genre could. There was literally nothing which it could not turn to account, and dramatize. In "The Future of the Novel" (1899), he had insisted upon the resilience and hospitality of the genre, for it had verily "the whole human consciousness" for its subject. Though James is keen to emphasize the value of the directness of impressions and the holiness of experience, he feels that beyond a point, the appropriating imagination turns into an imagination of proxy and indirection. The individual strains and the universal in human life then come together to form a cohesive paradigm of vision and values. What is more, one's interior life has an experiential richness and vitality of its own, and the mind, feeding like the birds of the air on invisible manna, goes back "homing" to the life of the senses—"the aesthetic life" of Kierkegaard.

Again, James views the novel as an organic entity answerable to the laws of its own nature and growth. The repeated use of the organicist metaphors of "germ" and "seed" etc., shows a settled awareness of the novel's economy in terms of its potential and fruition. James, it appears, saw at an early stage that the form was but the idea or substance made manifest, and that the technique was but a mode of discovery, and a way of organizing experience. It is thus he envisaged an organic link between vision and style. It may be noticed, then, that in all his aesthetic gropings and strivings, "the search for form" almost turns into a mystic quest, an unsleeping pursuit of the holy grail of fiction.

Above all, James is fascinated by the novel as a form of fabulation best suited to bring out the moral energies of man. In that running argument that broadly distinguishes the English Novel from the French in scores of reviews and articles, he keeps elaborating the point that the very genius and spirit and structure of the novel suggest a sustained and strenuous employment of the moral imagination. The moral imagination is an imagination of earned insights through a continual "dialogue with experience." And since the novel stipulates a web of human relationships, it cannot but generate a grammar of accommodations and adjustments, of discoveries and recoveries, in short, an ethic of action and deed. It becomes, in the process, an instrument of perception and judgement. In short, the novel's cognitive and epistemological aspects make it compulsively a moral document. And when the moral element assumes a lyrical quality as with a George Eliot, the novel emerges as a Shakespearean artifact in range and tone.

There is, to be sure, no hard-and-fast theory of the novel in James. His frequent use of a mixed critical lexicon based on analogies from painting, architecture, geometry, tapestry, music, etc., would testify to his unending quest. The things he looked for in the novel—dramatic intensities, moral energies and poetic expression—are not really a new charter, but such is the grandeur and sweep of his critical imagination that even the ordinary assumes an aspect of the extraordinary in James. The manner, so to speak, becomes the message.

Though what James looks for in a writer is finally much more than the energies of language, there is no doubt the question of style has for him an importance that simply tops everything else. This is because, for him, style is not only the signature of the writer's psyche, carrying the aroma of the personality in action, it is at once a mode of comprehending reality, and an aspect of reality. It has a cognitive function, and it is in this sense that style *becomes* insight, that it informs a writer's *Weltanschauung* in the end. All these ideas which are now a commonplace of stylistic criticism are naturally not aired with any kind of doctrinal belief or urgency in James's own comments on the style of the writers he takes up for consideration, though the underlying assumptions lead one inevitably in that direction. In the essay on Gabriele D'Annunzio, for instance, he observes that "there is no complete creation without style any more than there is complete music without sound,"[7] and he goes on to talk even of the "style of substance as well as of form."[8] My purpose here, however, is to confine the question to the "poetic" aspects of style insofar as poetry relates to the essence of things, and to the uniqueness of language. I trust a sampling of James's comments should suffice to settle the issue.

On Carlyle's style: James felt in Carlyle's writing an "avalanche movement," "as if a mass of earth and rock and vegetation had detached itself and come bouncing and bumping forward." It has "the quality of race and soil"[9] Clearly it is the turbulent Protestant and Scottish personality with its moral monism and the imagination of indignation which James wishes to highlight in relation to the rhetoric and style of Carlyle.

On Shakespeare: Referring to Shakespeare's style in his essay on *The Tempest,* James touches upon "the resources of such a style," which come from obscure but happy and secure "energies of every sort." Commenting upon "the lucid stillness of his style" in the final play after a stormy passage in life, he adds that the Bard of Avon "points for us as no one else the relation of style to meaning and of manner to motive."[10]

On Stevenson: James refers, among other things, to Stevenson's romance of words, "a kind of gallantry as if language were a pretty woman." Extending the metaphor (and that is how James gives a poetic form to his critical comment), he goes on to talk of the "absence" of women, otherwise, and adds wittily: "But Mr. Stevenson does not need, as we may say, a petticoat to inflame him: a happy collection of words will serve the purpose, or a singular image, or the bright eye of a passing conceit, and he will carry off a pretty paradox without as much as a scuffle."[11] The jauntiness of Stevenson's style is seen as his engagement with "the romance of boyhood"[12]—the sense of youth and the idea of play. And he sums up this singularity thus: "This special stock of association, most personal style, and most unteachable tricks fly away again to him like so many strayed birds to nest, each with the flutter in its beak of some scrap of document or legend, some fragment of picture or story, to be retouched, revarnished and reframed."[13] How true this is of James's own style!

On Alphonse Daudet: The French writer's light impressionistic style is something that is a feast for the eye and a music for the ear. Daudet, he says, "discovers everywhere the shimmer and the murmur of the poetic."[14] Commenting on the element of local colour and ambience in Daudet's rich, sensuous prose, he observes, "His style is impregnated with the southern sunshine and his talent, has the sweetness of a fruit that has grown in the warm, open air. . . ."[15] And yet James is also conscious of the nervous energies of this style: "The author's style has taken on bone and muscle, and become conscious of treasures of nervous agility."[16]

On Théophile Gautier: Gautier, observes James, loved words for their "aroma" and for their "colour"—"a bit of Keats gallicized."[17] For James, a writer's style had great attraction if the imagination could strike a new phrase or give an old one a new twist. This is Gautier's appeal, and James adds, "Half the charm of his writing is in the mere curl and flutter of his phrase."[18] However, James is careful enough to add that his enjoyment of Gautier's style did not prevent him from seeing him as "a very philistine of philistines"[19] where the higher moral consciousness is concerned. The "gaiety" of Gautier's style, then, is purely and simply a question of his Gallic temperament.

On George Sand: In Sand's style, as well, James finds that typical Gallic virtue of earthiness, warmth, and wildness which makes French prose, at its best, "an affair" with the language. "Her language had to the end an odour of the hawthorne and the wild honeysuckle. . . ."[20] Even as James laments the "want of moral taste" in her, he admires her art, for it is "open to all experience, all emotions, all convictions."[21] Comparing her style with Balzac's, he adds: "Madame Sand's novels have plenty of style but they have no form. Balzac's have not a shred of style, but they have a great deal of form."[22]

On Pierre Loti: Loti's vivid and striking descriptions of the sea hold James's imagination in awe, and yet he notes with regret that "the French imagination has none but a sensual conscience."[23]

Though all manner of beauties and felicities are found lurking in James's critical pieces, and some of his remarks on the popular women novelists of his day and on a variety of other writers constitute their own kind and order of criticism, it is only in the case of his favourite novelists (his criticism of contemporary poetry being both meagre and insignificant, on the whole) that his imagination rises to meet the critical challenge in full faith and force. The EML book on Hawthorne and the essay on him and the essays on George Eliot, Trollope, Stevenson, H. G. Wells, Daudet, Gautier, Loti, Balzac, Flaubert, Maupassant, George Sand and Turgenev, in particular, carry his most valuable and pondered criticism, which in certain ways would always remain something rare and refined, a collector's criticism, if you like. That is how he sums up Hawthorne's genius in the concluding paragraph of his book on Hawthorne: "He combined in a singular degree the spontaneity of the imagination with a haunting care for moral problems. Man's conscience was his theme."[24] Later he describes him as "an aesthetic solitary" whose "beautiful, light imagination is the wing that on the autumn evening just brushes the dusty window."[25] And who but James could have so penetratingly seen that George Eliot "succeeds better in drawing attitudes of feeling than in drawing movements of feeling"?[26] Even at the age of twenty-two when he set out to review books, James observed that Trollope was a master of "small effects,"[27] but that nothing in him "is infused." As for Balzac, James recognises the French passion for precision, completeness and symmetry in his work and "that huge, all-compressing, all-desiring, all-devouring love of reality."[28] But to reach this conclusion, he uses one of his favourite forms of criticism—comparative criticism. "When we approach Thackeray and George Eliot, George Sand and Turgenieff[29] it is into the conscience and the mind that we enter, and we think of the writers primarily as great consciences and great minds. When we approach Balzac we seem to enter into a great temperament—a prodigious nature. He strikes us half the time as an extraordinary physical phenomenon."[30] In a late essay, "The Lesson of Balzac" (1905), James shows how absorbed he was in the great globe of French life through tireless observation on the one hand, and through intuition and economy of art on the other. Though the spiritual life of Balzac's characters remains largely costumed, his mastery of the interlocking determinants and of the chemistry of social relationships and societal pressures makes him an unrivalled chronicler of the Gallic temperament and character. Again, in a handsome and high tribute to that "beautiful genius," Turgenev, James admires the marriage of realism and poetry in the work of the great Russian writer. He thus calls him "the novelist's novelist"[31]—a master spirit in worshipful labour and supremely alive to the moral rhythms of life.

The manner and the style of James's criticism, as I have hinted earlier, changes almost imperceptibly from phase to phase in the manner of his fiction. There is a continual shading off of colours and tints. While the earlier apprentice pieces have, at their best, a certain economy of line and shape, as in a pencil sketch, a crystalline purity and a water-colour impressionism characterise the criticism of the middle period. As we begin to view the heavy oils of the final phase, we realize that the earlier traits of economy and purity and lambency are not entirely lost; only they are now subsumed in the *chromatics* of his criticism. In short, James's criticism has been moving from the beauty and poetry of a Whistler to the intensity and visionary depth of a Rembrandt. While the earlier criticism is without cobwebs and codicils, on the whole, the later essays and critiques have a density of thought, imagery and style which constitute a kind of critical hieroglyphics. An effort of the imagination is needed to decipher the code, and to relate the ideas to their rhetorical resonance. In fact, the element of "muddlement" in his criticism has the same aesthetic sanction as it has in the novels of the final phase.

A part of the problem has recently been examined in insightful detail by William Veeder in "Image as Argument: Henry James and the Style of Criticism."[32] The critical method of the Master is seen in terms of the rhetorical energies of the developing style, and he shows how James uses images not as embellishment but as instrument, not as flourishes but as visionary vehicles. Or, to put it differently, the novelist develops "argument by image," as his muses seek to reach inwardly at the heart of the reality in a given book or writer. The mesh of images, changing and merging into patterns, thus indicate a suppleness of the responding imagination. What is more, the image is used in a dialectical manner, and both sides of the picture are sought to be comprehended through polarities. Such a double vision of things is hoisted gradually till *the drama of images* is completed. As Veeder sums it up beautifully, "Argument by image has become the argument of the image."[33]

To be sure, James's criticism also shows the same kind of weaknesses and limitations that his fiction does. A curious element of meretriciousness is perilously close to its riches and splendours, and an air of unreality seems to reduce certain pieces to a rhetorical exercise. There is in some of the earliest reviews even a patronising, presumptuous tone which is as exasperating in its own way as is the gratuitously involved nature of some of his later and larger essays. Also, there is a danger, here and there, of a volume under review disappearing altogether from the scene, leaving the reader with the critic's own whimsies and fancies. It is quite possible, particularly in some of the prefaces and in some later essays, that the reverberations we hear have a hollowness, or that in this piece or that, what we find at the end of a long ordeal of critical engagement is not "a jewel, but a vapour." But these are the hazards of James's criticism, and they are to be accepted as part of the Jamesian "effect." For when his critical imagination is in full cry, it goes ahunting with whip in hand, starting a whole school of hares and then running them to ground with an ease that leaves the reader gasping in awe and admiration. Even in the midst of all such detours and meanderings, so characteristic of the late style, there is a certain kind of intellectual tenacity and single-mindedness that is hard to come by in fiction criticism.

As in the animated and ambassadorial prose of the final phase, there is in his later criticism a tendency toward a very elaborate and complex type of imagery. Apart from a touch of intellectual colloquialism, there is a shift from the mechanical to the organicistic imagery. For instance, the earlier reviews and articles abound in the imagery of food, house, coin, carriage, etc., while the later essays are rich in the imagery of seed, blossom, fruit and tree, of germ, birth and growth. There are even "metaphysical" turns and twists and leaps quite in keeping with "the indirect vision" of the final years.

I have for obvious reasons, confined this critique to James's view of the novel and to his commentary on the novelists in question. There are, however, in this massive and magnificent compendium of criticism, variations on a variety of related subjects such as the energies of art and the life of the artist, the place of sex in literature, the theatre, the art form of the *nouvelle,* the epistolary art, the biographical art, the ethic of publishing and the reader's responsibility, the business and art of translation, women novelists and the dynamics of the popular romance, etc. Similarly, there are scores of comments on life, society, state and civilization that would constitute a revealing gloss on his own novels and tales. From the mystique of money and the romance of the ancestral houses and patrician families to the questions of marriage, politics, religion, culture, etc., there is little that does not hold our attention even when his opinions are tossed off in a casual comment, or aired elaborately in that characteristic mandarin style of the later years. In sum, it is only when his fiction and his criticism are read in tandem that we may truly realise the nature of the miracle called Henry James.

To sum up, it may be affirmed that James's genius has gone into his fiction and his talent into his reviews, critical essays, prefaces and so forth. In short, all that is greatest, strongest and most enduring is to be found in his creative writings, all that is collateral, redemptive and illustrative finds itself mirrored in his criticism. Each has its own unique charm and its own unique place in James's *oeuvre.* Together they make for an *order of writing* that has few parallels and fewer peers in the English language. Anyone who has savoured this criticism and lingered in those leafy and tangled arbours would come away with almost the same kind of awe, admiration and bewilderment as he would after a sojourn in the subtle and finely wrought novels and tales of intelligence. In fact, the *aesthetic* pleasure of James's criticism is not a small component of its appeal and effectiveness. The felicity of his "branched thoughts," to use a Keatsian phrase, is fetching.

Notes

Chapter 1

1. *The Opposing Self* (The Viking Press, New York, 1968 edition), p. 103.

2. Unlike Professor Wayne C. Booth who uses the word "rhetoric" in *The Rhetoric of Fiction* (The University of Chicago Press, Chicago & London, Phoenix edition, 1967) to mean all the linguistic, stylistic and *technical* devices used by a writer, I shall be employing it throughout this volume in its restricted sense; that is, in the sense of verbal energies and beauties.

3. This view evidently will be refuted by those who take humanism to mean simply a concern for Old World, classical pieties. Dorothea Krook goes on even to assert that James "might be counted as one of the greatest representatives of the modern Humanist tradition." (*The Ordeal of Consciousness in Henry James,* Cambridge University Press, paperback, 1967, p. ix). Again, William Troy in his essay, "The Altar of Henry James" (1943), pronounces him "one of our great humanists, the greatest perhaps because his humanism was grounded in such a rich tragic experience" (*The Question of Henry James,* edited by F. W. Dupee, Allan Wingate, London, 1947, p. 279). This is clearly a position I cannot accept. James's humanism was at best an extension of a fine vibrant sensibility.

4. *Politics and the Novel* (Meridian Books, New York, 1957), p. 23.

5. *The Portrait of a Lady* (The Modern Library, New York, 1951), p. 261.

6. *The Notebooks of Henry James,* edited by F. O. Matthiessen and Kenneth B. Murdock (Oxford University Press, New York, 1961), p. 133.

7. It will be noticed that James deals only with super-subtle psyches or intelligences and aristocratic natures on the one hand, with the hereditary rich on the other. The whole vast spectrum of life in between is simply a blank for him, one exception being *The Princess Casamassima*.

8. Quoted by S. Gorley Putt in *Henry James: A Reader's Guide* (Cornell University Press, Ithaca, 1967), p. 163.

9. *Stories of Writers and Artists* (New Directions, New York, paperback), p. 174.

10. Ibid., p. 272.

11. *The Short Stories of Henry James,* selected and edited by Clifton Fadiman (Random House, New York, 1945), p. 484.

12. David Kirby in a review of *The Crystal Cage: Adventures of the Imagination* by Daniel J. Schneider (The Regents Press of Kansas, Lawrence, 1978).

13. Quoted by Simon Nowell-Smith in *The Legend of the Master* (Constable, London, 1947), p. xvi.

14. H. G. Wells in *Boon*. See the relevant pages in *Henry James: The Critical Heritage*, edited by Roger Gard (Routledge & Kegan Paul, London, 1968), pp. 515–26.

15. Quoted by Simon Nowell-Smith in *The Legend of the Master*, p. xxi.

16. Edith Wharton in "The Man of Letters," *Henry James, Twentieth Century Views*, edited by Leon Edel (Prentice-Hall, Englewood Cliffs, N.J., 1963), p. 32.

17. *The Search for Form: Studies in the Structure of James's Fiction* (The University of North Carolina Press, Chapel Hill, 1967), p. 28.

18. Quoted by George H. Ford in *Double Measure: A Study of the Novels and Stories of D. H. Lawrence* (W. W. Norton & Company, New York, 1969), p. 22.

19. *The Tragic Muse* (Harper Torchbooks, New York, 1960), p. 321. Again, in the Preface to *The Golden Bowl*, James writes: "Among many matters thrown into relief by a refreshed acquaintance with 'The Golden Bowl' what perhaps most stands out for me is the still marked inveteracy of a certain *indirect and oblique view* of my presented action . . . " (italics mine).

Chapter 2

1. *The Conquest of London* (J. B. Lippincott Co., New York, 1962), p. 137.

2. In an article called "Henry James and the Dream of Fiction" (*The American Review*, Winter 1985, pp. 71–77) I have tried to evoke a picture of the Master at Lamb House in Rye in the context of "the masterful dream," etc.

3. *Stories of Writers and Artists*, "The Middle Years," p. 210.

4. Quoted by Leon Edel, epigraph, *The Middle Years* (J. B. Lippincott Co., New York, 1962).

5. Quoted by Leon Edel in "The Literary Convictions of Henry James " (*Modern Fiction Studies*, Henry James Special Number, Spring 1957), p. 6.

6. *Stories of Writers and Artists*, "The Death of the Lion," p. 222.

7. Ibid., p. 230.

8. *The Untried Years* (Rupert Hart-Davis, London, 1953), pp. 230–50.

9. *Henry James and the Jacobites* (Hill and Wang, New York, American Century Series, 1965), p. 95.

10. *Henry James: A Reader's Guide*, Introduction by Arthur Mizener, p. 7.

11. Conrad's obscure and confused impulses resulting from his alienation or expatriation, and Kafka's tortured relationship with his father could be regarded as psychological determinants, but I think in their work the epistemological and metaphysical aspects have clearly a more defined and independent basis.

12. See the details in the second volume of Henry James's autobiography, *Notes of a Son and Brother* (Criterion Books, New York, 1956), pp. 414–15.

13. *Literary History of the United States*, Robert E. Spiller and others (The Macmillan Company, New York, third edition, revised, 1966), p. 1040.

14. *The Selected Letters of Henry James*, edited by Leon Edel (Farrar, Straus & Cudahy, New York, 1956), p. 33.

15. Quoted by Leon Edel in *The Untried Years,* p. 330.

16. *The Complete Tales of Henry James,* Volume 12, edited and introduced by Leon Edel (Rupert Hart-Davis, London, 1964), p. 274.

17. *The Conquest of London,* p. 255.

18. Ibid., p. 255.

19. *The Expense of Vision* (Princeton University Press, Princeton, 1964), p. 41.

20. George Monterio, *Henry James and John Hay: The Record of a Friendship* (Brown University Press, Providence, 1965), p. 113. James's letters to John Hay are in the custody of the John Hay Library, Brown University.

21. Quoted by Leon Edel in *The Treacherous Years* (J.B. Lippincott Co., New York, 1969), pp. 64–5.

22. *Stories of Writers and Artists,* p. 253.

23. *Henry James and the Jacobites,* p. 167.

24. I emphasize this point, because for James all these values and virtues, though sincere enough in the context of the stories, have no universal connotations. The lower orders, so to speak, were almost entirely excluded from the ambit of his sympathies.

25. *The Art of the Novel: Critical Prefaces* with an introduction by R. P. Blackmur (Charles Scribner's Sons, New York, paperback, 1962), pp. 31–2.

26. Ibid., p. 18.

27. Daniel Mark Fogel, *Henry James and the Structure of the Romantic Imagination* (Louisiana State University Press, Baton Rouge, 1981), *passim.*

28. *Henry James: The Ibsen Years* (Vision Press, London, 1972), p. 15.

29. Ibid., p. 29.

30. *Henry James and Pragmatistic Thought* (University of North Carolina Press, Chapel Hill, 1974), pp. 73–86.

31. See *Hound & Horn,* Henry James Special Number, April-June 1934, "The School of Experience in the Early Novels."

Chapter 3

1. *James's Later Novels* (The William-Fredrick Press, New York, 1960), p. 14.

2. *Stories of Writers and Artists,* p. 78.

3. Henry James, *The Future of the Novel,* edited by Leon Edel (Vintage Books, New York, 1956), p. 5.

4. *Sex, Literature and Censorship,* edited by Harry T. Moore (Heinemann, London, 1955), "The Novel," p. 64.

5. *The Future of the Novel,* p. 30.

6. Ibid., p. 33.

7.   *The Art of the Novel,* p. 326.

8.   *The Future of the Novel,* p. 9.

9.   *The Art of the Novel,* p. 46.

10. *The Future of the Novel,* p. 9.

11. *The Sense of the Past* (Scribners, New York, 1945), p. 61.

12. *The Future of the Novel,* "The Art of Fiction," p. 20.

13. Ibid., pp. 19–20.

14. Ibid., pp. 12–13.

15. *The Art of the Novel,* pp. 64–65.

16. *The Future of the Novel,* "The Art of Fiction," pp. 15–16.

17. *Six American Novelists of the Nineteenth Century,* edited by Richard Foster (University of Minnesota Press, Minneapolis, 1968), p. 200.

18. *The Selected Letters of Henry James,* edited by Leon Edel, p. 171.

19. *The Future of the Novel,* p. 21.

20. *The Selected Letters of Henry James,* edited by Leon Edel, p. 107.

21. *The Art of the Novel,* p. 42.

22. *The Ordeal of Consciousness in Henry James,* p. 407.

23. *The Future of the Novel,* pp. 24–25.

24. Quoted by R. P. Blackmur in *The Lion and the Honeycomb* (Harcourt, Brace & Company, New York, 1935), p. 289.

25. *Sex, Literature and Censorship,* "The Novel," p. 66.

26. *The Future of the Novel,* "The Art of Fiction," p. 26.

27. Ibid., "The Future of the Novel," p. 39.

28. H. G. Wells, *Experiments in Autobiography* (London, 1934), p. 489.

29. *Henry James and H. G. Wells,* letters edited by Leon Edel and Gordon Ray (Hart-Davis, London, 1958), p. 264.

30. *The Future of the Novel,* "From 'The New Novel,'" p. 273.

31. Ibid., "The Lesson of Balzac," p. 104.

32. Quoted by J. A. Ward in *The Search for Form,* p. 3.

Chapter 4

1.   Henry James's phrase in "Greville Fane," *Stories of Writers and Artists,* p. 156.

2.   *Stories of Writers and Artists,* p. 68.

3.   For a comprehensive account of Paterism in relation to James's aesthetic and ethics, see Adeline R. Tintner's long essay entitled "Pater in *The Portrait of a Lady* and *The Golden Bowl,* Including

Some Unpublished Henry James Letters" (*The Henry James Review*, Winter 1982). It is Tintner's view that even as James absorbed the more valuable aspects of Paterism, he continued to battle against its sterile, passive and languid aspects. As she puts it felicitously, "James converted the *spectatorship* of art preached by Pater to the *doing* of art . . . " (p. 94).

4. *The Art of the Novel*, p. 326.

5. *Henry James, Twentieth Century Views*, "The Ambassadors," p. 72.

6. *The Notebooks of Henry James*, p. 165. James himself acknowledges the meagerness of some of his productions based on thin material, but given an elaborate treatment. In a letter to the Duchess of Sutherland in 1903, he says that in regard to his biography of Story, he has "served small beer with the effect of opening champagne." Quoted by Leon Edel in *The Master* (Hart-Davis, London, 1972), p. 166.

7. *The Art of the Novel*, p. 23.

8. *The Notebooks of Henry James*, p. 169.

9. *The Selected Letters of Henry James*, edited by Leon Edel, p. 33.

10. *The Art of the Novel*, p. 44.

11. *The Search for Form*, Preface, p. viii.

12. *The Art of the Novel*, p. 144.

13. *Rage for Order:* Essays in Criticism (The University of Chicago Press, Chicago, 1948), p. v.

14. Ibid., p. 159.

15. *The Art of the Novel*, p. 48.

16. See chapter 6 of *The Caught Image* by Robert L. Gale (The University of North Carolina Press, Chapel Hill, 1964 edition).

17. *The Ivory Tower*, New York Edition, pp. 148–9.

18. *The Art of the Novel*, Preface to *The Reverberator*,   p. 182.

19. *The Selected Letters of Henry James*, edited by Leon Edel, pp. 150–51.

20. *The Energies of Art* (Vintage Books, Random House, New York, 1962), p. 235.

21. *The Wings of the Dove* (A Signet Classic: The New American Library, New York, 1969), p. 497.

22. Henry James, *The Scenic Art* (Hill and Wang, Inc., New York, 1957), p. 3.

23. *The Art of the Novel*, p. 326.

24. *Henry James: Twentieth Century Views*, p. 39.

25. Quoted by Walter Isle in *Experiments in Form: Henry James's Novels, 1886–1901* (Harvard University Press, Cambridge, 1968), p. 45.

26. Ibid., p. 11.

27. Joseph Weisenfarth, *Henry James and the Dramatic Analogy* (Fordham University Press, New York, 1963), p. 39.

28. *The Art of the Novel*, p. 278.

29. Ibid., pp. 87–8.

30. *Henry James: Modern Judgements*, edited by Tony Tanner (Macmillan, New York, 1968), "Visual Art Devices and Parallels in James," p. 90.

31. For an extremely valuable discussion of the influence of the Impressionist painters etc., see Charles R. Anderson's book, *Person, Place, and Thing in Henry James's Novels* (Duke University Press, Durham, 1977). It is Anderson's view that the celebrated boat scene in *The Ambassadors* is really after Monet and not Renoir as is commonly supposed. He cites Claude Monet's *La Seine à Vétheuil*, painted in 1880, and presumably seen by James, as the source of the scene in the novel (pp. 273–74).

32. *Henry James: The Ibsen Years*, p. 121.

33. See R. P. Blackmur's well-known essay, "The Loose and Baggy Monsters of Henry James" in *The Lion and the Honeycomb*.

34. *The Complete Tales of Henry James*, Volume 12, edited by Leon Edel (Hart-Davis, London, 1964), p. 238.

35. *The Ivory Tower*, p. 124.

36. *To the Lighthouse* (Penguin, London, 1969), p. 194.

37. "Henry James" in *The Metamorphoses of the Circle* (Johns Hopkins Press, Baltimore, 1966), p. 317.

Chapter 5

1. Michael Egan offers the view that James's traumatic experience in the theatre, and the disaster of the *Guy Domville* episode made him turn to the theory of the central reflecting consciousness. This, to my mind, has a very limited relevance, for we know James started using this technique as early as *Roderick Hudson*. Still, it is possible to locate a Freudian base for the increased and complex treatment of this technique in his later novels. For instance, in his book, *Love and the Quest for Identity* (1980), Philip Sicker suggests apropos of "In the Cage" that the point of view technique was the outcome of James's own fear of self-entrapment. This Laingian view can be pursued up to a point.

2. Quoted by Richard Poirier in *The Comic Sense of Henry James* (Oxford University Press, New York, 1967), pp. 189–90.

3. *The Art of the Novel*, pp. 320–21.

4. This is one reason, among others, that may account for the spirit of the metafiction of today. The ideas of "game" and "play" and "cheerful deceit" are all part of the new aesthetic, and it is clear that the Jamesian aesthetic takes a nodding view of it in any case.

5. Krishna Baldev Vaid, *Technique in the Tales of Henry James* (Harvard University Press, Cambridge, 1964), p. 82.

6. *The Art of the Novel*, p. 16.

7. *The Search for Form*, p. 165.

8. *The Art of the Novel*, p. 37.

9. Ibid., p. 136.

10. *The Portrait of a Lady*, pp. 67–8.

11.   Ibid., p. 81.

12.   *The Art of the Novel,* p. 51.

13.   *Love and Death in the American Novel* (Dell Publishing Co., New York, paperback, revised edition, 1966), p. 344.

14.   For an exhaustive and perceptive account of the problem of "unreliable narrators," see Wayne C. Booth's book, *The Rhetoric of Fiction.* Some of Professor Booth's conclusions regarding particular narrators can be challenged, but the main thesis is incontrovertible.

15.   *The Art of the Novel,* pp. 63–4.

16.   Ibid., 142.

17.   Ibid., 142.

18.   Ibid., 143.

19.   Ibid., 146.

20.   *Henry James: The Major Phase* (Oxford University Press, Oxford, 1963), pp. 22–23.

21.   Sallie Sears, *The Negative Imagination: Form and Perspective in the Novels of Henry James* (Cornell University Press, Ithaca, N.Y., 1968), p. 21.

22.   *The Henry James Review,* Fall 1980, p. 38.

23.   *The Henry James Review,* Spring 1983, pp. 202–3.

24.   *The Art of the Novel,* Preface to *The Ambassadors,* p. 326.

25.   The Ambassadors: *Twentieth-Century Interpretations* (Prentice-Hall, Englewood Cliffs, N. J., 1969), p. 73.

26.   *The Art of the Novel,* Preface to *The Ambassadors,* p. 326.

27.   *The Rhetoric of Fiction,* p. 283.

28.   *The Madness of Art: A Study of Henry James* (University of Nebraska Press, Lincoln, 1962), p. 38.

29.   *The Search for Form,* p. 175.

30.   *The Art of the Novel,* Preface to *The Wings of the Dove,* p. 294.

31.   Ibid., p. 299.

32.   Ibid., p. 306.

33.   *The Art of the Novel,* Preface to *The Golden Bowl,* p. 330.

Chapter 6

1.   *The Art of the Novel,* Preface to *The Reverberator,* p. 186.

2.   Ibid., Preface to Volume XVIII in the New York Edition, p. 277.

3.   An appropriate tribute to Henry James inscribed on the tombstone of the novelist's grave in Cambridge, Massachusetts.

4.   *The Art of the Novel,* p. 195.

5. Ibid., Preface to Volume XIV in the New York Edition, p. 201.

6. *The Life of Hawthorne,* included in the volume *The Scarlet Letter* by Nathaniel Hawthorne (Asia Publishing House, Bombay, 1964), pp. 29–30.

7. *Stories of Writers and Artists,* p. 21.

8. *The Art of the Novel,* Preface to Volume XIII in the New York Edition, p. 194.

9. *The Sense of the Past,* p. 59.

10. *The Selected Letters of Henry James,* edited by Leon Edel, pp. 22–23.

11. *The Complete Tales of Henry James,* edited by Leon Edel (Hart-Davis, London, 1962), "The Point of View," p. 512.

12. *The Expense of Vision,* p. viii.

13. *Henry James* (Henry Holt & Co., New York, 1916), p. 9.

14. *Henry James: Man and Author* (Macmillan, Toronto, 1927), p. 347.

15. *The Question of Henry James,* edited by F. W. Dupee, "Henry James in the World," p. 148.

16. *Henry James and John Hay,* p. 87.

17. Quoted by Van Wyck Brooks in *The Pilgrimage of Henry James* (Dutton & Co., New York, 1925), p. 160.

18. *The Art of the Novel,* Preface to Volume XIV in the New York Edition, p. 198.

19. *The Novels of Henry James* (Macmillan, New York, 1961), p. 47.

20. *Roderick Hudson* (Harper, New York, 1960), Introduction, Leon Edel, pp. xiv–xv.

21. One is reminded of Ignazio Silone's remark to the Italian Communist leader, Togliatti: "The final struggle will be between the communists and the ex-communists." See *The God That Failed,* edited by Richard Crossman (Bantam Books, New York, paperback, 1952), p. 114.

22. Marius Bewley, *The Complex Fate* (Chatto & Windus, London, 1952), p. 8.

23. Quoted by J. A. Ward in *The Imagination of Disaster,* p. 37.

24. *The Opposing Self,* "The Bostonians," p. 59.

25. Quoted by S. Gorley Putt in *Henry James: A Reader's Guide,* p. 108.

26. *The Reverberator* (Charles Scribner, New York Edition), p. 102.

27. Quoted by L. B. Holland in *The Expense of Vision,* p. 52.

28. Edith Wharton, *Madame De Treymes and Others* (Charles Scribner's Sons, New York, 1970), p. 174.

29. *Madame de Mauves* (Scribners, New York), p. 277.

30. Ibid., p. 331.

31. *The Art of the Novel,* p. 269.

32. Ibid., p. 267.

33. *The Europeans* (Penguin, London, 1967), p. 33.

34. Ibid., p. 9.

35. *The Search for Form*, p. 109.

36. *The Europeans*, p. 154.

37. Ibid., pp. 60–61.

38. *The Art of the Novel*, pp. 198–9.

39. "Perhaps all art," writes Marius Bewley in *The Complex Fate*, p. 79, "represents a conflict between appearance and reality, but American literature is inclined to register the shock with peculiar earnestness and simplicity."

40. *The Reign of Wonder* (Cambridge University Press, 1965), pp. 266–67 and *The Notebooks of Henry James*, p. 28.

41. See the published address by Leon Edel, New York University, March 13, 1967, p. 8.

42. *The Search for Form*, p. 80.

43. Quoted in *The Ambassadors: Twentieth Century Interpretations*, edited by Albert E. Stone, Jr. (Prentice-Hall, Englewood Cliffs, N.J. paperback, 1969), p. 4.

44. Despite James's caricature of the image of Britannia in Aunt Maud of *The Wings of the Dove* and a few other random references to the Empire's lapses, he celebrates the imperial mystique and ethos in his letters and writings. In fact, imperialism had an emotional or spiritual pull for him. He refers to the "metaphysical magnificence" of the British Empire. See *English Hours* by Henry James (Horizon Press, New York, 1968), pp. 164–65 and p. 171.

45. The death-bed Napoleonic fantasy of James, dictated to his secretary, Miss Bosanquet, would surely indicate deep and dark urges in the direction of imperialist glory, grandeur and power. See *Henry James at Home* by H. Montgomery Hyde (Methuen, London, 1969), pp. 277–78. In "Owen Wingrave," however, James refers to Napoleon as an unmitigated monster. Obviously, it was at the unconscious level that he nourished visions of the Napoleonic mystique.

46. Quoted by Oscar Cargill in *The Novels of Henry James*, p. 62.

47. Quoted by Leon Edel in *The Selected Letters of Henry James*, p. 241.

48. *The Complex Fate*, Introduction, p. xiii.

Chapter 7

1. *The Future of the Novel*, p. 82.

2. *Love and Death in the American Novel* (Dell Publishing Co., revised edition, paperback, 1966), p. 302.

3. Henry James, *The Wings of the Dove*, p. 95.

4. *The Portrait of a Lady*, p. 72.

5. Ibid., p. 73.

6. Ibid., pp. 74–75.

7. *The Art of the Novel*, Preface to Volume XIII in the New York Edition, p. 187.

8. *The Reverberator*, pp. 16–21.

9. Ibid., p. 206.

10. It is a curious thing that nearly all the major American heroines of James—Catherine Sloper, Francie Dosson, Isabel Archer, Milly Theale and Maggie Verver—do not have mothers when we meet them. Could their spiritual "independence" be viewed partly as an aspect of this fortuitous circumstance? Or, was it a thematic strategy that suited James's *donneés?*

11. *The Art of the Novel,* pp. 188–90.

12. *The Wings of the Dove,* p. 88.

13. *The Art of the Novel,* p. 189.

14. *The Opposing Self,* "William Dean Howells and the Roots of Modern Taste," p. 103.

15. "The Muses," says Yeats, "resemble women who creep out at night and give themselves to unknown sailors and return to talk of Chinese porcelain." Quoted by Arthur Mizener in *The Permanence of Yeats,* edited by James Hall & M. Steinmann (Collier Books, New York, paperback, 1961), p. 141.

16. *The Opposing Self,* p. 90.

17. *The Art of the Novel,* p. 49.

18. *The American Henry James* (Rutgers University Press, New Brunswick, 1957), p. 126.

19. *The Art of the Novel,* Preface to *The Wings of the Dove,* p. 292.

20. *The Complete Tales of Henry James,* Volume 16, p. 293.

21. See Arnold Kettle's essay on *The Portrait of a Lady* in *An Introduction to the English Novel,* Volume II (Hutchinson University Library, 1974).

22. *The Art of the Novel,* Preface to *The Wings of the Dove,* p. 290.

23. *The Portrait of a Lady,* p. 23.

24. Ibid., p. 228.

25. Ibid., p. 235.

26. See "The Fearful Self: Henry James's *The Portrait of a Lady*" in *Henry James: Modern Judgements,* edited by Tony Tanner (Macmillan, New York, 1968), pp. 143–59.

27. See "Intimacy and Spectatorship in *The Portrait of a Lady*" (*The Henry James Review,* Fall 1981, pp. 25–35). O'Connor's reading suggests a very dubious Isabel, showing "the tragic configuration of convent, convention, and convenience" (p. 30).

28. *The Wings of the Dove,* p. 84.

29. *The Golden Bowl* (Dell, New York, paperback, 1964), p. 511.

30. Ibid., p. 417.

31. *The Portrait of a Lady,* p. 417.

32. Ibid., p. 261.

33. *Henry James: Twentieth Century Views,* edited by Leon Edel, p. 134.

34. *The Golden Bowl,* Introduction by R. P. Blackmur, p. 9.

35. *The Golden Bowl,* p. 134.

36. Ibid., 343.

37. Ibid., 345.

38. For a detailed discussion of the problem, see Reinhold Niebuhr's *Beyond Tragedy* (Charles Scribner's Sons, New York, paperback, 1965), pp. 155–69.

39. The term has been coined to denote a middle-aged person's "fixation" on a "nymphet." See Nabokov's *Lolita*. Manfred Mackenzie tends to see this eruption in James's old age as "a second go," and "the child debutante" as an agent of "a spiritual transformation" (*Communities of Honor and Love*, p. 137).

40. *The Portrait of a Lady*, p. 162.

41. *Henry's James: The Major Phase*, p. 179.

42. *The Ordeal of Consciousness in Henry James*, p. 368.

43. Ibid., 369.

44. *The Wings of the Dove*, p. 340.

45. *Madame De Mauves and Other Tales*, p. 229.

Chapter 8

1. The point is argued with considerable force by Lionel Trilling in his essay on Howells in *The Opposing Self*, pp. 98–103.

2. *The Golden Bowl*, p. 259.

3. Quoted by Harry Levin in *The Power of Blackness* (Vintage Books, New York, paperback, 1958), p. 26.

4. Ibid., p. 21.

5. *Washington Square* (The Modern Library, New York, 1950), pp. 195–96.

6. *The Portrait of a Lady*, Vol. II, p. 196.

7. Ibid.

8. Ibid., pp. 326–27.

9. Ibid., p. 379.

10. *Henry James*, edited by Tony Tanner, "Henry James at the Grecian Urn," p. 171.

11. *The Bostonians* with Introduction by Irving Howe (The Modern Library, New York, 1956), p. 79.

12. Ibid., p. viii.

13. Ibid., p. xxii.

14. Ibid., p. 464.

15. *The Golden Bowl*, p. 425.

16. I cannot agree with F. O. Matthiessen that the well-known statement of James establishes his repudiation of the Calvinistic past. "James," he writes, "did not have the heritage of American Puritanism." See *Henry James: The Major Phase*, p. 26.

17. James mentions the incident in his "Autobiography," and Leon Edel links up this malignant figure with the figure of his brother, William, who, in Henry's words, "was always round the corner and out of sight." See *The Untried Years* (Rupert Hart-Davis, London, 1953), p. 77.

18. For a fuller account of Henry James Senior's "Vastation," see Leon Edel's *The Untried Years*.

19. *The Energies of Art*, p. 243.

20. *Henry James*, edited by Leon Edel, p. 117.

21. Quoted by J. A. Ward in *The Imagination of Disaster*, p. 5.

22. Ibid., p. 5.

23. *The Other House* (Macmillan, London, 1897), p. 307.

24. Ibid., p. 329.

25. *The Imagination of Disaster*, p. 168.

26. No wonder we have two opposed views of James's imagination. See J. A. Ward's *The Imagination of Disaster* and Sallie Sear's *The Negative Imagination* on the one hand, and *The Imagination of Loving* by Naomi Lebowitz on the other.

27. *Henry James* by F. W. Dupee (Methuen, New York, 1951), p. 125.

28. See chapter 3 entitled "The Patter of Satan's Feet" in Eli Siegel's *James and the Children* (Definition Press, New York, 1968).

29. The question of evil in children remains a complex, difficult and controversial issue in James. Michael Egan traces this late interest to Ibsen's influence. In a long three-part essay in *The Henry James Review* (Winter and Spring 1980), Donal O'Gorman sees the Devil as the chief protagonist of *The Turn of the Screw*. With an overlay of Christian theology, the essay seeks to prove the idea that Satan seeks and finds lodgement in innocent and unwary souls. In O'Gorman's view, it's the governess who's the "possessed" soul. Referring to the Salem witch trials, he says, "Thus the history of witchcraft poignantly raises the question of the capacity for positive malice in the hearts of the young, whether as witches or as false accusers" (p. 233).

30. *The Imagination of Disaster*, p. 10.

31. *The Question of Henry James*, p. xiii.

32. *The Ivory Tower*, p. 141.

33. Ibid., p. 309.

Chapter 9

1. The idea of the defeat of rhetoric has lately received a great deal of critical attention, as in George Steiner's *Extraterritorial* (1968), James Guetti's *The Limits of Metaphor* (1967) and Tony Tanner's *City of Words* (1971). It may further be observed that this idea is also thematically used by several novelists, such as Melville in *Moby Dick*, Faulkner in *Absalom, Absalom!*, and Barth in *The Sot-Weed Factor*. In James this idea is vaguely at work in some later tales and novels, including the teasing fable, *The Sacred Fount*.

2. *Creative Sceptics* (Scientific Book Agency, Calcutta, 1969), p. 316.

3. *The Art of the Novel*, "Preface to *Roderick Hudson*," p. 16.

4. Since writing this chapter, I have come across an interesting article, "*Roderick Hudson:* The Role of the Observer" by Peter J. Conn in *Nineteenth Century Fiction,* June 1971. Although I cannot fully accept the thesis of Mr. Conn that Rowland Mallet is a "dehumanised observer" who "cannot be regarded as a personified surrrogate for James's moral imagination" (p. 66), the presence of a dark, secret wish that threatens to subvert his Calvinistic conscience may not be ruled out. This will perhaps explain the willed vision of Roderick's death in the Alps which Rowland Mallet has.

5. *Roderick Hudson,* p. 253.

6. *The Comic Sense of Henry James,* p. 31.

7. *Washington Square,* p. 81.

8. Henry James's phrase in *The Other House,* p. 5.

9. *The Art of the Novel,* p. 222.

10. *The Fields of Light* (Oxford University Press, New York, paperback, 1962), p. 52.

11. *The Compass of Irony* (Methuen, London, 1969), p. 14.

12. Ibid., p. 218.

13. Ibid., p. 219.

14. For a most perceptive and exhaustive study of the problem, see *The Rhetoric of Fiction,* chapter 12.

15. *The Short Novels of Henry James* by Charles G. Hoffman (Bookman Associates, New York, 1957), p. 67.

16. *The Expense of Vision,* pp. 99–100.

17. Ibid., p. 103.

18. See James W. Gargano in "James's *The Sacred Fount:* The Phantasmagorical Made Evidential" (*The Henry James Review,* Fall 1981, pp. 49–60). Gargano's argument has an element of freshness in any case. He seems to regard the Narrator of *The Sacred Fount* as a person deeply sincere at heart, and full of humane considerations. Thus all the "false" clues he provides and the false "scents" are there for a good cause, which is to save May Server, caught in a predicament. So, our Narrator now becomes a "visionary" liar!

19. *The Sacred Fount* (Macmillan, London, 1923), p. 242.

20. *Jamesian Ambiguity and The Sacred Fount* (Cornell University Press, Ithaca, 1965), p. 18.

21. This is not the only slighting reference to "The Turn of the Screw" in James's writings. See *The Letters of Henry James* (Macmillan, 1920), Volume I. While in his letter of October 21st, 1898 to Dr. Louis Waldstein, James calls it a "bogey-tale" (p. 112), in his letter of Dec. 9th, 1898 to H. G. Wells, and in his letter of Dec. 19th to F. W. H. Myers, he styles it as "a pot-boiler" (p. 306) and "a shameless pot-boiler" (p. 308) respectively. The idea of Heilman and others that James was "meditating upon an aesthetic problem" (*Technique in the Tales of Henry James* by K. B. Vaid, p. 273), to my mind, does not quite explain why James has repeatedly dismissed the tale as something essentially contrived and superficial.

22. See Edmund Wilson's well-known and controversial essay, "The Ambiguity of Henry James" in *Psychoanalysis and American Fiction,* edited by Irving Malin (Dutton & Co., New York, 1965, paperback), p. 185.

23. *Henry James: The Treacherous Years* (Lippincott Company, New York, 1969), p. 206.

24. *The Ironic Dimension to the Fiction of Henry James* (Duquesne University Press, Pittsburgh, Pa. 1965), p. 41.

25. Quoted by K. B. Vaid in *Technique in the Tales of Henry James,* p. 122.

26. Ibid., p. 96.

27. *The Art of the Novel,* p. 147.

28. Ibid., pp. 141–2.

29. James's repeated use of the "sweet-shop" metaphor may strike a Freudian critic as another example of his own suppressed sexual hungers.

30. *The Novels of Henry James,* p. 258.

31. *The Negative Imagination,* p. 24.

32. *Henry James and the Jacobites,* p. 150.

33. *The Great Tradition* (Penguin, London, 1966), p. 173.

34. See *"What Maisie Knew:* The Evolution of Moral Sense" in *Henry James,* edited by Tony Tanner, p. 225.

35. *The Reign of Wonder,* pp. 279–84.

36. Ibid., p. 288.

37. *Henry James: A Reader's Guide,* p. 250.

38. *What Maisie Knew* (Penguin, London, 1966), p. 183.

39. James criticism has lately been busy tarnishing even some of the palpably innocent characters with a view to establishing the pervasive nature of the Jamesian irony. Of course, James does leave a dark hint here or there in these stories to lead the critics on to fanciful conclusions. However, what is taken as an ironic twist or turn is perhaps no more than a trick of thought and style.

40. Quoted by U. C. Knoepflamacher in *The Ambassadors: Twentieth Century Interpretations,* p. 107.

41. Ibid., p. 116.

42. *The Wings of the Dove,* p. 262.

43. Ibid., Afterword by F. W. Dupee, p. 508.

44. See T. S. Eliot's essay on Henry James (1918) in *Literature in America,* edited by Philip Rahv (Meridian Books, New York, 1957), p. 222. Though Eliot is here talking of James the critic, I think, this is true of James the novelist as well.

45. *Henry James* by F. W. Dupee, p. 4.

46. *Creative Sceptics* by Margaret L. Wiley; see the chapter "Henry James, Incomplete Sceptic," pp. 248–75.

47. Ibid., "Introduction," p. 15.

48. *The Fields of Light,* p. 15.

49. *The Negative Imagination*, pp. 192–3.

50. *Creative Sceptics*, p. 273.

51. *The Rhetoric of Fiction*, p. 85.

Chapter 10

1. "Henry James" in *Six American Novelists of the Nineteenth Century*, edited by Richard Foster, p. 224.

2. Quoted by F. O. Matthiessen in *Henry James: The Major Phase*, p. 4.

3. Ibid., p. 136.

4. Ibid., p. 145.

5. *The Question of Henry James*, edited by F. W. Dupee, p. viii.

6. "The Thematics of Interpretation: James's Artist Tales" (*The Henry James Review*, Winter 1984), p. 122.

7. *Stories of Writers and Artists*, pp. 29–30.

8. *Introduction to Roderick Hudson*, p. xiii.

9. *Roderick Hudson*, p. 152.

10. Ibid., p. 322.

11. *The Tragic Muse*, p. 261.

12. Quoted by Elizabeth Stevenson in *The Crooked Corridor* (Macmillan, New York, 1949), p. 128.

13. "The Lesson of the Master" in *Stories of Writers and Artists*, p. 140.

14. "James's *The Tragic Muse—Ave Atque Vale*" in *Henry James*, edited by Tony Tanner, p. 197.

15. *The Art of the Novel*, p. 79.

16. "The Lesson of the Master" in *Stories of Writers and Artists*, p. 106.

17. "The Madonna of the Future" in *Stories of Writers and Artists*, p. 26.

18. *"The Princess Casamassima"* in *The Liberal Imagination* (The Viking Press, New York, 1950), p. 80.

19. Quoted by Dorothea Krook in *The Ordeal of Consciousness in Henry James*, p. 409.

20. "The Author of Beltraffio" in *Stories of Writers and Artists*, p. 68.

21. See *Henry James: The Major Phase*, pp. 147–49.

22. *The Ordeal of Consciousness*, pp. 399–400.

23. In a perceptive book, *The Limits of Metaphor* (Cornell University Press, Ithaca, 1966), James Guetti, discussing Melville, Conrad and Faulkner, shows how the human language, incapable of rendering the full burden of experience, becomes ultimately a decoy and a trap. Beyond a point, it begins to sabotage the structure of thought and reality. The later James, I believe, could be profitably studied, particularly, the theme of incommunication, in the light of Dr. Guetti's insightful observations. *The Sacred Fount*, for instance, might well be studied as an extended enquiry into the instability of human language.

24. "The Lesson of Balzac" in *The Future of the Novel*, p. 114.

25. *The Art of the Novel*, Preface to *The Wings of the Dove*, p. 320.

26. *Henry James: A Reader's Guide*, p. 363.

27. *The Short Stories of Henry James*, selected and edited by Clifton Fadiman, p. 393.

28. Ibid., p. 405.

29. Ibid., pp. 415–16.

30. *Henry James* (Minerva Press, New York, 1969), pp. 50–51.

31. "The Middle Years" in *Stories of Writers and Artists*, p. 210.

32. *The Liberal Imagination*, p. 77.

33. *The Expense of Vision*, p. 123.

34. *The Creative Process* (New York, Thomas Yoseloff, 1958), p. 146.

35. Quoted by Helen Horne (Marburg, 1960), Harvard Ph.D. Thesis, p. 132.

36. *The Complete Tales of Henry James*, Volume 8, edited by Leon Edel (Rupert Hart-Davis, 1961), "Collaboration," p. 408.

37. Quoted by Naomi Lebowitz in *The Imagination of Loving* (Wayne State University Press, Detroit, 1965), p. 31.

38. *Henry James*, p. 87.

Chapter 11

1. *The Great Tradition*, p. 23.

2. *The English Novel From Dickens to Lawrence* (Oxford University Press, New York, 1970), pp. 13–14.

3. *The Moral Philosophy of William James*, edited by John K. Roth (Thomas Y. Crowell Company, New York, Apollo edition, 1969), p. 35.

4. *Henry James: Twentieth Century Views*, "The Man of Letters," p. 32.

5. *Henry James*, p. 93.

6. *Henry James: The Major Phase*, p. 26.

7. *Henry James: The Critical Heritage*, edited by Rogert Gard, p. 233.

8. *Henry James: Twentieth Century Views*, "An Appreciation," p. 15.

9. The excerpt is from my paper "The Moral Vision of Arthur Miller" included in *Indian Essays in American Literature*, edited by Sujit Mukherjee and D. V. K. Raghavacharyulu (Popular Prakashan, 1969), pp. 85–86.

10. *Henry James: Modern Judgements*, "Henry James: The Poetics of Empiricism," p. 56.

11. *The Ordeal of Consciousness in Henry James*, pp. 59–60.

12. *The Method of Henry James* (Albert Saifer, Philadelphia, 1954), p. lxxvi.

13. Ibid., pp. 131–2.

14. *The Moral Philosophy of William James,* p. 41.

15. *Washington Square,* pp. 149–50.

16. Ibid., p. 184.

17. *Confidence* (Grosset and Dunlap, New York, 1962), pp. 136–37.

18. *The Portrait of a Lady,* p. 319.

19. *The Ethics of Ambiguity* (The Citadel Press, New York, paperback, 1968), p. 73.

20. *Eros and Civilization* (Vintage Books, New York, paperback, 1962), p. 48.

21. *The Art of the Novel,* Preface to *The American,* p. 22.

22. *The Imagination of Loving,* p. 59.

23. *Communities of Honor and Love in Henry James* (Harvard University Press, Cambridge, 1976), p. 152.

24. Ibid.

25. *The Moral Philosophy of William James,* p. 179.

26. *The Ethics of Ambiguity,* pp. 15–16.

Chapter 12

1. Although no James critic can avoid dealing with "the question of style" in some form or other, I am referring here to the work of such critics as Vernon Lee, R. W. Short, Ian Watt and David Lodge, who have examined the word, sentence and paragraph structure of James's prose to bring out its peculiar kinetics or energies. It is again interesting to note that *The Ambassadors* remains a favourite book for the purposes of illustration.

2. *Theory of Literature,* "Style and Stylistics," (Penguin Books, London, 1963), p. 180.

3. See "Metaphor in the Plot of *The Ambassadors*" by William M. Gibson (*Henry James,* edited by Tony Tanner), *The Caught Image* by Robert L. Gale and *The Development of Imagery and Its Functional Significance in Henry James's Novels* by Alexander Holder-Barell (Franke Verlag, Bern, 1959).

4. Quoted in *The Problem of Style,* edited by J. V. Cunningham (Fawcett Publications, Greenwich, Conn., paperback, 1966), p. 16.

5. *The Problem of Style,* p. 27.

6. In an article, "Henry James and the 'Transcendent Adventure': The Search for the Self in the Introduction to *The Tempest*" (*The Henry James Review,* Winter 1982, pp. 145–53), Lauren T. Cowdery seems to think that Shakespeare's imagination as the novelist sees it in the Introduction to *The Tempest* is "unlike his own," and goes on to add, "James's Shakespeare, in contrast, is above all things verbal; his wealth of figurative language, his similes and metaphors and imagery of all kinds, group themselves perforce into points of view and thus inevitably into characters. Nothing could be less like the creative activity at work in James's notebooks" (p. 153). But the point to press here is that we are not really concerned with "the creative activity in the notebooks" (though even there, the situation is not exactly the way Cowdery sees it), but with the achieved works of art. And there when we examine James's style, we find it highly and constitutively metaphorical as in Shakespeare. In fact, this is precisely what makes people think of James as

"the Shakespeare of fiction" at times. It may also be helpful to recall here James's own view of Shakespeare's style. It is "imaged creative Expression" which is the "first and rarest of his (Shakespeare's) gifts," a quotation picked up by Cowdery to describe the novelist's view of style *qua* style (p. 150).

7. *Theory of Literature*, p. 184.

8. *Against Interpretation and Other Essays* (Dell, New York, 1969), p. 41.

9. *Watch and Ward* (Rupert Hart-Davis, London, 1960), p. 110.

10. Ibid., p. 81.

11. *Roderick Hudson*, p. 287.

12. *English Hours*, with Introduction by Marius Bewley (Horizon Press, New York, 1968), p. xxx.

13. *The Bostonians*, Introduction by Iriving Howe, p. xiv.

14. *The Portrait of a Lady*, Volume I, p. 117.

15. The Bostonians, p. 27.

16. Ibid., p. 35.

17. *The Portrait of a Lady*, Volume I, p. 72.

18. Ibid., p. 235.

19. Ibid., p. 396.

20. Ibid., Volume II, p. 196.

21. Ibid., p. 391.

22. *Henry James: The Critical Heritage*, p. 335.

23. Ibid., p. 427.

24. See the Introduction to *The Method of Henry James*.

25. *Henry James at Work* (Hogarth, 1924), p. 247.

26. *The Complete Tales of Henry James*, No. 12, pp. 339–40.

27. Tzvetan Todorov in his influential book, *The Poetics of Prose* (Cornell University Press, Ithaca, 1977), says some very acute and penetrating things about Henry James. On the subject of the Jamesian "blanks" and "silences" he comments, "The absence of the cause or of the truth is present in the text—indeed, it is the text's logical origin and reason for being. The cause is what, by its absence, brings the text into being. The essential is absent, the absence is essential" (p. 145).

28. *The Wings of the Dove*, pp. 496–97.

29. *Rage for Order*, p. 147.

30. "The Birthplace" (New York Edition, Volume XVII), p. 212.

31. See these remarks in *Hardy The Novelist* (Constable & Co. Ltd., London, 1956), p. 86. Here Lord David Cecil is discussing Hardy's characters and their "manner of speech."

32. *Henry James: A Reader's Guide*, p. 355.

33. *Henry James,* p. 193.

34. I am quoting from Professor Lionel Trilling's letter of November 16, 1971 in which he makes some observations about James's "colloquialism." Earlier, I had briefly discussed the problem with him during a meeting at Harvard.

35. *Henry James: Twentieth Century Views,* p. 72.

36. *The English Novel* (Penguin Books, London, 1962), p. 278.

37. Selected Essays (Faber & Faber, London, 1963), p. 289.

38. *Mannerism and Anti-Mannerism in Italian Painting* (Schocken Books, New York, paperback, 1966), p. 9–10.

39. See *The Expense of Vision,* pp. 77–78.

40. *The Tragic Muse,* p. 437.

41. The later style of James is peculiarly susceptible to parody because of its marked oddities. See Owen Seaman's parody (1912) of the style of *The Sacred Fount* (*The Critical Heritage,* pp. 309–16), and Max Beerbohm's well-known piece, "The Mote in the Middle Distance" (The Hart Press, Berkeley, 1946), etc.

42. *The American* (Eurasia Publishing House, New Delhi), p. 333. I think Matthiessen is nearer the truth than Professor Edel in this respect. James, he writes, "made these revisions at the plenitude of his powers, and they constituted a *re-seeing* of the problem of his craft." (*Henry James: The Major Phase*) p. 152.

43. Ibid., p. 79.

44. *The American* (Mladinska Knjiga, Ljubljana, Yugoslavia, 1966), pp. 121–22. In the manuscript corrected by James (now in the Houghton Library, Harvard University), the page no. is 95. A perusal of the manuscript shows how James was ceaselessly trimming, hemming, embroidering and stitching up the tapestry of words with a view to bringing the text closer to his essential vision.

45. *The American* (Eurasia), p. 205.

46. *The American* (Mladinska Knjiga), p. 339.

47. Quoted by Cornelia Pulsifer Kelley in *The Early Development of Henry James,* p. 145.

48. See *Language of Fiction* (Columbia University Press, New York, paperback, 1966), pp. 46–47.

49. *Henry James: The Critical Heritage,* p. 392.

50. Ibid., pp. 393–94.

Chapter 13

1. I have touched upon this problem in some detail in chapter 10, "The Quest of Art," pp. 150–51.

2. Since the imagination in James has been recognized as a major phenomenological element, we have had a number of insightful studies including *The Imagination of Disaster* (1961) by J. A. Ward; *The Imagination of Loving* (1965) by Naomi Lebowitz; *The Negative Imagination* (1968) by Sallie Sears; *The Grasping Imagination* (1970) by Peter Buitenhuis; and *Henry James and the Requirements of the Imagination* (1971) by Philip M. Weinstein. And we may remember that Lionel Trilling's well-known collection, *The Liberal Imagination* (1950), carries his influential essay on *The Princess Casamassima.*

3. Henry James, Preface to the New York edition of *The Portrait of a Lady*. Of course, James is talking here of the form of fiction, whereas I have used the phrase in an altered sense and situation.

4. From Max Beerbohm's cartoon "The Rage of Wonderment" and Faulkner's gag about James being "the nicest old lady" to Hugh Walpole's report to Stephen Spender about the Master's horrified "I can't; I can't," we have had a number of cracks at his expense in this regard.

5. As we know, Eliot's poem was possibly spawned by James's late story "Crapy Cornelia" (1908), and White-Mason, the hero of that story, is a typical Jamesian character, diffident and passive, drained by scruples. In a perceptive essay, "Jamesian Being" (*The Virginia Quarterly,* Winter 1976, pp. 115–32), Millicent Bell touches upon this problem in passing. The question of sex in James is certainly an aspect of the retreat from "doing" into "being." Savouring sex as a state of mind amounted for him to a kind of participation, such being the intensity of his imagination.

6. Richard Ellmann, *Golden Codgers* (Oxford University Press, London, 1973), pp. ix–x.

7. Also see page 12 where the problem has been touched upon.

8. Sigmund Freud, *The Problem of Anxiety* (W. W. Norton and Company, New York, paperback, 1963), p. 15.

9. In his book, *Henry James at Home* (Metheun, London, 1969), H. Montgomery Hyde quotes Hugh Walpole on the subject of a possible "affair" with a young woman. Walpole says in this regard; "I remember him [James] telling me how he had once in his youth in a foreign town watched a whole night in pouring rain for the appearance of a figure at a window. 'That was the end. . . ,' he said and broke off . . . " (p. 228).

10. Mrs. Humphrey Ward with whom James was staying during an Italian holiday records how during an excursion to the blue lake of Nemi, he found himself spell-bound by the beauty of a boy called Aristodemo who was "straight, lithe and handsome as a young Bacchus." (Quoted by Leon Edel in *The Treacherous Years,* Lippincott, New York, 1969, p. 298.)

11. "The female principle," of course, denotes the passive, receptive, contemplative side of James. It is interesting, however, to note that one Dr. Collins who looked after the novelist during his American visit found "an enormous amalgam of the feminine in his make-up." (Quoted by Leon Edel in *The Master,* Rupert Hart-Davis, London, 1972, p. 456.)

12. Evelyn J. Hinz, "Hierogamy versus Wedlock: Types of Marriage Plots and Their Relationships to Genres of Prose Fiction," *PMLA,* October 1976, p. 905.

13. In her article, "Marriage and the New Woman in *The Portrait of a Lady,*" *American Literature,* 47 (3), Annette Niemtzow observes that deep down, Isabel Archer is conscious of her latent and troublesome sexuality. "Isabel," she writes, "gets a frightening vision—an unveiling of herself as a 'loose woman' . . . she possesses an almost obscene—curiously not frigid—imagination." (p. 386). This is rather an extended Freudian view of the matter, but there is sufficient ground for such a surmise. Niemtzow is referring here to the Goodwood kiss.

    On the other hand, Dennis L. O'Connor insists on Isabel's dread of sexuality and of raw male passion. The way James shows her with "set teeth" suggests, according to him, "a vagina dentata as well as a portcullis . . . her implacable resistance to noetic and to sexual penetration." (*The Henry James Review,* Winter 1981, p. 25.)

14. Allen F. Stein, "Marriage in Howells's Novels," *American Literature,* January 1977, p. 503.

15. Henry James, *Roderick Hudson* (Harper, New York, 1960), p. 322.

16. Herbert Marcuse, *Eros and Civilization* (Vintage Books, New York, paperback, 1962), p. 45.

17. The idea of virgin worship which Leon Edel sees in James's later fiction is a widespread religious practice in India. For instance, there is in the northern states a day in the calendar when young girls below the age of puberty are ceremoniously washed and feasted. In the Punjabi language, such girls are called *kunjiks*. In the Nanda-Longdon affair in *The Awkward Age,* in particular, James seems to be emphasizing the mystic power of young female beauty to transform life.

18. Henry James, *What Maisie Knew* (Penguin, London, 1963), p. 18.

19. Henry James, *The Awkward Age* (Penguin, London, 1966), p. 181.

20. Ibid.

21. Maxwell Geismar, *Henry James and the Jacobites,* p. 167. One is reminded of the eruption of dark and repressed sexuality in Edith Wharton when, in her mid-forties, she told her lover, Fullerton, how her well-tended personality had "crumbled to a pinch of ashes in the flame!" (Quoted by R. W. B. Lewis in *Edith Wharton: A Biography,* Harper and Row, New York, 1975, p. 218.)

22. Robert L. Gale has noticed over 1300 water images in Henry James. See *The Caught Image* (University of North Carolina Press, Chapel Hill, 1964 edition), p. 17.

23. Lyle Glazier, "Henry James: Sex and Self-Knowledge," in *Asian Response to American Literature,* edited by C. D. Narasimhaiah (Vikas Publishing House, Delhi, 1972), p. 235. This article deals with *The Ambassadors* only.

24. Ibid.

25. Philip M. Weinstein, *Henry James and the Requirements of the Imagination* (Harvard University Press, Cambridge, Mass., 1971), p. 63.

26. Henry James, *English Hours* (Horizon Press, New York, 1968), p. 7.

27. Quoted by Leon Edel in *The Treacherous Years* (Lippincott, New York, 1969), pp. 64–65.

28. Norman O. Brown, *Life against Death* (Wesleyan University Press, Middleton, Connecticut, paperback), p. 69.

29. Henry James, *The Wings of the Dove* (New American Company, New York, paperback, 1964), p. 222.

30. Henry James, "Guy de Maupassant," in *Selected Literary Criticism,* edited by Morris Shapira (Penguin, 1963), pp. 143–44.

31. Ibid., p. 341.

32. André Gide, "Henry James," in *The Question of Henry James,* edited by F. W. Dupee, p. 258.

33. Leon Edel, *The Master,* p. 121.

34. Quoted by Gorley Putt in *Henry James: A Reader's Guide* (Cornell University Press, Ithaca, 1967), p. 92.

Chapter 14

1. *The Selected Letters of Henry James,* edited by Leon Edel (Farrar, Strauss and Cudahy, New York, 1956), p. 76.

2. *Fictions, the Novel, and Social Reality* (Penguin Books, London, 1976), pp. 11–15.

3. Ibid., p. 41.

4. *Real and Imagined Worlds: The Novel and Social Science* (Harvard University Press, Cambridge, 1977), p. 82.

5. For a detailed discussion of this Marxist idea in Fredric Jameson's *The Political Unconscious: Narrative as a Socially Symbolic Act* (1981), see "The Traces of Capitalist Patriarchy in the Silences of *The Golden Bowl*" by Mimi Kairschner, *The Henry James Review,* Spring 1984, pp. 187–88.

6. *The Political Novel: Its Development in England and America* (Oxford University Press, Oxford, 1924), p. ix.

7. *The Political Novel* (Doubleday, New York, 1955), p. 2.

8. *Politics and the Novel* (Horizon, New York, 1957), p. 17.

9. Ibid., p. 21.

10. In Marxist circles, the subject continues to be vigorously debated. While Arner Zis paraphrases Ernest Fischer as arguing that ideas hardening into ideologies become "petrified moulds of intellectual stereotypes serving to promote the interests of the ruling classes," the view is effectively disputed by Zis and others. See *Foundations of Marxist Aesthetics* (Progress Publishers, Moscow, 1977).

11. *Politics and the Novel,* p. 23.

12. *The Novels of Henry James* (Macmillan, New York, 1961), p. 137.

13. It is believed that James modelled Rosy on his own invalid and hypersensitive sister, Alice, though in the process he inverted the latter's world-view. Nearly all the references to her in James's letters, as well as her own published diaries, clearly establish her radical, anti-imperialist sympathies.

14. James has, it appears, in several striking images used the Keatsian motif throughout the book in relation to Hyacinth's sensibility and aesthetic "mysticism." For a full discussion of this motif, see Adeline R. Tintner, "Keats and James and *The Princess Casamassima,*" *Nineteenth-Century Fiction* 28 (1973) pp. 179–93. The famous passage about looking at "the good things of life through the glass of the pastry-cook's window" is, incidentally, echoed in Yeats's poem "Ego Dominus Tuus." The poet sees Keats as "a schoolboy" "with face and nose pressed to a sweet-shop window."

15. *"The Princess Casamassima"* in *The Liberal Imagination* (Viking Press, New York, 1950), p. 86.

16. In a comprehensive and insightful essay on *The Princess Casamassima,* Martha Banta applies Fredric Jameson's Marxist views on the relationship between history and fabulation in an elaborate manner. It is her argument that James uses the Hegelian concept of history as "the realization in matter of World Spirit" and that Hyacinth Robinson experiences the pull of "two other allegiances: an *aesthetic of history* . . . and an *ideology of history."* ("Beyond Post-Modernism: The Sense of History in *The Princess Casamassima,*" *The Henry James Review,* Spring 1982, p. 100.) Without entirely accepting her application of Jameson's ideas, I must nonetheless say that I largely share the premise of her larger formulations, though I doubt if James himself had any coherent, integrated and enveloping sense of history in the manner of Shakespeare or Tolstoy. His "sense" of such things and phenomena is, at best, Balzacian. In the works of such writers, the historicism of the books stems less from a truly historical imagination

than from an instinctive grasp of the sociological changes their aesthetic and ethical antennae pick up. I believe that it is in this sense that Lukács considers both Balzac and Scott as having a prognosticative consciousness despite their avowed reactionary world-view.

17. For a detailed treatment, see Manfred Mackenzie, *Communities of Honor and Love in Henry James* (Harvard University Press, Cambridge, 1976).

18. *The Tragic Muse,* edited by Leon Edel (Harper Torchbooks, New York, 1960), p. 40.

19. Ibid., p. 86.

20. Ibid., p. xii.

21. *Covering End* in *The Two Magics* (Macmillan, New York, 1907), p. 316.

22. Ibid., p. 318.

23. *English Hours,* edited by Marius Bewley (Horizon, New York, 1968), pp. 73–74.

24. Ibid., p. 171.

25. *The American Scene,* edited by Irving Howe (Horizon, New York, 1967), p. vii.

26. Ibid., p. 5.

27. Ibid., p. 75.

28. *The Art of the Novel* (Scribner's, New York, 1962), p. 193.

29. *The Selected Letters of Henry James,* pp. 45–46, 214.

30. *Literary Reviews and Essays,* edited by Albert Mordell (Grove, New York, 1957), p. 266.

31. Quoted by Marius Bewley in the introduction to *The American Scene,* p. xvii.

32. Quoted by Leon Edel in *Henry James: The Master, 1901–1916* (Hart-Davis, London, 1972), p. 33.

33. *Henry James: The Middle Years, 1882–1895* (Lippincott, Philadelphia, 1962), p. 114.

34. See *Communities of Honor and Love in Henry James,* chapter 2.

35. Whereas in the Dreyfus affair and in the Parnell case James's sympathies were on the side of the victims, in the case of John Brown he displayed a typical racist and reactionary attitude.

36. *The Development of Imagery and Its Functional Significance in the Novels of Henry James* (Franke Verlag, Bern, 1959), p. 5.

37. *The Caught Image: Figurative Language in the Fiction of Henry James* (University of North Carolina Press, Chapel Hill, 1964), p. 91.

38. Ibid., p. 172.

39. See chapter 12, "The Question of Style."

40. *Puritans and Pragmatists* (Lyall Book Depot, Ludhiana, 1968), pp. 415–16.

Chapter 15

1. James's criticism continues to attract, bemuse and fascinate all manner of students and scholars. A recent full-length study, *The Literary Criticism of Henry James* (Ohio University Press, Athens, 1981) by Sarah B. Daugherty, oddly enough, excludes the celebrated Prefaces. That the

Prefaces do distress certain people is true enough, but no other novelist has, at the same time, left behind such a remarkable body of comment on his own work, and on the processes of fiction in general as James has done.

2. *Henry James: Literary Criticism* edited by Leon Edel & Mark Wilson, The Library of America, New York, 1984. Volume I: Essays on Literature, American Literature, English Writers. Volume II: French Writers, Other European Writers, The Prefaces to the New York Edition.

3. Ibid., Vol. I, p. 98.

4. Ibid., Vol. II, p. 522.

5. Ibid., p. 524.

6. Ibid., p. 804.

7. Ibid., p. 914.

8. Ibid., p. 933.

9. Ibid., Vol. I, pp. 246–49.

10. Ibid., p. 1211.

11. Ibid., p. 1233.

12. Ibid., p. 1237.

13. Ibid., p. 1271.

14. Ibid., Vol. II, p. 217.

15. Ibid., p. 232.

16. Ibid., p. 244.

17. Ibid., p. 363.

18. Ibid., p. 385.

19. Ibid., p. 358.

20. Ibid., p. 718.

21. Ibid., p. 725.

22. Ibid., p. 730.

23. Ibid., p. 486.

24. Ibid., Vol. I, p. 457.

25. Ibid., p. 467.

26. Ibid., p. 926.

27. Ibid., p. 1315.

28. Ibid., Vol. II, pp. 66–67.

29. James uses another spelling "Turgenev" in his major essay on the Russian novelist (Vol. II, pp. 968–1034).

30. *Henry James: Literary Criticism,* Vol. II, p. 46.

31. Ibid., p. 1029.

32. *The Henry James Review*, Spring 1985, pp. 172–81.

33. Ibid., p. 178.

Select Bibliography

1. Novels

Watch and Ward (1871). *Roderick Hudson* (1875). *The American* (1877). *The Europeans* (1878). *Confidence* (1879). *Washington Square* (1880). *The Portrait of a Lady* (1881). *The Bostonians* (1886). *The Princess Casamassima* (1886). *The Reverberator* (1888). *The Tragic Muse.* (1889). *The Other House* (1897). *The Spoils of Poynton* (1897). *What Maisie Knew.* (1897). *The Awkward Age* (1899). *The Sacred Fount* (1901). *The Wings of the Dove* (1902). *The Ambassadors* (1903). *The Golden Bowl* (1904). *The Outcry* (1911). *The Ivory Tower* (Uncompleted) (1917). *The Sense of the Past* (Uncompleted) (1917).

2. Tales and Nouvelles

Poor Richard (1867). The Romance of Certain Old Clothes (1868). A Most Extraordinary Case (1868). A Passionate Pilgrim (1871). The Madonna of the Future (1873). Madame de Mauves (1874). Four Meetings (1877). Daisy Miller (1878). An International Episode (1878–79). The Pension Beaurepas (1879). A Bundle of Letters (1879). The Siege of London (1883). Lady Barbarina (1884). Pandora (1884). The Author of Beltraffio (1884). The Aspern Papers (1888). The Liar (1888). A London Life (1888). The Lesson of the Master (1888). The Pupil (1891). Brooksmith (1891). The Chaperon (1891). The Real Thing (1892). Collaboration (1892). Owen Wingrave (1892). Greville Fane (1892). The Wheel of Time (1892–93). The Middle Years (1893). The Death of the Lion (1894). The Coxon Fund (1894). The Next Time (1895). The Altar of the Dead (1895). The Figure in the Carpet (1895). The Friends of the Friends (1896). The Turn of the Screw (1898). In the Cage (1898). Europe (1899). The Great Good Place (1900). The Abasement of the Northmores (1900). The Beast in the Jungle (1903). The Birthplace (1903). Julia Bride (1908). The Jolly Corner (1908). The Velvet Glove (1909). Mona Montravers (1909). Crapy Cornelia (1909). The Bench of Desolation (1909–10). A Round of Visits (1910).

For other tales and *nouvelles,* see *The Complete Tales of Henry James* Volumes 1–12), Rupert Hart-Davis, 1961–1964.

3. Autobiography

The Middle Years (Criterion Books, New York, 1956).
Notes of a Son and Brother (Criterion Books, New York, 1956).
A Small Boy and Others (Criterion Books, New York, 1956).

4. Criticism, Travel and Letters

The American Scene (Horizon Press, New York, 1967).

The Art of the Novel, Critical Prefaces, with an Introduction by R. P. Blackmur (Scribner's, New York, 1962).

English Hours (Horizon Press, New York, 1968).

The Future of the Novel, edited, with an Introduction, by Leon Edel (Vintage Books, New York, 1956).

Henry James and H. G. Wells, edited by Leon Edel and Gordon N. Ray (Hart-Davis, London, 1958).

Henry James and John Hay, edited by George Monteiro (Brown University Press, Providence, 1965).

Henry James Letters Vols. I, II, III, IV, edited by Leon Edel (The Belknap Press of Harvard University Press, Cambridge, 1974–1984).

Henry James: Literary Criticism, 2 Volumes, edited by Leon Edel & Mark Wilson (The Library of America, New York, 1984).

The Letters of Henry James, edited by Percy Lubbock, 2 volumes (Macmillan, London, 1920).

The Notebooks of Henry James, edited by F. O. Matthiessen and Kenneth B. Murdock (Oxford University Press, New York, 1961).

The Painter's Eye, edited by John L. Sweeney (Hart-Davis, London, 1956).

The Scenic Art, edited by Allan Wade (Rutgers University Press, 1948).

Selected Letters of Henry James, edited by Leon Edel (Farrar Straus, New York, 1955).

5. Bibliography

Henry James, compiled by Leon Edel and Dan Laurence (Hart-Davis, 1957).

Henry James, 1866–1916: A Reference Guide by Linda J. Taylor (G. K. Hall, Boston, 1982).

Henry James, 1917–1959: A Reference Guide by Kristin McColgan (G. K. Hall, Boston, 1979).

Henry James, 1960–1974: A Reference Guide by Dorothy Scura (G. K. Hall, Boston, 1979).

Henry James: A Bibliography of Secondary Works by Beatrice Ricks (Scarecrow Press, Metuchen, N.J., 1975).

6. Critical Biography and Memorabilia

Leon Edel, *The Untried Years* (Hart-Davis, 1953).

―――― *The Conquest of London* (Hart-Davis, 1962).

―――― *The Middle Years* (Hart-Davis, 1963).

―――― *The Treacherous Years* (Lippincott Company, New York, 1969).

―――― *The Master:* 1901–1916 (Hart-Davis, London, 1972).

Clinton H. Grattan, *The Three Jameses.* (New York University Press, New York, 1962).

F. O. Matthiessen, *The James Family* (Knopf, New York, 1947).

H. Montgomery Hyde, *Henry James at Home* (Methuen, London, 1969).

Simmon Nowell-Smith, *The Legend of the Master* (Scribners, New York, 1948).

7. Criticism

Charles R. Anderson, *Person, Place and Thing in Henry James's Novels* (Durham, Duke University Press, 1977).

Quentin Anderson, *The American Henry James* (Rutgers University Press, New Brunswick, 1957).

Ramakant Asthana, *Henry James: A Study in the Aesthetics of the Novel* (Associated Publishers, New Delhi, 1980).

Louis Auchincloss, *Reading Henry James* (University of Minnesota Press, Minneapolis, 1975).

Joseph Warren Beach, *The Method of Henry James* (Albert Saifer, Philadelphia, 1954), first published in 1918 by the Yale University Press.

Marius Bewley, *The Complex Fate* (Chatto and Windus, London, 1952).

Jean Frantz Blackall, *The Jamesian Ambiguity and the Sacred Fount* (Cornell University Press, Ithaca, 1965).

R. P. Blackmur, *The Lion and the Honeycomb* (Methuen, New York, 1956).

Wayne C. Booth, *The Rhetoric of Fiction* (The University of Chicago Press, Chicago, 1967; first published in 1961).

Theodora Bosanquet, *Henry James at Work* (Hogarth, 1924).

Nicola Bradbury, *Henry James: The Later Novels* (Clarendon Press, Oxford, 1979).

Van Wyck Brooks, *The Pilgrimage of Henry James* (Dutton and Co., New York, 1925).

Peter Buitenhuis, *The Grasping Imagination: The American Writings of Henry James* (University of Toronto Press, Toronto, 1970).

Peter Buitenhuis (Ed.), *The Portrait of a Lady, 20th Century Interpretations* (Prentice-Hall, Englewood Cliffs, N.J., 1968).

Oscar Cargill, *The Novels of Henry James* (Macmillan, New York, 1961).

John A. Clair, *The Ironic Dimension in the Fiction of Henry James* (Duquesne University Press, Pittsburgh, 1965).

Frederick C. Crews, *The Tragedy of Manners* (Yale University Press, New Haven, 1957).

Sarah B. Daugherty, *The Literary Criticism of Henry James* (Ohio University Press, Athens, 1981).

Stephen Donadio, *Nietzsche, Henry James, and the Artistic Will* (Oxford University Press, New York, 1978).

F. W. Dupee, *Henry James* (Methuen, 1951).

F. W. Dupee (Ed.), *The Question of Henry James* (H. Holt, New York, 1945).

Leon Edel, "Henry James" in *Six American Novelists of the Nineteenth Century,* edited by Richard Foster (University of Minnesota, Minneapolis, 1968).

Leon Edel (Ed.), *Henry James, 20th Century Views* (Prentice-Hall, 1953).

Pelham Edgar, *Henry James: Man and Author* (Macmillan, Toronto, 1927).

Michael Egan, *Henry James: The Ibsen Years* (Vision Press, London, 1972).

Leslie A. Fiedler, *Love and Death in the American Novel* (Dell Publishing Co., New York, 1966).

Daniel Mark Fogel, *Henry James and the Structure of the Romantic Imagination* (Louisiana State University Press, Baton Rouge, 1981).

Robert Gale, *The Caught Image* (University of North Carolina Press, Chapel Hill, 1964).

David Galloway, *The Portrait of a Lady* (Arnold, 1967).

Roger Gard (Ed.), *Henry James: The Critical Heritage* (Barnes and Noble Inc., New York, 1968).

Maxwell Geismar, *Henry James and the Jacobites* (Hill and Wang, New York, 1965).

Charles Hoffman, *The Short Novels of Henry James* (Bookman Associates, New York, 1957).

Alexander Holder-Barell, *The Development of Imagery and Its Functional Significance in the Novels of Henry James* (Franke Verlag, Bern, 1959).

Laurence B. Holland, *The Expense of Vision* (Princeton University Press, Princeton, 1968).

H. Montgomery Hyde, *Henry James at Home* (Methuen, London, 1969).

Walter Isle, *Experiments in Form* (Harvard University Press, Cambridge, 1968).

D. W. Jefferson, *Henry James and the Modern Reader* (Oliver and Boyd, London, 1964).

Susanne Kappeler, *Writing and Reading in Henry James* (University of Columbia Press, New York, 1980).

Cornelia Pulsifer Kelley, *The Early Development of Henry James* (Revised Edition, University of Illinois Press, Urbana, 1965).

Dorothea Krook, *The Ordeal of Consciousness in Henry James* (Cambridge University Press, Cambridge, 1967).

F. R. Leavis, *The Great Tradition* (Penguin, London, 1966, first published by Chatto and Windus, 1948).

————— *The Common Pursuit* (Penguin, London, 1963, first published by Chatto and Windus, 1952).

Naomi Lebowitz, *The Imagination of Loving* (Wayne State University Press, Detroit, 1965).

Brian Lee, *The Novels of Henry James: A Study of Culture and Consciousness* (St. Martin's Press, New York, 1978).

Ellen Douglas Leyburn, *The Relation of Comedy to Tragedy in the Fiction of Henry James* (The University of North Carolina Press, Chapel Hill, 1968).

Robert Emmet Long, *Henry James: The Early Novels* (G. K. Hall, Boston, 1983).

Percy Lubbock, *The Craft of Fiction* (Viking, New York, 1957).

Manfred Mackenzie, *Communities of Honor and Love in Henry James* (Harvard University Press, Cambridge, 1976).

Darshan Singh Maini, *The Portrait of a Lady: An Assessment* (Oxford University Press, New Delhi, 1977).

Robert Marks, *James's Later Novels* (The William-Frederick Press, New York, 1960).

F. O. Matthiessen, *Henry James: The Major Phase* (Oxford University Press, 1944; Galaxy Book, 1963).

Harold T. McCarthy, *Henry James: The Creative Process* (Yoseloff, New York, 1958).

Bruce R. McElderry Jr., *Henry James* (Twayne Publishers, New York, 1965).

Susan Reibel Moore, *The Drama of Discrimination in Henry James* (University of Queensland Press, St. Lucia, 1982).

Ralf Norrman, *The Insecure World of Henry James* (Macmillan, 1982).

Sergio Perosa, *Henry James and the Experimental Novel* (University Press of Virginia, Charlottesville, 1978).

Richard Poirier, *The Comic Sense of Henry James* (Oxford University Press, New York; Galaxy Book, 1967; Chatto, 1960).

————— *A World Elsewhere* (Oxford University Press, New York, 1966).

Joel Porte, *The Romance in America* (Wesleyan University Press, Middletown, 1969).

S. Gorley Putt, *Henry James: A Reader's Guide* (Cornell University Press, Ithaca, 1967).

Shlomith Rimmon, *The Concept of Ambiguity—the Example of James* (University of Chicago Press, Chicago, 1977).

Daniel J. Schneider, *The Crystal Cage: Adventures of the Imagination in the Fiction of Henry James* (The Regents Press of Kansas, Lawrence, 1978).

Sallie Sears, *The Negative Imagination* (Cornell University Press, Ithaca, 1968).

J. N. Sharma, *The International Fiction of Henry James* (Macmillan, New Delhi, 1979).

Sister Carona Sharp, *The Confidante in Henry James* (University of Notre Dame Press, 1963).

Philip Sicker, *Love and the Quest for Identity in the Fiction of Henry James*. (Princeton University Press, Princeton, 1980).

Stephen Spender, *The Destructive Element* (Houghton and Mifflin Co., Boston and New York, 1936).

Mary Doyle Springer, *A Rhetoric of Literary Character: Some Women of Henry James* (University of Chicago Press, Chicago, 1978).

Elizabeth Stevenson, *The Crooked Corridor* (Macmillan, 1961).

Albert E. Stone (Ed.), *The Ambassadors, 20th Century Interpretations* (Prentice-Hall, 1969).

Tony Tanner, *The Reign of Wonder* (Cambridge University Press, Cambridge, 1965).

Tony Tanner, (Ed.), *Henry James, Modern Judgements* (Macmillan, New York, 1968).

Lionel Trilling, *The Liberal Imagination* (Viking, New York, 1950).

————— *The Opposing Self* (Viking, New York, 1968).

Krishna Baldev Vaid, *Technique in the Tales of Henry James* (Harvard University Press, Cambridge, 1964).

William Veeder, *Henry James—The Lessons of the Master* (University of Chicago Press, Chicago, 1979).

Edward Wagenknecht, *Eve and Henry James: Portraits of Women and Girls in His Fiction* (University of Oklahoma Press, Norman, 1978).

———— *The Novels of Henry James* (Frederick Unger, New York, 1983).

J. A. Ward, *The Imagination of Disaster* (University of Nebraska Press, Lincoln, 1961).

———— *The Search for Form* (The University of North Carolina Press, Chapel Hill, 1961).

Austin Warren, *Rage for Order* (The University of Chicago Press, Chicago, 1948).

Philip M. Weinstein, *Henry James and the Requirements of the Imagination* (Harvard University Press, Cambridge, 1971).

Joseph Weisenfarth, *Henry James and the Dramatic Analogy* (Fordham University Press, New York, 1963).

R. B. J. Wilson, *Henry James's Ultimate Narrative: The Golden Bowl* (University of Queensland Press, St. Lucia, 1981).

Walter Wright, *The Madness of Art* (University of Nebraska Press, Lincoln, 1962).

Ruth Bernard Yeazell, *Language and Knowledge in the Late Novels of Henry James* (University of Chicago, Chicago, 1980).

8.   Journals: Special Number, Henry James

Horn & Hound (April-June, 1934).
Modern Fiction Studies (Spring 1957).
Modern Fiction Studies (Spring 1966).
The Henry James Review (1979–1987).

Index